BENEATH THE DOME

BENEATH THE DOME

Stories and Vignettes from Our Time at
Pennsylvania Military College, 1954 to 1973

Edited by three Rooks from Echo Company
William Speer, William J. Troy
& James H. VanSciver

Deeds Publishing | Athens

Copyright © 2023 —William Speer, William J. Troy & James H. VanSciver

ALL RIGHTS RESERVED—No part of this book may be reproduced in any form or by any electronic or mechanical means, including information storage and retrieval systems, without permission in writing from the authors, except by a reviewer who may quote brief passages in a review.

Published by Deeds Publishing in Athens, GA
www.deedspublishing.com

Printed in The United States of America

Cadet artwork by Rex Newman
Cover and interior design by Deeds Publishing

ISBN 978-1-961505-02-5

Books are available in quantity for promotional or premium use. For information, email info@deedspublishing.com.

First Edition, 2023

10 9 8 7 6 5 4 3 2 1

Dedicated to preserving and celebrating the legacy of Pennsylvania Military College and the men who used their experiences there to make the world a better place.

PENNSYLVANIA MILITARY COLLEGE

CHESTER, PA

NATION'S SECOND-OLDEST MILITARY COLLEGE

FOUNDED 1821; COLORS CASED 1972

TO FOREVER HONOR AND REMEMBER

THE LEGACY OF

EVERY GRADUATE OF THE CORPS

DEDICATED FOR ALL PMC CADETS

BY THE CLASS OF 1972

VIRTUE, LIBERTY, AND INDEPENDENCE

CONTENTS

Foreword	ix
Preface	xiii
Rook (Freshman) Year	1
Sophomore (Third Class) Year	147
Junior (Second Class) Year	179
Senior (First Class) Year	233
Odds & Ends	319
Reflections	365
About the Authors	385
Index	401

ALMA MATER

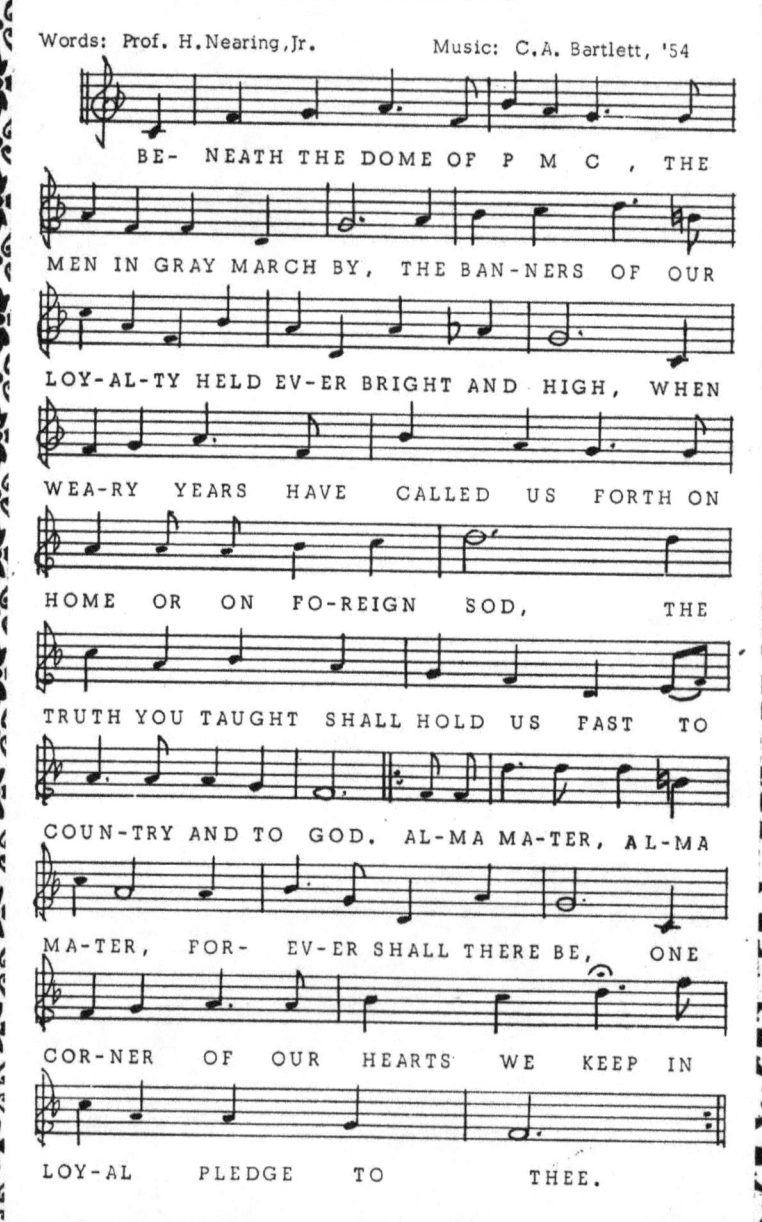

Words: Prof. H. Nearing, Jr. Music: C.A. Bartlett, '54

BE- NEATH THE DOME OF P M C, THE MEN IN GRAY MARCH BY, THE BAN-NERS OF OUR LOY-AL-TY HELD EV-ER BRIGHT AND HIGH, WHEN WEA-RY YEARS HAVE CALLED US FORTH ON HOME OR ON FO-REIGN SOD, THE TRUTH YOU TAUGHT SHALL HOLD US FAST TO COUN-TRY AND TO GOD. AL-MA MA-TER, AL-MA MA-TER, FOR- EV-ER SHALL THERE BE, ONE COR-NER OF OUR HEARTS WE KEEP IN LOY-AL PLEDGE TO THEE.

FOREWORD

What can a mosquito teach you about leadership? Read on and James H. VanSciver, PMC Cadet #466 will tell you.

Throughout my career in the Army, most of the officers I met earned their commission through ROTC at a college (as I did) or from the United States Military Academy at West Point. I served with many West Point graduates, and we became close friends through shared experiences. On long tours of duty and longer deployments, I listened to many stories of their time at the Academy, and I got a sense of what life was like for a USMA Cadet. Rarely, I'd meet someone who would say they attended Norwich, Virginia Military Institute, Virginia Tech, The Citadel, Texas A&M, or U of North Georgia, and it was evident that they were fiercely proud of their institutions. These are the six senior military colleges remaining in the US, but for a long time, the Pennsylvania Military College was the second oldest military college in the nation. These are their stories. This body of work exemplifies the lines in the PMC Alma Mater; "The truth you taught us will hold us fast...." and "One corner of our hearts we keep in loyal pledge to thee."

The reasons one might attend a military college are as varied as the students who make the decision, but the result, the product, the alchemy that in four years takes these young high school graduates through college to graduation and perhaps earn a commission as a military officer is remarkable. This book will help you understand what it is like to attend a military college, more specifically, what it WAS like in the '50s, '60s and early '70s while attending PMC. Be forewarned, you will do yourself a disservice by reading this with our 21st century globalized societal norms. The stories are snapshots of the times, but the lessons these Cadets learned lasted a lifetime.

This book is not a collection of war stories or tall tales. It is a collection of memories of a shared formative experience, through which life lessons were learned. For those who have experienced boot camp, attended a military academy, or attended any of the military "schools" (Airborne, Ranger, etc.) you will "get it" immediately and be reminded of similar experiences. (OK, for you folks, these memoirs will read like war stories.) You will find excitement, uncertainty, doubt, pride, creativity, and help from unexpected sources ("won't be long now").

James goes on to say, "Be on time. Be supportive. Be dependable. Do the right thing in the right way for the right reason… These expectations are fundamental if a military is to be successful. They are also important if one is to live a prosperous, successful, and happy life. Not abandoning your post until relieved is more than a soldierly value. So, too, are dependability, teamwork, dedication, focus, and hard work."

Read this and you will be enlightened and amused, but you will also learn how the immutable values of Loyalty, Duty, Responsibility, Selfless Service, Honor, Integrity, and Personal Courage are developed, and how Leadership, once thought a trait of personality, is learned.

About LTC (Retired) Jon Peterson

LTC Jon Peterson attended Dickinson College on an ROTC scholarship and subsequently served 25 years of Active duty in the Army as a helicopter pilot, unit commander and strategic planner. Major tours of duty include the 7th Infantry Division (Operation Just Cause, Panama), the 82nd Airborne Division, (Operation Uphold Democracy, Haiti), 1st Armored Division (Germany, Task Force Hawk, Kosovo), 18th Airborne Corps (Operation Iraqi Freedom), and was the Professor of Military Science at Widener University. Upon retirement from the Army, Mr. Peterson worked as the Associate Director of the Oskin Leadership Institute at Widener University, teaching leadership to students and developing leadership programs for local, national, and international organizations. During this time, he was inducted into the Phi Beta Delta society, which recognizes scholarly achievement in international education. Jon is a past commander of American Legion Post 405 in Philadelphia and has been recognized for his work by the City of Philadelphia. He is also a life member of the VFW, the DAV, and the Association of the US Army. (AUSA)

Jon is married to his wife Kristin, and they have three grown daughters. He and Kristin are now enjoying retirement and enjoy travelling and time with family and friends.

—*LTC (Retired) Jon Peterson*

PREFACE

This book is a labor of love by the cadets and spouses of Pennsylvania Military College. In the past year, we have been gathering memories, the kind you tell your grandkids and friends (or maybe you don't!) These vignettes date from 1954 to 1973. No matter how much time a cadet spent "Beneath the Dome" those times are indelibly etched into our souls and very being. We all grew as a result of our experience at PMC, just in vastly different ways.

It has been at least fifty years since all these cadets graduated and, as it always does, memories fade. With the Class of 1972, Pennsylvania Military College was relegated to the dustbin of history. The institution is now Widener University with an ROTC detachment known as the Dauntless Battalion. As a former Professor of Military Science at Widener put it eloquently, "During my tenure, I discovered the John Philip Sousa march "Dauntless Battalion" and I realized that we had to change the battalion's name to Dauntless. Unfortunately, I ran out of time on my tour, but I convinced my successor to make the change. What other ROTC unit can claim a Sousa March and a Civil War [Gettysburg] Campaign Streamer? Awesome!"[1]

According to pennsylvaniamilitarycollege.com (which we high-

---

1. LTC (Ret) Jon Peterson

ly recommend you explore), over the years only two cadets wrote in detail of their experiences at PMC. Roy Eaton, Class of 1969, wrote *Soldier Boy, An Autobiography*. He was the only student in college history to be elected student government president, senior class president, and Brigade Honor Court president; it is an excellent read. Noted poet Gil Fagiani, Class of 1967, wrote *Rooks* a collection of poetry about his time at PMC. As one reviewer wrote, "*Rooks* is a stunning, sobering, blueprint of a corner of the militarized mind…"

The institution has produced numerous other authors; Horace Hobbs (Class of 1897) *Kris and Krag: Adventures among the Moros of the Southern Philippine Islands*. *Adventures among the Moros of the Southern Philippine Islands* is recognized as a classic work on the little-documented Philippine Insurrection. Eugene Hoopes (Class of 1901) wrote *Silent Friends, Tales of a Dude Wrangler*, a series of fictional stories told, as one reviewer put it, "by the type of wrangler one may find at any roundup, at any 'dude' ranch, or around any campfire where stories of the rangeland and its lore were told." Karl Wettengel (Class of 1921) *The Ghost of Paddy O' and other Poems*. Written in free verse while at PMC, it illustrates the continuity of the spirit of PMC.

And then there was George Bjotvedt Class of 1965. After George's time in Korea where he was a German Shepherd Scout Dog handler, from 1972 to 1982 he wrote show scripts for the one of the greatest television shows of all time, *M*A*S*H*. Mervyn Harris (Class of 1957) wrote *A Brief History of Nether Providence*. His book traces the history of Nether Providence Township, Pa, from its original Lenape Indian inhabitants. Louis Horner (Class of 1962) in *Who Will Water the Flowers*, chronicles his life as an African-American during a turbulent time in U.S. history and examines the friendships he forged, beginning with those built at PMC. Charles E. Merkel (Class of 1967) wrote *Unraveling the Custer Enigma*, which contains information about the court martial of George Armstrong Custer.

Edward Marolda (Class of 1967) *The U.S. Navy in the Vietnam War, An illustrated History*. He has authored, coauthored, or edited nine works on the U.S. Navy's experience in Vietnam.

Tom Vossler (Class of 1968) *A Field Guide to Gettysburg* as well as a piece on Antietam. Brian Kates (Class of 1968), as a reporter and editor at the New York Daily News, won numerous awards for journalistic excellence, including a Pulitzer Prize for editorial writing. His non-fiction book, *The Murder of a Shopping Bag Lady*, the story of a homeless woman slain on the streets of New York, won a Special Edgar Allan Poe Award from Mystery Writers of America. David Fiedler (Class of 1968) wrote a book on radio physics that is still in use today and used extensively in the Gulf War / Afghanistan and being incorporated into official Signal Corps doctrine. He is one of the authors of numerous stories included herein.

Mark Richards (Class of 1969) *Legions of the Forest*, which opens in 9 A.D., and centers around a clash between Roman legions and the German people. Bill Speer (Class of 1972) *Broomsticks to Battlefields: After the Battle, the Cadets of Delaware Military Academy*, The story of Henry C. Robinett and David Vickers reminds us that historians and psychologists have barely begun to study the question of post-traumatic stress disorder and traumatic brain injury among Civil War veterans, issues we are still tackling with today's military.

And finally, Jim VanSciver (Class of 1972) a prolific writer whose works include *About Lewes, Hi! I'm Elvis: Ain't Nothing but a Hound Dog*, and *Generalities of Distinction: Leadership, Learning, Limitations*. You will find the last two also have contributed to this collection of stories. All these fine authors have enriched the PMC story.

Reflecting on the past is a delicate process. Some look back to bygone years seeing what they want to see, not what really was. Others, it is reported, have the ability to remember circumstances that really did not happen. That is the beauty of this tome. Whether it actually did take place, whether the writer wished it had, or whether it really happened on the campus of what was Pennsylvania Military College matters not as much as that it will spur a reaction from the reader. That is our purpose. We have created a kind of "Chicken Soup for the Cadets" work that will absolutely serve its purpose with each page that is turned. And, for that, we are thankful to all of those who have contributed to our bibliophiles' enjoyment.

It was our desire by collecting these tales to bring back memories long faded into history. To allow everyone who reads this to travel back to the day when we were young and full of unlimited energy, some positive, some, well…you will see. Keep in mind, memory is a fickle mistress and loves to play tricks on us all. These stories are the unvarnished memories of those who wrote them. We have made no attempt to verify the "facts" or to seriously edit the content or context of these stories. The only changes that the editors made are related to spelling, grammatical, and other such issues. The opinions expressed herein are those of the individual writer and do not reflect those of the editors.

We organized these stories by class year (Rook, Sophomore, Junior, Senior, Odds and Ends) and the years listed are approximate in some cases. We hope that this collection of anecdotes will enhance your understanding of life at a military college. We are sure those from other such institutions will find some common ground. We sincerely hope you enjoy the antics, hijinks, exploits, and escapades of the cadets from Pennsylvania Military College. [2]

---

2. Inspirational credit for this volume belongs to Vietnam Veteran Bob Babcock, his Deeds Publishing has produced two fascinating volumes by Vietnam Veterans "I'm Ready to Talk" where members of the Atlanta Vietnam Veterans Business Association share experiences about serving during the Vietnam War. We strongly recommend it for an insight you can get nowhere else. Thanks Bob!

ROOK (FRESHMAN) YEAR

Alan Hilkene:
Getting There

Graduated high school on 23 June 1950. On June 25 1950 the N. Koreans invaded S. Korea. Pres. Truman asked the UN to call it "A Police Action." An armistice was declared in mid-Summer 1953.

I was bestowed a four-year full scholarship to Cornell U. in Ithaca NY and started in late August 1950. By mid-term, I sensed that I was not going to complete the semester and told my parents so! I left for the Christmas break while my dad, looking through a National Geographic mag inside rear cover noted a PMC ad. In early January 1951, we drove down and went through the drill of signing up!

I was dropped off on January 15 to begin attendance and lodging. My roommate was Al Lerner who had attended prep school before. Soon after, as I was walking down the 3rd corridor of Old Main, I saw a familiar face!!

It was Peter Marx, a dorm mate with me at Cornell some five doors down!! He hooked up with Ray Long for the entire time they both were there. Because there were over 20 new cadets, PMC opened Summer classes for us in Wyman hall and Andy Velichko became my roommate for the remaining spell at PMC! In truth, I let my parents down by flubbing my opportunity at Cornell—I carry a stain on my soul forever for being such a jerk and irresponsible then. I needed discipline and obedience to stiffen my backbone and to understand responsibility for the remainder of my life! Thank you all for being my helpers along the way!!

Larry Liss:
Joining the Corps of Cadets — With permission, Excerpts from The Forgotten Mission by Jack Swickard

Larry said his first military memory was just after World War II ended. "When I was five or six years old, one day all these men showed up in uniform. My uncle Sammy was there, he was in the Navy, and he had his ribbons on. My uncle Sid was in the Army, he had all his ribbons on. They wore their uniforms for weeks." When Larry was eight years old, misfortune struck. On Mother's Day 1949, a laundry truck struck him as he darted into the street from between two parked cars. Larry had crossed the street to pick flowers for his mother and was returning to give them to her. Larry had been in a coma for two months.

While he was hospitalized with the coma, some of his young relatives would visit him. "My cousins tell stories about putting mustaches and funny hats and wigs on me while I was in the hospital," Larry said. "When I came out of the coma, I couldn't speak very well. When I look back on it now, I was like a walking zombie. They didn't have CAT scans or MRIs or anything like that. They just had x-rays," he said. "I had a major concussion. I was like a zombie for two or three years. So I was way behind everybody else. I had tutors. I didn't really wake up until I was about 11.

"One day, everything was silent. Then there was this noise and I looked up and there was this woman's face next to my face—I could see her eyes, her makeup, and her red lipstick—screaming at me. "Then it was, 'Larry Liss, you're always looking out the window. I'm tired of this! Go to the principal's office now!' She pulled me up by my collar and pushed me. I walked out of the classroom, and I walked around the halls. I swear to God, I had no idea where I was.

"Then I saw daylight and I walked toward the doors and opened them. All I know is, I sat on the steps. I remember sitting there and looking at cars for the first time. Trees for the first time. It was spring. Grass. Clouds. People talking, walking. I could hear footsteps. I was like a stranger in a strange land. I felt like an alien," he said. "My parents came, and my mother and father were crying. I remember my father hugging me and asking me if I was OK. Then my mother crying and saying, 'Thank God!'"

Larry said, "Years later they told me I was quiet and walked around like a zombie. But I attended school and got picked on. I don't remember anything for three years. I was totally blank until the moment that teacher was yelling at me. And, you know, if that teacher had not yelled at me, who knows how long I would have been like that." Larry received tutoring and attended summer school. "I guess parts of your brain develop, while other parts shut down. When I took my college boards, I maxed the literature part of it and bombed on the math part," he said. "I think I got a 299 in math and 800 in literature. You get 200 points from putting your name on a piece of paper."

"So, if you put the two scores together, it was still like 1,000 or 1,100, and you needed 1,200—1,400 to get into a good school, so I got turned down by every school except for Pennsylvania Military College and Swarthmore, of all places, which is a really highly regarded academic university. They wanted to take me because I was a really interesting character. I was like a savant in some areas. They wanted to put me on probation," Larry said.

A friend, a guy named Lenny Ellenstein, who had been flunking out in college, went to Pennsylvania Military College and wound up getting all 'A's.' He said, 'Look, you've got to come visit this place because it's great.' So I went to Pennsylvania Military College on Mother's Day 1958, when I was a senior in high school. They had a big parade. I got hooked. It was like 2,200 cadets. They had horse cavalry, and they had the infantry, and the drums and the band were playing. The Corps of Cadets was behind the stadium, all lined up, and I was watching these guys and they blew me away. Some of them were my age and I was still blown away," he remembered.

"Then I got in the stands, and they marched out onto the field. That was the day they gave awards to certain people or promotions and stuff. It had been cloudy, and the sunlight was hitting the sabers, and the horses were there, and I said: 'I got to do this.' So I told my father, 'Look, I've got to go to this school because I'll flunk out of college. If I go to any college, I'll flunk out and I don't want to do that.' My father said, 'OK.'

Larry remembered coming home for the first time during his Rook year at Pennsylvania Military College. "I was in my uniform, and my mother fainted. She just collapsed into a heap. She was scared to death." Larry loved life at the military college and was a distinguished military graduate. "I was like a fish in water. The Rook year was kind of rough, but I went into the Pershing Rifles Drill Team. We became the national champions in 1961, 1962 and 1963. As a Rook, I was part of Pershing Rifles, which was 36 brothers out of a cadet corps of 2,200, so it was a very elite group." Nevertheless, his first year was rough. In addition to keeping up with his academic studies, Larry arose every morning at 4:30 to drill with the Pershing Rifles.

Because the college was a cavalry school, most of the graduates went into the Armor Branch. Larry was commissioned a second lieutenant in the Regular Army upon graduation in June 1963.

"After Armor school, I was assigned to the 2nd of the 9th Cavalry in Germany, on the Czech border, up against the Russian Special Forces (Spetznaz)," Larry said. He served as an armored cavalry platoon leader. "I used to race around in what was called a 114. I had a Jeep, a tank, and a 114, which was like the command track vehicle, about half the size of an armored personnel carrier. It had a .50-caliber machine gun on it. It was a cool little vehicle; it had a '70 Chevy Corvette engine in it. We raced all over Germany in that thing."

His first exposure to the Vietnam War occurred during this time. Larry was part of a study to determine how effective tracked vehicles would perform in the combat area. He remembered traveling to South Vietnam for six to eight weeks at a time on TDY—or temporary duty. "I was rotated in and out. I lived in Munich, so I would do the Czech-German border, come back, then rotate to Vietnam, then rotate back out, then go back to the Czech border," where he mainly performed scouting missions.

In December 1965, he volunteered for helicopter flight training. Larry recalled visiting with an Army helicopter pilot along the Czech border on a cold and snowy winter day that year. The pilot was in the warm cockpit of a UH-1 Huey, drinking a cup of coffee. Larry said the pilot told him, "Look at you. You're freezing your ass off. You ought to apply for helicopter flight school." Later, at the Officers Club, Larry saw a sign encouraging young officers to apply for flight training.

After four months of primary helicopter training at Fort Wolters, an Army post outside of Mineral Wells, Texas, Larry and his classmates were sent to Fort Rucker, Alabama, the Army Aviation Center. There, at Mother Rucker, the student pilots were taught to fly with cockpit instruments, transitioned from small training helicopters to the Huey, learned gunnery and formation flying, then spent time in the field learning escape and evasion.

Larry graduated from flight school in the fall of 1966. Within 30 days, he was in South Vietnam.

Rick Moller:
Unintentional Streaker

It was the Fall of 1961. I started as a Rook in my Fourth-Class Year at PMC. I had originally started as a Brother Rat (Fourth Classman) at VMI in 1959 but had to resign for health reasons. At PMC, I was assigned to HQ (The Band) Company as a Drummer in the Drum Line. All HQ Rooks were quartered on the East and West Sides of the First Floor of Howell Hall.

The First floor PMC quarters were a surprise to me. When I was at VMI, all Rats (Fourth Classmen) were quartered on the Barracks Fourth Floor, Third Classmen were on the Third Floor, 2nd Classmen were on the 2nd Floor, and First Classmen were on the First Floor. As a PMC Rook, I almost had First Classman Privileges! I was quartered with half of the HQ Rooks on the West side of Howell Hall and our PMC First Classmen Bruce Hanley '62 (RIP) (HQ

Company Commander) and Dick Johnson '62 (HQ Company Executive Officer). The remainder of the HQ Rooks were quartered on the East side of Howell Hall along with the PMC Cadre NCO's Nick Manente '64 (HQ First Sergeant) and Buzz Miller '64 (HQ SGT/Squad Leader). Separating the two sides of Howell Hall was the Corps Headquarters Lobby, the Officer-of-the-Day's Counter, and the Quarters of Bob Bellinger '62 (RIP) (Cadet First Captain and Brigade Commander).

The Howell Hall lobby was the focal point of the PMC Quadrangle. It had the only fully functioning TV, multiple sofas, and served as a lounge for PMC visitors and guests. It was a well-used lobby and, during any given day, was well occupied. Entry was from the front doors and the from the doors of the west and east side HQ Rook corridors. Each corridor had Gang Showers. On Saturdays in the Fall of 1961, after Mess 1 (Breakfast), Saturday Morning Inspection, Mess 2 (Lunch) when we had a home football game, the Corps of Cadets, led by HQ Company prior to the game, would conduct a Pre-Game Corps March-On. Following the game, we would somewhat relax and rest before Mess 3 (Dinner). We would take advantage of our free time to hit the showers and clean-up.

Well, as luck would have it and boys being boys, on one occasion there was a wet towel snapping contest in the Gang Shower on the west corridor. The snapping spilled into the corridor. Now, all we had on (apparel-wise) were those wet towels. The contest quickly got out of control. First Classmen Hanley and Johnson were not around. NCO's Manente and Miller were in the other corridor. the west corridor floor was slick with shower water. Rook Mike McCloy '65 (RIP) started running toward the lobby doors. He slipped on the wet floor and couldn't stop himself. He went flying through the doors, totally butt-naked, into the Howell Hall Lobby to the astonishment of all those waiting there. It was quite the scene. Mike recovered and did a rapid exfiltration back inside the west corridor. I recall we all did multiple pushups and multiple green chairs as a result of that escapade. I don't believe Howell Hall was ever the same after that.

Jack Wilson:
(As told to son Tom Wilson) Coke

My Dad, Jack Wilson, PMC 1965, used to tell a story about hazing a freshman during the first week. The freshman was in a dorm room with a bottle of coke. My Dad came in and saw the coke, proceeded to grab the coke, and yell at the newbee for having a bottle of coke in my Dad's dorm without permission. As he's chewing out this freshman, he's slowly shaking the bottle of coke. Dad finishes chewing the kid out, hands the kid the coke and tells him he has two minutes to drink the coke. Dad slams the door to the dorm...hears the pop of the bottle cap, followed by the sound of volcanic soda gushing all over the place...and an "Oh My God" from the kid.

According to my Dad, he made sure the kid remained demerit free for the next two weeks. This is as I remember it, and as accurate as I remember. It was one of the signature stories he told. He also said they used to paint the dome on the library flesh color like a boob.

Bruce David Hubbell:
The Privilege of being a PMC Rook

I always considered a privilege to have become a PMC Rook...irrespective of my early departure from Company C...Walking into Old Main for the first time finding my room 209 and my roommate, Bob Boltz, and my cadet number 291...I felt I had finally made it...I had become a PMC Rook...Class '66... It was everything I'd dreamed it would be..

I had the upper bunk and it made it easier for me to make my bed because I could sit on my roomies bed and pull my sheets tight through the springs before inspection...and those sheets had to have no wrinkles in them...I got used to gently sliding into my bed at night so as not to disturb the tuck I had worked so hard to make...I learned to sleep on my back at PMC.

And it was my shoes...shoot...I practiced and practiced and practiced spit shining my shoes for three months before I got to campus...but nope just could not get that shine...and then some guys had patent leather shoes that were always shined...Grrrrrrr

But THEN: I got The Uniform...the authentic West Point Academy Grey Line uniform with the tight neck wool greys and the sharp-edged white-collar rim... (keeps your chin up—neck straight) and the wool pants with the broad black stripe...man, I was in uniform heaven!!

Bruce David Hubbell:
At the Urging of a Fellow PMC Facebook Friend

I share with all of you my PMC story I've held inside for over 50 years...maybe now I can forgive myself and rest from my guilt of abandonment.

I was in the class 1966...entering the Fall of 1962...I left that November...I just had lost my love, trust, and excitement for PMC after years of preparation, planning and anticipation of the privilege of becoming a PMC Rook...long story and some of you were there with me...I was roommates with Bob Boltz...2nd floor, Old Main.

Here's what happened...We had one upperclassman on our

floor, supposedly a state champ wrestler, who was always being much meaner than necessary and unusually unkind in his bracing of us to the point of finally pushing my edge by verbally disrespecting my girlfriend and that was it. I just lost my cool, he and I broke into a full-on fist fight outside my room: we were given 15 demerits and walked the yard: that was my breaking point. I experienced for the first time, knowing I could never trust him as a comrade. I so deeply disliked this guy and how he treated many of us and this caused such an emotional conflict in my 18-year-old self that I left PMC…broken hearted…

I wondered for years what it was and why I gave up my chance to stay at PMC and what it meant to me. It was all I had ever wanted all through high school. I had my destiny set: that of being a soldier in arms with my fellow men protecting our country, just like my brothers and my grandfather Capt. Stuart D Hubbell; he died in WWI leaving my dad at 13 and his four siblings and my Beloved grandmother. That was so very difficult for my father emotionally he spoke about that loss many times. I was always inspired by my grandfather's commitment. He was wounded by shrapnel and came home, but because of his dedication, he then went back to France to be with his men…and that's where he is buried.

But later on in life I saw what it was! As a football coach and father of three boys to men. I had seen it often; he was that type of individual who was abused or bullied as a child. So he seemed to have a compulsive enjoyment and need to provoke others as a way of having their punishment satisfy a place inside of himself so he could feel he was getting even. It's that kind of guy who holds a grudge and I sensed he would be that type who would shoot you in the back in battle. I've thought about that moment so often. I still have a sort of wound that I've carried with me: missing my Army career!

And, as life would have it in 1968, and as you know it was Vietnam and my number was called and I was sent the draft notice, even though then, I was a college sophomore, with a wife and two children. I passed the mental test but when I got to the physical part which I was passing, at the very last station where the Doctor behind the screen jamming his finger in my groin telling me to cough causing me to yell at a deep pain he created. I asked, "What the hell is that?" He said, "Let's see, you're in college, married with two kids?"… "Yes sir"… "Well for you, that's a hernia and is a 1Y deferment…go home son!"

…thus ended my soldier's life.

That's it…thanks for being here…

W. David Eckard:
Summer of 1962, Pre-PMC

I had a part-time job which afforded me a lot of free afternoons. My family belonged to the Tri-State Yacht Club as social members, and it had a wonderful swimming pool which I used whenever weather permitted. During one of my visits, I struck up a conversation with the lifeguard. He told me that he had just graduated from PMC and was awaiting his final orders to report for active duty. When he learned that I was going to start my Cadet journey, he very kindly gave me a lot of good advice. Such as build up some polish on my shoes, get the belt and remove the varnish from the buckle with Brasso, get my gray shirts asap and have them 'bloused' by a tailor. Plus others, all of which held me in great stead. So: A very fond Thank You to Franklin H. Andrew, Jr., Class of 1962, for taking the time to provide this apprehensive Rook-to-Be some very helpful advice. As a side note — in preparing this I stumbled across the fact that Franklin H. Andrew (I assume Sr.) was in the Class of 1933!

W. David Eckard:
A Rook "Whoops"

As the Rook Period progressed during Fall 1962 the 'bracing' took on a new twist: By early-November we had to maneuver with our back to the wall of the hallway while being at a full brace. Not fun at all, inching along the wall. My room, Turrell 206, was in the center of the hallway so we had the longest distance to go to get out of the dorm. One morning, I left my room a few minutes early to make sure I was on time for breakfast formation. I made it all the way to the stairwell door. All of a sudden, bursting out of his room was my squad sergeant, Bob Gardill, a very sturdy gentleman who was a lineman on the football team. He accidentally (I think) stepped square on the toe of my right shoe, causing a spider-web like effect of the layers of Kiwi. So much for the spit shine! Anyway: The formation was held, and the announcement was made that there would be an inspection of the ranks. SGT Gardill proceeded to inspect the members of the squad, got to me, looked down at my shoes and said quite loudly: "Five demerits, Eckard, unshined shoe." I think they were my only demerits in all four years!

Al Peck:
Atlantic City, The Little Army Navy Game

In 1963, the admissions department of Pennsylvania Military College welcomed me into the freshman class of Cadets. A proficient enough football player, I made the starting team at the right guard during the third game when fate intervened, and the starting right guard endured an injury. Played my entire Freshman and Sophomore year but sadly, I blew out my left leg my junior year, ending my career.

Back in the day, PMC and the Merchant Marine Academy based on Long Island played what was dubbed the "Little Army Navy Game." The protagonists confronted each other in Convention Hall in Atlantic City, NJ. Yes, in the Hall. Back in the sixties, Convention Hall was a big deal. The Convention Hall hosted The Miss America Pageant and received conventions, conferences, and a variety of events during the year. The Miss America Pageant has absolutely dwindled in popularity in recent years, but it had substantial TV ratings. The Convention Center floor was just spacious enough to incorporate a football field. When you entered the building and cleared the ticket booth, the mezzanine stairs and the end line of the field greeted you. If a player ran through the end line, they had to avoid the ticket booths. It was tight. The other end zone finished at the stage, which held the Pageant. A facade of about five feet rose from the floor, holding the stage. Grounds crew protected the front of the stage with hanging green mats. Only short plays could be planned for that goal line. Sod was brought in and placed on the concrete floor, covering the field. Some under matting was under the sod to make it relatively softer when you struck the ground.

The big game was on Thanksgiving weekend, and it was televised on a local Philadelphia CBS station. No ESPN+, we had seven channels on regular TV to choose. My mother not a big fan of watching me play football. Because I played right guard, I usually found myself in the middle of the pile, and she would hold her breath until 67 appeared on two feet. As a result, she, and thus my father, did not come to many games. Since this game was on TV, they preferred to watch from their hotel room.

In 1965, PMC was the home team so we were clad in our white uniforms with red and gold trim, and red helmets. The reason I mention this is the colors stood out easily on TV. This final game, televised, tradition, and ample pageantry took place before the game.

Both teams' band marched, and PMC's highly accomplished Pershing Rifles Drill Team demonstrated its prowess. With no opportunity to practice on the field before the game, our cleats hit the sod for the first time during pregame warmups. As we tried out the field, the TV commentator interviewed the team captains. I did not worry about being interviewed as a sophomore.

If memory serves me right, the kickoff was at 3 pm. The game started when the director standing next to the camera motioned to the referee. We won the toss, I remember, because I was on the kickoff team. As the game progressed, we were not doing well. Our defense was holding up, but the offense could not move the ball. Suddenly, on a screen pass, our halfback broke free. I was part of the screen and when he started down field, I followed him. One of the Merchant Marine closed fast. Rules for blocking were considerably relaxed in those days. We could cross block and leave our feet. I set up the angle of trajectory and threw my body in front of his. The defender crashed into me, and the halfback scored. The TV producers showed the play on replay a couple of times. Notice I did not say instant replay. I took the TV crew time to set up the replay. We scored.

At the beginning of the second half, we were behind by a couple of touchdowns and backed up against our own end zone. The quarterback took the snap. He handed off to the fullback. A Merchant Marine came flying through the line and slammed into the fullback. The pig skin dislodged and bounced into the end zone. If one of them fell on the ball, they would have another touchdown. I happened to be the closest Cadet to the elusive football. I took a few steps and dove onto the prize.

The force of my landing dislodged the sod and propelled me forward. We were at the stage end of the field. The protective green mats that covered the stage wall were curled at the ends, exposing the concrete wall. The brown ball, the green sod and the red white and gold me careened headfirst between the two curled mats, smack into the stage. I bounced backward, but the oncoming Marines pushed my dazed body, still clutching my captive, back into the platform. All the Marines ran into the mats. Not me—back into the stage. I lay motionless for a few seconds as the coaches and medics came rushing on the field. Taken off the field on my own power, I sat out a few plays and then returned to the field to finish the game.

This was my great moment. What makes this disastrous "touch back" a great moment? The TV producers stepped in and made a replay of the event in agonizing slow motion. My head bouncing off the stage and then bouncing back, followed by half the Marine team jumping on my back, and the mass of humanity crumpled against the stage. CBS replayed the incident several times during the game, during the post-game show, and on the evening news that night. Everyone, including my mother, saw it.

My mother, by all reports, became frantic. No cell phones and no way of contacting me, she had to wait. This was one of her worst nightmares. She calmed down when she saw me walk back onto the field. Little did she know I apparently had a concussion. With no concussion protocols, I have no personal memory of the game or disaster. The only reason I can report my great moment in any detail is I viewed every minute of the replay that night.

Brian P. LaBar:
Freshman Football

Despite what the yearbook says, I only played one year of football and that was by mistake. I will explain a little later. I am from the Allentown, Bethlehem, Easton (ABE) area of Pennsylvania where we had some great high school football teams and very talented players.

My recollection is that there were six freshman players from the ABE area, and we all started. I loved the game of football; however, I originally did not intend to play at PMC. I used to go to practice every day and throw the football around with the team managers. Eventually, the Freshman team had a scrimmage and during the game one of the running backs (Dusty Miller, Hellertown, PA) sustained a double ACL tear from a horse collar tackle. I played against Dusty in high school.

From what I was told, the coach (a local high school teacher) visited Dusty in the hospital, and they were discussing who would replace him at his running back position. This is when Dusty mentioned my name, that he played against me, and that I was at practice every day. The next practice, which I believe was the following Monday, I was at practice doing my thing with the team managers when the coach came over and asked if my name was LaBar. We talked a little and he eventually told me to go get some equipment and come back out to practice. This was the beginning of the most enjoyable football season I played. There was some great talent on the team that went 8/9-0-1. Just to name a few: McGuiney, Baum, Grove, Fiesta, Anderson

Dick Anderson was great broken-field runner who played left halfback, and watching him run was something to behold. Nick Fiesta was a tackle and our punter; he eventually left PMC and went to West Chester University to play. I played defense, special teams, and right halfback, which was the position that was used as the blocking back and to run plays into the game.

My recollection of the season was that the coach didn't expect us to win because after each game he would say that we played above our heads. We went on to be undefeated, whether it was eight or nine games, I don't remember. The season didn't end with our last scheduled game. They wanted to keep the freshman team intact to scrimmage the varsity and help them prepare for the Boardwalk Bowl. This meant we were going to have to practice with no incentive to do so for an additional two weeks. So, they scheduled one more game for us in order to keep us interested in practice to be beat up by the varsity.

They told us that we had one more game to play and to suit up in our game uniforms on a Saturday morning. We were out on the field warming up when the buses pulled up with our opponent. It was the University of Penn (obviously not their starting units). This game was a little faster and harder hitting than I had ever played in. We played them to a 0-0 tie.

David Fiedler:
The Seven Nickels

The day that the 4th class system was put into effect for the class of '68, I was called out into the hallway on the 2nd floor of Turrell Hall. At the end of the hallway was an old-fashioned pay phone, the kind with coin slots on the top. If you remember, for local calls you deposited a dime for three minutes, for out of the area calls a recording came on telling you to deposit additional money, and for long distance the operator came on and told you how much to deposit. As the coins went in, different audio chimes were heard so the amount of money you put in would tally in the system. For long distances, the operator could hear the chimes and know how much you deposited. The whole process was manual and depended on mechanical coin slots and the audio chimes in order to charge for the call. The upper classmen gave me seven nickels and I was told to deposit them in the nickel slot and either hang up or hit the coin return, get the money back, and keep repeating until told to stop, OR when the nickels fell into the return slot WITHOUT any other action.

I kept this up for days along with other classmates until one day the seven nickels came back to the coin return slot WITHOUT doing anything else. The upper classmen knew that this meant that the mechanical balance in the phone was worn out, but the system would still hear the chimes as you dropped in the money. Instead of the money going into the money box, it would pop out into the coin return. All coins, not just nickels, would come right back to the coin return slot on the bottom of the phone.

After this action, there was always a long line of cadets in the hall making free phone calls. I watched a classmate call Hawaii and drop the same quarters over and over again into the phone from the return slot. I did the same with my calls home to New York. The phone company could never figure out how we were doing it. First, they thought we had a key to the money box since there were no jimmy marks on the box, but it was empty. They put a jimmy proof coin box on the phone, but that didn't work. They then put an "armor" box around the phone, but that didn't work either! Then they replaced the phone, but we did the same thing over with the seven nickels.

I don't know how many free phone calls were made from that phone, but there must have been hundreds. Finally, the phone company removed the phone, but we just went on to another one on the 3rd floor and did it again. When you have unlimited manpower (4th class), you can do this stuff!!!

David Fiedler:
Cadets and their M-1 Garands

Upon reporting for cadet basic training, a new PMC cadet began a very close relationship with his M-1 Garand rifle. When they issued it to you, it usually came with a little ditty that said, "US Rifle caliber .30, always rusty, always dirty." It became your job to make sure that neither happened to the rifle that PMC gave you! The good part of that was that if you were working on your rifle, the upper classmen would not harass you. Your rifle was your constant companion for at least two years since privates and corporals carried one. If you got promoted in your last two years, you had a sword or a saber and no longer had your M-1 to worry about. Four-year privates, like me, had one for all four years. You trained with it, you kept it in perfect shape, and if you screwed up you slept with it!!!

PMC Cadet basic training began with learning the manual of arms in accordance with Army Field Manual 22-5, supplemented by PMC regulations. One of the drill movements was "inspection arms" where you brought your M-1 across your chest, grabbed the operating rod handle, and threw the bolt open so that an inspecting officer could look into the inner workings of the weapon. The next movement was "order arms" where you closed the bolt, pulled the trigger to release the firing pin spring, and lowered the weapon to your side. In order to close the bolt, you had to insert your thumb into the receiver and push down on the magazine follower to release the bolt. We were very carefully instructed that when lowering the magazine follower, you MUST keep the heel of your hand against the operating rod handle very tightly or the bolt would close on your thumb with the full force of the operating rod spring.

If you screwed this up, you would get a nasty bruise under your thumb nail that would be very painful and last for weeks. This bruise was known as M-1 thumb! In my company as the cadre went down the line ordering each cadet to "order arms" at least five screams could be heard as rifle bolts slammed into thumbs. These five were then made to fall out in front of the company where they were chewed out for not following instructions. Talk about learning the hard way!!

In my company, we had a very sharp cadet corporal (a classmate) who thought he was the sharpest cadet ever. He was in the Ranger

Platoon, the Pershing Rifles, and on the rifle team. We had an ROTC rifle inspection scheduled one Saturday morning and the night before he made sure that his M-1 was perfect. That night after taps a few of the jokers got into the rifle rack and disconnected the magazine follower from the latch that held it. They then tied a string around the follower and tied the other end to something in the ammunition well. When the "perfect" cadet came to inspection arms in front of the ROTC officer (a major), the magazine follower flew out, almost hitting the major in the eye, bounced off his cap brim, bounced off the cadet's chest, and then hung by the string about a foot from the rifle. All around tried to keep a straight face, but the major broke up. It was pretty funny, but a message was sent.

One of the most feared events in a cadet year was the annual inspection by the First U. S. Army headquarters (HQFUSA). FUSA was the higher headquarters to which our ROTC detachment reported, and the inspection was an important rating factor for ROTC. Part of the inspection included an "in ranks" inspection of the Corps of Cadets. In my rook year the cadet chain of command decided that we would look "super sharp" for this inspection, but we resented that we would be inspected by some junior officer from FUSA. The word was passed that if the open ranks inspecting officer was not a captain or higher, then we would do what was called "thumb" our M-1's at the inspector.

The drill was that we would open ranks and the inspecting officer would march down the ranks and randomly turn in front of a cadet and reach for his rifle to inspect it. Our instructions were that if you were the one the inspector chose, as soon as his hand started to move up to take the M-1, you would flip the rifle with our thumbs right at his chest with all the force you could muster. Thumbing the rifle that way was commonly done in the Pershing Rifles drill team, and it looked sharp because the inspecting officer was prepared for it.

Sure enough, in my Rook year FUSA sent a new lieutenant to do the in ranks inspection. As luck would have it, the lieutenant stopped and turned in front of the best "flipper" in my company! As soon as his arm moved, the M-1 flew at his chest and he was not prepared for it. The guy caught the rifle by the front sight and held it before it hit the ground. All could see that the sight gave him a small cut on his hand. The lieutenant was actually pretty cool. He returned the M-1 properly and marched on down the ranks. He NEVER stopped and turned in front of another cadet. In my next three years, the inspecting officer was always a captain or a major. Message sent and received, I guess. No one in the ROTC detachment ever said a word about it, but I am sure that they knew!

If you lived like we lived (the reason for your effort), you did these things for entertainment I suppose!!!!

Byron Wood Daniels:
Lessons Learned

I came from a very patriotic, lower middle-class home with a Mother's shielding protection from most of the exposure I believed my peers experienced growing up in rural Kansas. So, when we moved to Northern Virginia, I left behind my plans to attend the University of Kansas and eventually found PMC. Its restrictions on all of us offered me the opportunity to learn to compete on an equal basis so that I could acquire the skill sets to survive in the adult world. I knew that my parents would not be able to provide attractive clothing, an automobile, or funds for dining, dating, or entertainment. So the uniforms, marching, restrictions to campus, and to foot travel were equally attractive to my parents and to me.

After surviving the rigors of my Rook year, I needed to make up some classes in the more relaxed Summer Sessions. There I met and became friends with a cadet in the year ahead of me, Gilbert Fagiani. This was the first Upperclassman in my life that I could talk with as well as do things with in a relaxed, normal manner. Gil later was graduated from PMC, got into trouble with drug addiction, turned his life around, and became a Counselor helping other addicts overcome their addiction. Before he passed away, he wrote a book about his cadet life, which he autographed for me. The book described a Life Lesson which I remembered that he had passed onto me on how to deal with the predations of Upperclassmen.

When he was a Rook, he would frequently skip eating the Mess Hall Meal III, and get a Cheesesteak ETB (Everything But Peppers), which still is a fond memory for me from Fran 'n' Nan's. However, its enticing aroma would draw one of his Cadre Corporals who would follow his nose to Gil's room. When he'd enter, Gil would of course, have to brace to attention and then watch with dismay as the purposefully left unnamed, Cadre Corporal would eat most of Gil's dinner with glee in his eyes. This seemed as if it would never cease, so Gil came upon the plan to order his next cheesesteak WITH EXTRA, EXTRA PEPPERS.

The next night, true to the pattern, the Corporal came down, grabbed the cheesesteak, and wolfed down a couple of bites before he realized that something was dreadfully wrong and bolted out of the room. When they next encountered, the Corporal asked about why Gil had changed the cheesesteak. Gil just replied that he'd discovered that he liked peppers. He never ordered a cheesesteak with peppers again but was never bothered by the Corporal either.

A couple of years later, I was a Cadet Sergeant in my second semester and pretty much a "Made Man" as a Fraternity Frater. I'd acquired some social skills to survive in an all-male military school, but I was still financially poor. One of my delights was treating myself to a $.15 grape soda for evening study hours from the vending machine on First Floor Howell. My roommate, Bulldog, was my Fraternity Brother and Cadet Sergeant, but was a little more equal than me as a double letterman in varsity wrestling and football. That and the money provided from his parents in addition to our $40/month ROTC contract money helped him have a larger social life as well. Bulldog was a massive presence in our small room and would always take his turn first in such things as combing his sparse hair in front of the mirror and so forth. However, one night he started crossing the line. He would enter our room, snatch my still sweating grape soda and gulp most of it down while looking at me. Why? Because he could.

Eventually I remembered one of the lessons that Gil had passed onto me for this sort of situation. I took the empty grape soda can that I had saved from the previous night and urinated into it. I set the can into its usual place and the trap was set. I wondered if Bulldog would sense the difference in temperature or the lack of condensation on the can. The door opened and I waited. Sure enough the Bulldog took the bait. After several sips instead of gulps this time, he stopped. He looked at the can and said, "Tastes kinda salty." Then the look of realization spread to his countenance of what had just happened. He asked me why I had a can of urine on my desk? I replied that the can was left over from the night before and I'd used it to relieve myself instead of walking down the hall to the latrine. Later he repeatedly denied that he'd commented on the salt content of the liquid in the grape soda can and I never asked him how he knew what urine tasted like.

Although, the Bulldog would later joke about him swiping the grape soda can on my desk, he never drank from it. We ran into each other decades later at a Widener Homecoming Football game and he told me of some resentment he had against me for something involving my wise mouth used against him in our room. I didn't recall at all but deeply apologized for hurting him so and we still remain friends and Fraters, 54 years after Graduation and Commissioning.

David Fiedler:
South American multi-millionaire

Among the Rooks of "C" Company in 1964 was the real-life son of a South American multi-millionaire named Armondo Irrizary. This guy was a true South American playboy!!! For the two months he stayed at PMC, I knew him quite well.

Armondo was sent to PMC by his parents, believing that PMC discipline would cure him of his playboy ways and prepare him for a spot among the highly wealthy society that he came from. Armondo had no desire to change his ways and did everything he could to get thrown out. I believe the school turned a blind eye to his antics because they were after a large donation and possibly more South American cadets. Many of his shortcomings were officially attributed to language difficulties, claiming that he just did not understand his instructions, yet in the classroom he performed quite well. He was far from a dummy. Even the ROTC instructors laid off him, probably because the government did not want to piss off a powerful South American ally. The same with the Commandant's staff and the cadet chain of command. After all, he was not an American citizen so ROTC could care less. I hung out with him quite a bit and can tell you he always spoke perfect English to me.

One day his wish finally did come true. He discovered the one cadet sin that would not be tolerated was stealing. Lying and cheating maybe not so much. SO, one day down in the cadet store in front of "Doc" the retired professor who ran the store, he shoplifted a couple of bars of soap. Doc of course turned him in to the Commandant

(General Biddle) who of course took the action required since Armando was only too happy to confess to the crime.

The next day he was gone, and many wondered why a guy who was heir to such immense wealth had to steal 30 cents worth of soap. I knew the answer. He was very clever and knew how to use the system to get what he wanted.

Byron Daniels:
Won't be Long Now

Due to my Father's career at the Federal Aviation Administration, we moved from rural Kansas to northern Virginia during my senior year in high school. The plan to go away to the University of Kansas was as gone as my parents' promise to give me a car that year. It appeared as if I would never escape my mother's apron strings. The new plan that seemed to be shaping up was for me to walk to George Mason Community College. Then it was a one building institution, literally within sight of our new apartment. I was going to be walking to school as I'd done my entire life. This very protective upbringing did not include much beyond walking everywhere and studying so I could go to away to college.

Furthermore, I could never convince my parents of my need for more than two school shirts for each season and three sets of underwear. Want to go on a date? If Dad was off shift work, my parents would drive my date and me. I knew I needed socialization or as an Admiral, I later worked for called it, "wire scrubbing."

Somehow, I convinced my parents to send me to PMC instead. This was what I thought would be a more difficult path than the one my parents were contemplating. Our mutual goal was for me to be the first college educated offspring from amongst my Father's generation of siblings which was descended from their Assyrian immigrant parents. It also had the lesser but included goal of becoming an officer when it came time for me to perform my two years of military service. Dad loved his time of service in WWII, but not how he was treated as enlisted.

I was assigned to be a Bravo Company Rook. Unlike other companies, our Rooks were housed in two locations: 1st floor Turrell Hall and 3rd floor Howell Hall. On 1st Floor Turrell, I recall there were about ten of us Bravo Rooks but most from Charlie Company Rooks. That was somewhat isolating because the bonding, friendship, and consolation that comes from shared misery during the early Rook period was confined to our small group of ten. The rest of the Bravo Company Rooks were forming its own cohesive unit up on Howell Hall.

Then one of those life's learning opportunities that I'd yearned for in my quest to become wire scrubbed presented itself. I'd been assigned to be the roommate of our future Fourth Class President, but future end of year dropout, George. George seemed more mature, had a great military bearing, and seemed to have gone through every grade in military schools. So, he knew how to march; press his pants; shine his shoes, and generally look superior, especially compared to awkward me. Sometime during the Fall, as classmates would drop out, George decided he would complain about me and end up with a private room.

I don't know what he said, but I ended up far away from my little support group and on Third Floor Howell with a trail of at least rumors about me in those days before social media in those days before cyber bullying. I never heard but only kind of assumed they existed, although I could not imagine what they could have been about. My new roommate, Jimmy McBride, also a product of military schools, was wary of me. Later we became friends, and I became his Fraternity Brother, but at that room reassignment made me the F**king New Guy or FNG.

So, I became isolated and almost shunned by my peers. I struggled militarily and found college classes more difficult than rural Kansas high school classes were. I felt lonely, blue, and running out of hope on this long, almost impossibly arduous path of my choosing. One gray Pennsylvania day slipped into another. What had I done?

It was then that I was told of this security guard on Third Floor Howell, Ernie, who would offer a cheery phrase of hope. He seemed the only person older than us who was not looking to correct or punish us. In fact, he'd offer a friendly smile and a phrase of encouragement. Huh? Who was this Angel boosting cadet morale? Then one evening, as I was squaring around the fire extinguisher to return to our room from the bathroom before Lights Out, I encountered him.

Ernie was a slim black man about 5'8" or more who would walk quickly between stations where he would retrieve a key that he would insert into this drum that hung over his shoulder. He always seemed to wear a black leather jacket and a matching Outer Hebrides style cap. Ernie always seemed clean but not in the smooth-shaven department. His gait was quick and stiff legged, almost as if he was falling forward, drug down or towards the next key station by either the weight of his drum or its mysterious magnetic pull towards the next key station. I remember telling Jimmy that night that I'd seen Ernie. He asked, "What did he say?" I answered that he's said, "Won't be long now" and kinda smiled. Jimmy said that he always said that. We both wondered what he meant by the statement, but sleep enshrouded us before we figured it out.

Eventually, survivors of that ongoing Rook year would talk about him and to him and on until our commencement. We'd learn that he never said anything other than, "Won't be long now." Sometimes, early on, we'd wondered if there was a dorm fire would he have done anything but walk past it to turn the next key. Eventually, when we became non-Rooks or Old Men of The Corps we initiated the exchange greetings with Ernie, "Won't be long now." It became a phrase we used amongst ourselves. Eventually, I think most of us knew he was watching out for us and lifting our spirits with his greeting that filled us with a bit of a smile. I know he helped a number of us to be cheered so that our difficult paths would be. "Not too long now." Our class came to quip "Won't Be Long Now" and one class had a yearbook page dedicated to him. I thank Ernie and wish him to know that his greeting helped me though.

My first roommate, George, decided to quit going to classes his second semester and just lift free weights in his private room. He told me he'd decided during the Spring semester of 1965 to enlist in the US Marines and fight in Vietnam and so he was exercising to be in good shape for that. Jimmy became a civilian in Penn Morton College. I don't think he graduated with our class. The last I talked with him, he'd become a representative of expensive socks for men on the Eastern Seaboard and then he died young. Ernie was there when we were graduated on May 26, 1968. I still thank him, and I hope to see him in Heaven. "It won't be long now."

David Fiedler:
So It Begins

The class of 1968 reported to the campus in late August 1964. At first, things were relatively quiet, we received several orientation briefings on the school facilities, we were introduced to key faculty and administration personnel, were sworn into ROTC, given tours of the campus facilities and the still under construction Kirkbride Hall, taught the elements of close order drill (IAW FM 22-5 (Dismounted Drill (School of the Soldier)), and given endless batteries of tests to determine our math and writing skills. We were issued our M-1 rifles and taught how to clean, assemble, and disassemble them. We were also given classes on how to wear the uniforms and what their configurations were, issued our infamous "red book" of cadet regulations, introduced to our roommates, and learned how to make our beds and polish shoes and brass to PMC cadet standards. All this was done quietly with barely a voice being raised by our ever-helpful cadre. We even had free movies shown to us in the alumni auditorium.

After about a week of this, we were all marched into the "Old Main" Assembly Room and given a pep talk about how we were the largest class in history. Then a senior member of the cadre addressed us and said, "Class of '68 congratulations, you have matriculated into the best of seven colleges that the Department of the Army has designated as 'Senior Military Colleges.' This institution will like all the others now take away from you all of your God given rights and we will give them back to you one by one as privileges. Gentlemen of the class of 1968, the 4th class system is now in effect!!! Good luck, I hope you have the courage to survive!"

Then all hell broke loose! We were marched back to the barracks where the previously friendly cadre had us bracing against the walls and we were told just how low we were! We performed numerous pushups and sit-ups as the cadre tore up our neatly arranged rooms. The corporals screamed at us, "You ain't Joe College anymore, mister, that dream is over, and that boat has sailed!" Our 1st Sergeant took a more philosophical approach and stated, "This is the life you chose, so deal with it."

The rest is history, some dropped out and left, some failed academically and left, the rest of us became a band of brothers and lived together as soldiers for the next four years. When we started, cadets could not leave the Corps without sitting out a semester and reapplying to Penn Morton College. BUT after our first year or so, Dr Moll changed that policy and you could just walk across the street after you had a bad day and become a civilian student. We lost a few brothers that way, which really hurt the rest of us.

For the majority of the class of 1968, we adapted, adjusted, and overcame until graduation.

David Fiedler:
The Paper

In 1964, like every other Rook, I was enrolled in MS-I (military history). Our teacher was LTC Henry Phillips, the PMC PMS himself. On the first day of class, Phillips showed up with a large cardboard box full of little slips of paper. He then broke us up into two-man teams, my teammate was Karl Kotch who was in my company (C) and was also a science/engineering major. Every slip of paper had a topic on it.

Our slip of paper says, "The German invasion of France in 1914 has failed to take Paris and defeat the French army. Tell me why and name the officer responsible, minimum paper length 10 pages (typewritten)." Philips also made some crack about how since we both had German names, this should be easy for us! Well, Karl and I were both science majors. We had no time to write a 10-page paper on military history. Time marched on and then we realized that the semester was coming to a close and we had no paper to submit to LTC Phillips. On the weekend before the paper was due, we finally took action. I went to the library and took out every book on World War I they had. Karl had a typewriter, so I dictated, and he typed. I grabbed paragraphs and facts from a dozen different books, threw in a lot of plain bull analysis, and we stopped when we reached 10 pages. We did name a German Field Marshal as the officer responsible, and we had lots of quotes from both contemporary and later German Field Marshals on the subject and on the officer responsible. We even threw in some quotes from Kaiser Wilhelm III on the subject because the quotes helped greatly to fill up the pages.

Well, Phillips grades the papers and returns them to us at the end of the semester. And even though it was one afternoon's work full of bulls**t and quotes from obscure German Field Marshals, we not only got an A we got an A+. You should have heard the nasty remarks from our classmates about that and how it "pulled up the grade curve." The average grade was between C+ and B-, except for us. After a bunch of this harassment, Karl finally shot back and said, "Don't look at me, I only typed, the Field Marshal over there was the one who dictated the paper." Well after that, the name stuck for the next three and one half years I was either THE FIELD MARSHAL, or FIELD MARSHAL FIEDLER among the class of 1968. I thought it was quite funny!

It gets better, fast forward about 25 years and I am working at Fort Monmouth on a major project called the Army Battle Command System (ABCS). I am working closely with the British exchange officer who was Major Mark Vincent who also just happened to be the son of Field Marshal Vincent, chief of the British Imperial General Staff. I was asked to brief the Field Marshal (a very nice guy by the way) who came to Fort Monmouth under the cover of visiting his son on the ABCS. Over lunch I told the above story when talking about my cadet days at PMC. He laughed and said, "Well, it is always nice to meet a colleague." I guess the class of 1968 was correct.

David Fiedler:
Food

In 1964, I was working in the MacMorland Center as a waiter and later (1965-1968) as an assistant cook. As such, I was very familiar with how the Slater/ARA food system worked.

In the Fall of 1964, my friend Brian Kates said to me, "I have an old high school girlfriend who is going to Swarthmore. Let's go over there and impress the girls with our uniforms and other cool military stuff." Little did I know that Swarthmore was a Quaker school, and the girls were not impressed at all. Anyway, we are sitting on the Great Lawn talking to the girlfriend and her friends and the subject of college food comes up. One of the girls said to me, "We have the Slater food system, and the food is great!!!" I said to her, "We have a Slater food system also, and we hate it."

The next day I go back to my kitchen job, and I have a conversation with the Slater guy about why Swarthmore food is so much better than ours. Turns out Slater had three levels of food service (A, B, and C) and Swarthmore had A level and PMC had C level. This meant they got steaks and chops, and we got hamburgers, pasta, and potatoes, except for special occasions. The conversation also revealed that Slater had an algorithm that predicted the number of meals to be served, the number of students who would not show up for meals, the reduced number of meals on weekends, etc.

Unfortunately for Slater, the algorithm did not match the cadet lifestyle. Slater's algorithm did not reflect that cadets did not have to go to class, but they did have to go to meals. It also did not recognize that instead of taking off on weekends like civilians did, the cadets had military training on Saturday so for sure the breakfast and lunch calculations for Saturday were out of whack with Slater's plans...and dinner probably was also. I asked him what this meant for us since Slater was trying to make a profit after all was said and done.

He said it means you cadets get more hamburger, potatoes, and pasta. It also meant the Fran and Nan's sub shop was going to make a fortune keeping us fed!! And they did. I had at least one cheese steak a week for four years!!

What finally made things change somewhat was the famous PMC food riot of November 1967. The poor quality of the food continued for years. I know because I helped to prepare it. One day, the cadets had hot dogs with all the fixings for lunch. Dinner that night was meat loaf which was not a popular dish. At one of the tables, it was discovered that the meatloaf contained chunks of hot dog left over from lunch. This discovery caused the pot to boil over. First words and then food began to fly. Tables were lifted and then dropped, Slater employees behind the steam tables brought out from the kitchen to serve additional food were bombarded with all sorts of missiles. The first shot fired in their direction was a baked potato thrown by a cadet 2LT (platoon leader). Things got worse seconds later when the Brigade Adjutant announced from the command group table that "You may leave when you are finished rioting." I do not recall who the Military Officer In Charge was that evening, but he was nowhere to be seen. The cadet chain of command also went into hull defilade.

The next morning when I reported for work, I expected to see a wrecked cadet dining hall, but to my amazement, everything was back in its place as if nothing had happened. Full time Slater/ARA staff hardly talked about the riot at all. I had no clue who put the dining facility back together from the wreck that it was. I was usually on the cleanup crew in order to make some money, but not that night. The Corps marched into breakfast as normal, and the breakfast was slightly better than it had been.

The next day a delegation went to see Dr. Moll. I have no clue who appointed them or how they were chosen (probably by the Commandant who I think was Colonel O'Hara at that time). The delegation had with them a sample of the hotdog meatloaf (don't ask me how, no clue). After that, the quality of the food improved, but not by much.

Alfred J. Peck:
Service Agencies. My Cannon Let Me Down

On my high school 1964 senior trip to Gettysburg, I purchased a miniature smoothbore, Civil War 1857 Field Gun, 12 Pounder, Napoleon Cannon. I arranged the ordnance on my dresser at home to remind me of an extremely successful trip. There it rested through high school graduation and the summer. In August of 1964, as I was packing to travel to Pennsylvania Military College, the cannon suggested an obvious military image to bring. It slid into my suitcase. Eventually, the little black cannon with the brass barrel became an ornament on my desk at PMC.

For the uninitiated, Freshman at PMC became designated Rooks. Rooks ranked lower than whale dung. We had no privileges except those granted us by the upperclassmen. Inspection of your room, clothing, and rifle occupied a good part of the first three weeks after arrival. Unexpectedly, every so often we would be rousted out of bed at 3 am to have a mattress check. The idea is to strip our beds and bring the mattresses into the hall to insure you had a mattress. After that, you lugged your mattress back to your bunk.

No sleeping yet. Immediately, the command was given, "Prepare the rack military style and stand for inspection." The cadre would inspect your efforts. Unfortunately, the Cadre all looked so wide awake. If they could not bounce a quarter off the bed, the inspector would pull your rack apart. You obediently remade the space you profoundly wished to lie in and formerly stood inspection again.

You can ask any PMC cadet about their red blanket. There are many stories. White glove inspections were on every Saturday morning. The inspections were known as white glove because the cadre sported white gloves. The room had to be spotless. Shoes must be spit shined until the officer viewed his reflection while standing in front of you. Floors meticulously shined, clothing properly hung or folded. Of course, bunks perfectly made. In our lowly station as Rooks, perfection was a distant dream. The upper classmen always found something out of place or overlooked.

Rooks' bondage ended on Lincoln's birthday. Three Saturdays before Freedom Day, the Corps, as usual, conducted a Saturday White Glove inspection. By this stage, the Rooks understood all the tricks the upperclassmen would perpetrate during inspection. The top of the door produced dust. The bottoms of your shoes and boots are dirty. Pay attention Rook, these uniforms are 3cm out of line. Your laundry bag did not belong at the end of your bed. Nothing should be on the windowsill. Your desk chair is out of line. Waxing, spit shining, button, and belt buckles polishing, and checking each other's uniform alignment developed into a routine. My bunk mate, Pat Quinn, and I turned into shining stars for Saturday inspection.

Prior to this upcoming inspection, we endured physical discipline for rule breaking. Any infractions of the rules or protocol, you received pushups or extra duty. "Drop for ten" became a command heard around the campus. The punishment could be doled out for looking at an officer the wrong way. The only place safe from pushups became the classroom. "Drop for ten." Unfortunately, starting this week, added to our retribution could be demerits. An infraction of any reason warranted demerits. You received one demerit or multiple demerits, depending on the transgression. The possibility of gaining demerits from cadet with higher rank loomed. Lower than whale dung, anyone might give a Rook a demerit, even a senior private.

A captain, lieutenant, and a Sergeant from another company formed an inspection team. The Sergeant, the designated recorder, penned for any violation announced. The room occupants stood at rigid attention, bracing, one at either end of the bunk as a crashing open, hoping for the best. God forbid you looked at the entering group while the entourage arrived with exemplary dignity and intent purpose. At that moment, the inspection would begin. Pat and I had worked extra hard and long for this inspection. We did not want demerits. The inspection progressed well for as uttered a little, very tiny, acknowledgement of our efforts. As the team readied themselves to exit, it looked like we were home free.

At that moment of our triumph, the captain peered at my desk. With his best military bearing, he approached my desk and ceremonially raised my cannon. Knowing the cannon wheels were dust catchers, I took extra care to clean the spokes. All brass must be polished, so the brass barrel reflected sunlight. The captain twirled the cannon around like inspecting a rifle on the drill field. As he looked down the barrel, the little voice in my brain started me worrying.

While holding the cannon, the captains' eyes grew dim, and the corners of his mouth quivered. His attitude revealed disgust, as the captain unceremoniously returned the cannon to the desk. He turned sharply toward me. His eyes pierced mine, proclaiming, "Sergeant, three demerits, dirty bore."

With that order, the captain pivoted toward the door and marched out with the Lieutenant and Sergeant in hot pursuit. My souvenir from Gettysburg just cost me my first demerits. They would not be my last. As the inspection team disappeared through the door, I relaxed and stared at my cannon. Pat consoled me on my demerits, while I plucked up the cannon from my desk and spied down the bore. Without doubt, in the smooth bore, minute flakes of dust became visible. I had no argument. Even if I complained, no one but Pat would listen. The bore received a Q-Tip on every inspection after that. The cannon remained on my desk all four years.

David Fiedler:
The Phantom (authored by Bill Luckenbill)

A small part of PMC history that is often overlooked is the existence of the "phantom." Every class had one that seemed to materialize and be the champion of justice or in some cases a practical joke. He is responsible for painting the Dome pink one year and various other activities of a like nature. He also handed out justice when someone broke the code of loyalty, character, and integrity. The phantom would place well documented information into the hands of the military administration so that the wrongdoer could be punished properly. When someone was too overzealous in hazing or failed to maintain respect of their classmates, the phantom would sometimes intervene.

I can recall one occasion during my freshman year in Cann Hall when two cadre NCO's who roomed on the 2nd floor in the next building, Dorm 5, were on the list to be dealt with by the phantom, but the human fly, who still serves in a reserve component unit, scaled the corner of the building and went from windowsill to windowsill until arriving outside their room. He presented them with a food bomb, containing mustard, ketchup, onions, milk, and other things in a milk carton containing a black powder ignition device. I saw the flash, heard the bang, and watched the human fly drop from the windowsill and disappear. Sounds like a strange story, but Everitt and Dave Fiedler will verify it.

David Fiedler:
The Human Fly

As my roommate and I were studying for finals in the Spring of 1965 in our room on 2nd floor Turrell Hall, we looked across the quad and saw on the 2nd floor of Cann Hall someone open the end window (this was the latrine) and climb out. The cadet then pushed his leg out to the room next to the latrine window, balanced himself and stepped across the gap using the widow frame as a hand hold. He then opened the room window and disappeared inside the room. This kind of action was usually the precursor of a room wreck (common among the Corps jokers). This usually meant filling the room with crumpled newspaper or worse the feared BABO BOMB! The BABO bomb was a can of Babo powered cleanser wrapped with M-80 grenade simulators the result of which was white Babo powder all over everything in the room. Quite a mess. As we waited for the explosion, we were amazed to see the cadet return to the latrine window the same way he exited. We thought, why didn't he just leave by the room door. He didn't because he didn't want to be spotted. About a half hour passed, we were still at our desks, and we saw the cadet return and repeat the window climbing trick. We thought the fuse on the bomb must have gone out and he was back to fix it. In a few minutes he returned to the to the latrine window and was gone with still no explosion. The next day at dinner was read an expulsion order and then we found out the real story.

    The cadet who I can still name went into the room and stole a term paper that he knew was there. He then copied the paper. He then went back into the room and returned the paper. The next day he went to his professor and told him that he had lost the original of his paper BUT luckily, he had made a copy and was it okay for him to turn that in. The professor said sure, so he did. This professor had a reputation for not reading term papers. That was false, he did. The cadet was so stupid that he stole a paper from a cadet taking the same course with the same professor. The professor realized that he was reading the same paper twice, one original and one a copy with a dummied-up cover sheet.

He beat feet over to the Commandants office with the evidence. And that was the end of that. I think he was gone the next day. Pretty dumb to assume that the professor was not reading the term papers. The guy was a sophomore or a junior and should have known better. He also had a reputation for doing the window trick so often in order to trash targeted rooms that he was known in the Corps as the "human fly." Knowing both parts of the story, it didn't take the Commandant long to determine what happened and who it was.

David Fiedler:
Freak Out

There was another cadet that was a year ahead of me at PMC (class of '67). This guy seemed like the rest of us, but I guess he was a little bit nuts. The year was 1965 and we got the news that John Geoghegan, a former First Captain of the Corps had been killed in Vietnam while fighting with the 1CAV in the Ia Drang Valley. There was another former cadet also killed or seriously injured in the same battle.

The news about Geoghegan really freaked the guy out and he had a premonition that if he continued on with ROTC and got a commission he would be killed in Vietnam. In addition, he reasoned that if he left ROTC, they would change his draft status from 1ID (member of reserve component) to 2S (student) and this would get him drafted and again he would get killed in Vietnam.

He was in total freak-out mode so he went into the army regulations (AR's) in order to find out what would keep him out of the army. Too bad there was no Google in those days, his search would have been a lot quicker, but he dug out two reasons the army would reject him. Turns out that you can't be in the army if 1—you are "grossly ugly" or 2—if you are "morbidly obese." It was pretty hard to prove the ugly reason, judging by some of the characters I saw in the army, this regulation was not strictly enforced. The second reason (morbidly obese) was a lot easier to prove. The army defined morbidly obese as being 80 to 100 pounds above normal weight for your height.

This being the situation, this cadet decided to eat his way out of the army. He did not keep quiet about his plan, and it became widely known among the Corps. The Corps being the Corps immediately swung into action.

All kinds of food began to appear for him, particularly high fat and high sugar foods and snacks, in huge amounts. The waiters in the mess hall made sure that he had double and triple portions of everything. Everyone was in on the plot. The guy's weight just ballooned because he consumed everything in sight!!! He did manage to gain 80+ pounds over most of the academic year. He did not go to ROTC summer training at the end of his 3rd year and when he returned to campus senior year, he was truly morbidly obese. Willy Bell, the college tailor, made him uniforms that fit but just barely.

In the end, his plan was a success! ROTC dropped him, his local draft board didn't draft him, and he graduated from PMC!! My takeaway from this was to always read the Army regulations, knowing them can really help you under certain circumstances.

David Fiedler:
On The Run

In the Spring of 1965, I attended a PMC "mixer" held in MacMorland Center. I had no luck with the girls, but I did get a job cleaning up after the "mixer," thanks to the cadet cleanup crew employed to put the Center back together for mess-I the following day.

Around 2330 hours, I left the Center to put on my work uniform (gray chinos and gray shirt that made us look like gas station attendants, later replaced by army fatigues). Around 2350 hours, I left Turrell Hall for the short walk back to the Mac Center. Just as I was coming up to the ramp that led to the entrance to the dining room, a figure that I recognized as a popular football playing upperclassman ran past me heading down 14th street toward the Hyatt Armory at a high rate of speed.

I then heard a voice that I immediately recognized as General Biddle, the Commandant of Cadets yelling, "You there stop, halt where you are!" The reply from the speeding cadet was obscene as he passed the Armory, turned, and headed up Melrose Avenue in the direction of the parade ground. The General who was in his sixties but had the body of a 30-year-old athlete (even though we all thought his mind was gone) was in hot pursuit. The cadet football player though had quite a lead on him, and he too was fast.

Of course, the first thing out of my mouth to the few cadets around was, "What the hell is going on?" Turns out that the cadet football player was at the mixer and was a bit tipsy since a few of his classmates had snuck a bottle into the mixer. Drinking on or near campus (the so called "blue zone" at that time was grounds for instant dismissal). After the tipsy cadet left the mixer, he then decided to urinate in the street almost in front of General Biddle's house (since torn down) that was right next to MacMorland Center. As luck would have it, he was urinating just as the General came out to walk his dog.

It was later revealed to me that Biddle chased the cadet all the way down to the end of the campus and the cadet then made a right turn into what was then called Washington Park but is now the Widener field house and stadium area. Since we used Washington Park as a military training area, the cadet knew the terrain very well and managed to lose the pursuing General in the dark.

I and the others in the area all went quickly into MacMorland

Center so that if questioned we had an alibi as to where we were. We also prepared the Sergeant Schultz defense for ourselves. We saw nothing, we knew nothing, we were not in the area, we were inside the building. Also as it turned out, a cadet service cap was found in the street near the General's house, but it quickly disappeared along with the upperclassmen that had it.

The next day was Sunday and it passed quietly except the story got out in spite of instructions from the cadet chain of command to "dummy up." This was no problem since the cadet culprit was a very popular guy!

On Monday morning, the General and some of his staff came to morning formation, which was rare. They may have been trying to identify the transgressor or maybe they were looking for a cadet with no service cap, but it was to no avail. Nothing was ever officially said about the incident, and it just blew over. I kind of thought that some of the upper-class harassment eased up on those cadets who saw what happened, but it really did not matter since Mother's Day and recognition was only a few weeks away.

David Fiedler:
Cadet 1st Captain Norman Goldberg

Norman Goldberg '65 was appointed cadet 1st Captain in the middle of the 1st semester of academic year 64/65. He replaced the originally appointed cadet 1st Captain which was considered a very unusual event. Norm was an interesting guy. He was a sincere cadet that wanted to go to law school and also into the Army, and he did both.

One very cold Saturday night, probably in early November 1964, two cadets returned to campus via the train. They got off in Chester and took a cab from the train station to the campus. Got out of the cab and then took off without paying the driver. The driver, being pretty smart, went into the guard room in Howell Hall and rousted out the cadet OD. Apparently the MOIC was either not there or was not aware of what happened because no official report ever reached the Commandant, and no official action was ever taken, to my knowledge.

Unofficially, the cadet OD woke up Goldberg, the 1st Captain who made a beeline to Howell Hall before the cab driver could call the Chester Cops. Goldberg paid the driver out of his own pocket plus a handsome tip in order to keep him quiet, according to my sources who were privates of the guard that night.

Then all hell broke loose. Goldberg rounded up every cadet officer and NCO still on the campus that night. He then had them roust out every cadet on the campus. We were told to get to the quad in front of Howell Hall, "RIGHT NOW…no matter how you were dressed." Many reported with very little on and it was very cold! I was lucky, I managed to put on my rubber overshoes, my overcoat, and grab my scarf before they threw me out into the cold. When several hundred of us were out there in front of Howell Hall freezing, Goldberg appeared and started to harangue us about what kind of low life would steal from a working man. He then moved on to what an honor and privilege it was to be a cadet at PMC, then on to how the culprits had besmirched the reputation of the college, how anyone who could do such a thing deserved not to graduate and never to get a commission, how lucky we were to have the resources to go to PMC, and a few dozen other things. That speech still impresses me, I agreed with it all. After the speech, he said that we would all remain here until he found out who did it.

We stood there in the cold for I would say almost an hour, freezing our butts off. No one said a word because 99% of us could not have known who it was. Suddenly, Goldberg went into the guard room, came out a few seconds later, looked at us, and said, "You people and your code of silence piss me off. Dismissed!" We all went back to bed to thaw out.

The next day we all assumed that the two culprits must have been made known to Goldberg so there would be an SPO or worse in the next few days. I asked my 1st Sergeant about a week later and was told Goldberg was handling it within the cadet chain of command. Nothing was ever said after that. Apparently, the whole thing was kept within the Corps of Cadets and the school officially knew nothing about it.

Goldberg for this action in this instance, I think we all admired him. He probably saved the futures of two cadets and protected the reputation of the school and the Corps by his actions! Bravo, brother Norman!!

Thomas D. Caracciolo:
Memories

Who can forget Fran & Nan's cheesesteaks. He had that old station wagon loaded with boxes of food to be delivered to the dorms. The store had a shelf on one of the walls lined with PMC service caps that had been left to him. I admit, he made many deliveries to my room. I used much of my $50 monthly ROTC pay for it. Didn't like how many guys he extended credit to that he had to chase down at the end of the year to collect.

I have a vivid mental picture of the day we received our uniforms Rook year. Hung the garments in the closet, placed our shoes and boots on the bottom rack, caps and hats on the shelf, stuffed the cabinet with our sheets, towels, underwear, etc. That evening, members of the cadre came by for inspection! Everything, and I mean everything, ended up in a pile in the middle of the floor. We found out all clothing had to be zipped, buttoned, shoes and boots laced and tied. Items in the cabinet had to be folded behind 3x5 cards folded in thirds, and books lined up by height, and everything was organized by our cadet number. The cadre said they'd be back later for a re-inspection, what a night!

One snowy day we were assembled and marched out to the parade ground, 1st Battalion on one side, 2nd on the other, the two battalion staffs in the middle. They proceeded to make snowballs, yelled charge, and a great snowball fight ensued.

In November 1965 when we assembled for breakfast, we were informed of the death of John Geoghegan (*We were Soldiers Once*) at the Battle of Ia Drang and LZ X-Ray. It was a reminder of life's uncertainties. (six years later, I was called into the office of then MG Harold Moore, where he discussed Geoghegan when the general read in my folder that I also graduated from PMC).

John W. Stealey:
College and Scholarships

My four-year ROTC scholarship was good at any school that the Army would approve their engineering degrees. I really thought I would be going to the US Air Force Academy as I had good grades, played Sports on a B+ level, and was Squadron Commander of three different Civil Air Patrol Squadrons.

When I got the letter that said First Alternate, I still thought I was going. My Stepdad, West Point, Class of 1953, told me I better enlist and keep trying. A few days later, he said that there was a new program with two full ride scholarships for each state for engineering interested applicants. I applied and was told I was accepted if I could get accepted at three schools from the list they provided me within the new three days.

My Guidance counselor got me into all three schools, Michigan State, Valparaiso, and PMC. My Stepdad, since the family was at Ft Dix, suggested PMC. He had gone to VMI for one year before West Point.

My guidance counselor got me in by calling each school, with me sitting next to him at our high school. Great guy, retired military, and really went to bat for me. Besides, my high school girlfriend lived in Browns Mill and I figured we could see each other often! Incentive!

John W. Stealey:
Church

After I got to PMC, I did not see any college girls? I liked girls in high school, even if I was not good at talking to them.

I decided to go to Sunday School at the Provident Avenue First Methodist Church because I thought there had to be pretty girls there? Turned out there was! I met a redhead who drove her Daddy's car, a 1965 GTO Convertible, built just as great as I thought she was! We had a disagreement about something, and she decided to go on the Church hayride in October with another guy. Devastated!

While we were on the hayride, my redhead friend was necking with her date. I was sitting with a skinny Temple nurse at home for the weekend and decided to make her jealous by doing the same. That hayride date and I reconnected during my 2nd Class Year at USAFA. I was married to that good lady for 27 years! We have three great kids and 10 wonderful grandkids, and 1.5 great grandkids, with many more coming over the next 10 years, I am sure!

John W. Stealey:
Exam Time and Grades

Okay, getting called on the carpet by the head of ROTC at PMC is not a good thing! As I reported in, he said, "Cadet, Attention!" I guess I was not standing properly for him but after that order I was!

"About Face!! Pull down that map of Vietnam. Point out Tan Son Nhut on that map!"

"About Face!"

"Cadet, I see you are failing calculus!"

"If you don't at least get a B, I will have you shipped to Vietnam with a rifle in the next three months! Do you understand?"

"Yes, Sir!"

"Dismissed!"

The back story is that three of my friends did not regard Mrs. Wolfe, our calculus professor, very highly. Trying to be in with my friends, my roommate and two exact twins in our class, I went along with it. We would march in, do a left face, and say, "Take seats!" We would do that, never paying any attention to the lectures. I had passed calculus in high school and knew most of it anyway, and I was just being a smarty pants.

By the way, the Lt. Colonel scared me good enough that I got that B grade where I don't believe my classmates did. They would not be thrown out as I was already enlisted in the US Army and if they took away my scholarship, I would be heading to SE Asia, ASAP.

John W. Stealey:
Christmas Decorations

My roomie and I were told by upperclassmen to go "collect" some

Christmas decorations. We were told it was a tradition that had long been practiced at PMC. We did, tried not to damage anything, and brought back a wreath and a few lights. We then went back to our racks.

Suddenly the upperclassmen were in the hallways screaming for us to come out and stand in front of our rooms. We did. Fred was marched off and I was told to go to bed? Why did I get off? I had remembered to clean my face of the black paint we had put on for camo and Fred did not. When he went to join the formation, it was clear that he had been out in the night!

Small things can really get you in trouble sometime.

John W. Stealey:
West Chester State Teachers College

My roommate from Lancaster, Fred Sample, met a young lady from West Chester. He wanted to go on a date with her to a dance at that school. She would not go without her friend. Fred asked me to escort her friend. He told me I had to get my best dress uniform with all 42 buttons shiny and the girls would pick us up behind Old Main.

I got my uniform, ensured I was looking like the put together Cadet I was trying to be, and walked with Fred to the parking lot. As we approached, Fred said, "Look your date is in the front seat and she is already sitting on your side!" I was to drive, so Fred could neck with his date in the back. Yes, she was already sitting on both my side and her side! Fred's date told me she was the best cook she ever met! Great! Right??

As I got into the car, the young lady elbowed me and said, "We are going to a fun motel party after the dance!" I did not know at that time what a motel party was! We went to the dance and danced a lot, even swinging away the sash we borrowed from the upper classmen!

Off to the motel party with my date that probably outweighed me. She was pleasant and nice, but not my type! We were sitting together on the floor of the motel near the Philly airport when she asked if I would get her a beer.

Certainly. I marched over to the drinks and was getting her a beer when one of the civilian guys says, "Drink this first??" It was a bourbon chaser I had never ever had before. I drank it, took two beers for my date and I and sat down. I think I did that two more times?? Yikes!

I remember standing on the bed in my Dress Uniform, defending the guys in the Vietnam War where my Stepdad had served, from the anti-military rants of a few of the civilian guys there! I let them have it and then decided it was time to leave!

My date drove us back to PMC, and was very disappointed that I was on the Alpha roster and had to be in early??? The next day my parents came to a parade we were having for some holiday. As Right Guide, mom knew where I was standing. She said, "Honey your face is very red. Are you OK?"

"Certainly Mom, just hot in the sun!" or "Gee Mom, hangovers are GREAT!"

John W. Stealey:
Getting My Appointment to USAF Academy

Sometime in early May 1966, I learned my congressman, John O. Marsh, future Secretary of the Army, gave me the appointment to USAFA. He did confront my Stepdad, asking him if he had a son who wanted to go to USAFA. My Stepdad was a training officer at

Ft. Dix and often went to supervise Guard units on summer two-week active-duty stints.

A particular company commander had a company that did not do great during their two weeks active duty at Fort Lee, Va., according to my Stepdad. He berated the young captain about the company performance. The captain stood at attention and took it in saying, "Yes, Sir. We will try to do better Sir!" When my Stepdad said, "Dismissed," the captain asked, "Sir, may I ask a question?" My Stepdad was not happy with that but allowed him to ask his question. "Do you have a son that has asked for an appointment to the USAF Academy?" A bit shocked at that, my Stepdad asked him how he knew that. "Sir, I am your Congressman from Winchester, VA." WOW! Dad was a bit set back with that!!

Flash forward twenty years and I am a major in the J-5 at the Pentagon for Reserve duty when I get a message the Secretary of the Army would like to see me in his office ASAP. Not knowing what it was about, I hustle to his office, fixing my uniform as best as I could. As he greeted me, he said, "Guess you were one of my better appointments to USAFA." John O. Marsh bought me lunch!

John W. Stealey:
USAFA Academy Harassment

After PMC I moved to the BOQ at Ft. Dix as my folks were moving to Scofield Barracks, Hawaii. I got a military space A flight to visit them in late May 1966. I got another Space A flight back to Colorado Springs, Colorado in June 1966 wearing my PMC Uniform.

Needless to say, lots of questions of why I was wearing the PMC uniform on the way to USAFA. One of the Second Classmen, Paul G, noticed my uniform. He was a pain my entire Doolie year in my

Squadron. He was from Pennsylvania and was going to go to PMC if he did not get into USAFA.

He made me keep a demerit form for 60 hours of penalty marching in my wallet that said, "Gross Indifference to the 4th Class System" as I was already recognized once and knew I could get to my second recognition very soon. I could say "Yes, Sir, No, Sir. How many pushups would you like, Sir!" with the best of them.

Fast forward six years. I am now the Senior Instructor Pilot at Reese AFB pilot training base. Guess who comes to stand at attention in front of my desk. "Captain G. reporting to learn how to fly, Sir!" He is the only dollar ride, new flight student that enjoyed 10 spins on his very first Dollar Ride!

He said to me as he cleaned his mask. "Bill, I think we are now even, let's get down to flying." 15 years later he came to me for a job, and I helped him out. The world is a funny place. Try to be nice to everyone.

John E. N. Blair:
Alcohol

Early in my freshman year, I concluded that many cadets (all classes) in The Pennsylvania Military College Corps of Cadets were quite interested in the consumption of alcohol (all types). In my sophomore year, I was selected to become the cadet-assistant to a P.M.C. Dean/Professor and, in conjunction therewith, our travels sometimes led us to the "Voyager", a small, nautical-theme bar located at the intersection of West McDade Boulevard and Bullens Lane in Woodlyn about two miles/five minutes from campus. In order to be served alcoholic beverages there, it was necessary for me to convince Joe, the affable bartender, that I was 21 years old. Therefore, for my first underage alcoholic drink in April, 1968, I ordered a vodka martini with a twist of lemon 'up' and, because it required a bit of out-of-ordinary (for the 'Voyager') composition, he concluded that I was 21, concocted my drink, and served it to me.

Thereafter, I ordered either a 'Moscow Mule' (vodka, ginger-beer and lime juice) or a cold beer. Sadly, the 'Voyager" was closed and demolished in the early-to-mid-1970's to make way for the 'Blue Route' (I-476) feeder roads, such as Bullens Lane, which connected I-95 with the Pennsylvania Turnpike. On its final night of operation, my Dean removed the lighted 'MEN'S' sign from the bar's wall, took it home, and kept it until his death in 1994; whereupon his wife gave it to me. It now hangs on my office wall as a fond memory of the wonderful place where I consumed my first underage alcoholic beverage at the age of 19.

Stuart Perlmutter:
My First Time

One spring day in April of 1966, I visited the PMC Campus for the first time with my parents. While I grew up in a small town in eastern/central Pennsylvania, my mother and father knew of the school as both were born and raised in Philadelphia. They both knew of the fine reputation of PMC and wanted me to consider attending the school. My mother had been at a dance in the armory as a young lady, and my father was enamored of the famous PMC football player, William "Reds" Pollack.

We were interviewed by Vincent Lindsley, the admissions director, in his office in Old Main. I do not remember whether or not we were offered a "tour" of the school, but after the interview we chose to just walk around campus taking our own tour of the grounds surrounding Old Main. I do remember seeing two distinctive upper-class cadets who were walking in front of the Library toward Old Main that afternoon. Later, I would learn that their names were Dennis Grealish and Purnell "Jack" Sprigs. Their confident demeanor along with the smart military uniform they wore was impressive to me as an 18-year-old high school senior from a small town in Pennsylvania.

As we strolled along the grounds, my mother, father, and I heard music being played somewhere on campus. In search of the source of the music, we walked around the horseshoe in front of Old Main heading toward the Armory. Led by the sound of the music, we continued, and we made an immediate left at the end of the Old Main building and headed down a path that became a parade field entrance. As the field came into view, we viewed and heard a band practicing and playing an inspiring march called "The Olympians."

I stood in awed silence along with my mother and father as we all saw a band on the field, playing music and dressed in the same smart uniforms as were worn by the two cadets we had seen a few minutes earlier. While I did play an instrument in my junior and high school bands, I had never heard such a beautiful rendition of a marching song.

One year earlier, that PMC band had won the award of first place in the National R.O.T.C. marching competition. Sixty days before we visited the school, that same band had led the Mardi Gras Parade in New Orleans, Louisiana. As I stood listening to the marching music being played, I inadvertently glanced sideways to my immediate right and my eye caught the vision of large yellow sign on wooden posts in the ground near the pathway to the field with words that said:

"Upon this field of friendly strife are sown the seeds that, upon other fields and other days, will bear the fruits of victory. Douglass Macarthur.

Being so inspired by the beauty of Old Main, the sound of the march, the two cadets, the PMC uniformed band, and those inspiring words by General Douglass Macarthur, I knew at that moment in time that I had decided to attend Pennsylvania Military College.

Often times now when I return to our campus, while standing in the inspirational PMC memorial garden, I find myself looking across that same field gazing at that same parade entrance spot where I had stood between my mother and my father as we looked upon the parade field 57 years ago.

The Armory is gone as is the sign, but that "spot" is still there and that is alright with me as I will always have the memory of that day in April of 1966 when I made the decision to go to PMC. Five months later, I was a cadet at Pennsylvania Military College, and I joined that Band.

Mark L Richards:
A Flaming End to My Rook Year

It was late May of 1966. It was the end of a long, long Rook year that began the third week of August in 1965. I mean it was really bleeping long. All the Fourth Classmen were cramming for the last of our final exams, military science. We were all eager to put this behind us and move on to the graduation parades and then a leisurely summer as a civilian. A bunch of us had planned a celebratory beer party at the Jersey Shore the night before the upcoming graduation parades. Little did I know there was one more kick in the butt in store for my roommate, Walt Daly, and me.

I was in Bravo Company and was domiciled on the third floor of dorm six. I guess it was about midnight, and I had just come out of the shower when one of my classmates (cannot remember who) burst into the latrine, screaming that there was dark smoke coming out from beneath the door to my room. We hurried down the hallway to my room. Sure enough, there was thick, black, ugly smoke wafting from the gap between the floor and the door to the room.

I unlocked the door to my room and observed flames consuming the closeted area where our uniforms were hung. Someone raced down the hall and got one of the fire extinguishers and someone called the Chester Fire Department. The flames were partially extinguished by the valiant efforts of Bravo Company, and within minutes, a bright, red fire truck with sirens, and whistles was out front of my dorm. They finished the task.

The military officer in charge (MOC) Captain Hubbard, also known as Zeus, appeared at the scene. Amid the excited chatter, it did not take long to determine the cause of the fire. Apparently two fellow cadets, who shall remain nameless, were engaged in what they thought were some harmless shenanigans involving matches. Captain Hubbard took it all in and quickly concluded the blaze was attributed to careless smoking, and that the wind had blown a lighted cigarette from an unattended ashtray to the closet where some of the uniforms had plastic wrap from the dry cleaners. This in turn ignited, causing the fire. The other members of Bravo Company all nodded sagely at Captain Hubbard's official explanation of the fire.

I do not believe any of us slept that night. The next morning, the Commandant, Colonel Menard, appeared at the scene. He observed the damage and shook his head with a forlorn expression. He did not say much and walked away.

I muddled through the military science exam and salvaged what uniforms I could from the blackened closet. Thus ended my rook year, down in flames.

Stuart Perlmutter:
Corps 'Snap Outs'

Sometime, in the late-winter/early-spring of 1970, in the quadrangle consisting of Cann, Howell, and Turrell Halls, a few unparalleled as well as spontaneous events occurred. It all began with an announcement, over the public-address system linking all six of the cadet-barracks: **"BRIGADE, 'SNAP-OUT."**

Anyone standing in front of 'Old Main,' on 14th Street in Chester that night, would have observed a group of military college cadets singing, yelling, and acting out in an outrageous manner!

Whether it was the pressure of final examinations, the possible closing of the military college in the near future, the Vietnam War, a general sense of emotional turbulence, the doldrums of winter or, perhaps, something else, no one is completely certain of the origin of the events that led to Corps "Snap-Outs." No alcohol was involved—it was probably just a group of cadets "blowing off steam."

Perhaps some of the local residents, living in homes near the dormitories, complained about the noise, confusion, and the students "carrying on." On at least two occasions, officers of the Chester Police Department responded to the scene on 14th Street to investigate the source of these unusual and unprovoked disturbances.

At that time, Headquarters Company was comprised of all of the band-cadets, which were billeted in Howell and Turrell Halls in the aforementioned 'quadrangle.' Seeing the police approaching the young men from 14th Street, the band cadets, who had been wildly playing their instruments along with everyone else came up with an innovative idea.

The Band played the Star-Spangled Banner! The police had to stop in place, hand over their hearts, and stand at attention! As the anthem was being played, the students got a reprieve and ran back to their rooms.

Once the National Anthem had been completed, the cadets from the band frantically returned or better said, escaped while laughing all the way back to their rooms to prepare for another day at Pennsylvania Military College.

Gerald Ferguson:
M-1 Thumb

During my four years at PMC, the Corps was equipped with the Garand Rifle, M-1, a 10-pound, wooden stock beauty. Every cadet who was not a sergeant or officer, was issued a rifle that was used in drill, carried in parades, and occasionally fired. We had to be able to disassemble and clean the rifle without assistance and quickly. Routine rifle drills could take place on the parade field in formation and even, for Rooks, in the barracks' hallway. There was one drill command called "inspection arms" where the rifle was brought to your chest and the bolt opened and locked. The following command was "port arms" where the mechanism was pushed down with your right thumb and quickly released while removing the thumb, because the bolt would come crashing home. If the thumb lingered or slipped, you received a nasty bruise on the thumb nail, aka M-1 Thumb. M-1 Thumb usually happened only once per cadet! 4th Class "Rooks" were especially susceptible to M-1 thumb, not only due to inexperience, but because the occasional evening barracks manual-of-arms practice usually caused sweaty hands with predictable results.

Dave Esto:
The Beginning of the End

When we showed up for our Rook training in the last week of August 1966, it did not take long to realize that the Military "side" of PMC Colleges was not popular amongst some of the school's staff. During our parents' dinner on the arrival evening, I, along with my parents, sat with Gerry Ferguson and his parents. We never realized that evening that Gerry and I would remain lifelong friends when two out of three from that dinner never made it to graduation.

We had a member of the faculty sitting at our table, just as all others did. I won't mention the professor's name, but he was very clearly biased against the Corps and the military. When he asked why we chose the miliary side of PMC versus the civilian side, I was a bit put off that a staff member could be so outwardly biased during a time when we were supposed to be welcomed. The evening was billed that way, but our host made it anything but.

Over the next four years, we saw a growing lack of support for the Corps within the faculty, including the school's president and staff. It was at the height of the Vietnam War and the school was clearly feeling the effects. However, I will tell anyone who cares to listen, I learned more by way of preparation for a career and life after PMC from being a cadet than by being a student. The Military tenets are summarized:

- Passion
- Integrity
- Teamwork
- Accountability
- Achievement

The Corps lives on and always will.

Gerald Ferguson:
The Rack

I suppose all military colleges and some branches of the U.S. military refer to a bunkbed as "The Rack." During our Rook/4th Class orientation one of the first things taught and later emphasized in inspections was the correct appearance of the rack's sheet and blanket. The sheet had to be turned down a set number of inches from the pillow and the red PMC blanket had to have "hospital corners" of 45 degrees and pulled so tight that, optimistically, a quarter would bounce off it. New blankets didn't cooperate very well in this regard. For rooks and underclassmen in general, racks had to be inspection ready immediately after Mess 1. For me this meant I would sleep on top of the blanket, not under it. Luckily the barracks rooms were always hot, so I didn't suffer from the winter cold. I don't think I slept under the sheet/blanket at any time during my four years at PMC.

For some unknown and mysterious reason, our "racks" would cast a spell on cadets usually after a late night of "studying" or socializing. The spell caused the rack to capture many cadets, resulting in missed morning classes and, since sleeping during the day was not permitted, demerits for unauthorized rack time.

Dave Esto:
The First Week as a Rook

When we started our first week, the only uniforms we had were fatigues and our two pairs of black shoes and, of course, the civilian clothes we showed up with. Our uniforms were not ready, and we were told it would be another week or so until they were. Our Cadre Lieutenant (Curt Velsor) told us things would be a little more casual until we received our uniforms, but to not get too comfortable because things were going to get tougher over the next week or so.

On our first Sunday, about three days after arriving, our Cadre marched us over to Kirkbride Hall to watch a movie, "Where the Boys Are" starring Connie Francis. We were all having a great time and after the movie ended, we marched back to Howell Hall. Our Cadre, two of whom were Corporal Jim Hogg and Corporal George Duque, told us that when we got back to our rooms, we were going to have a party. I remember thinking to myself this military stuff isn't all that bad.

Within a few short minutes, we all found out that the party was a "bracing party!" Every Cadre member screaming in our faces, telling us how worthless we were, and insisting that we brace harder. An introduction to the "green chair" was included, as well as "assume the position" where we pumped out numerous pushups, numerous times. When the party was over, we went in our rooms. I remember looking at my roommate, Ray Pepper, and saying something along the lines of "is this how things are going to be?" It was the first time in three days that I began to wonder if I had done the right thing by accepting my offer.

And as the saying goes, the beatings continued. Uniforms arrived and more fun, removing all the lacquer from all of our brass, learning how to spit shine shoes, iron shirts and pants, and even how to tie our ties. This was all prior to classes starting, so the evenings were always spent organizing things, folding our underwear, rolling socks properly, and boxing up our civilian clothes which were to be shipped home. And of course, those loud Cadre commands, "third floor, Howell Hall, Charlie Company, STEP OUT!" The first time this was requested we did not respond fast enough so we went back and tried again and again and again.

What did we get ourselves into?

Gerald Ferguson:
Freshman (Fourth Class) Academics)

As 4th Class "Rook" cadets, the Class of 1970 reported to campus on September 6, 1966 to begin a delightful 10-day orientation. The first day of classes was Friday, September 16th. The orientation program was filled with activities to give us some basic military fundamentals, uniform fitting and issue, physical training, etc. In any case, we looked forward to the end of the orientation and the start of classes.

A few of the class, myself included, had some limited experience with college level work, but the thing that wasn't anticipated by any of us was the impact the constant pressure rook training would have on our ability to deal with academics. In those years, cadets were expected to carry 18 credit hours per semester or more in order to ensure graduation in four years.

Mess 1 Reveille was 0700 hrs. All freshmen seemed to have classes at 0800 hrs., I suppose the upperclassmen got all of the later class times. The first class always seemed to be in a warm lecture hall that would make it almost impossible to stay awake after a night of "step outs," running around in the barracks, room cleaning, etc. The result of the many distractions and stresses was that many of the freshman had disastrous grades for the 1st marking period. I was "lucky" to hover just below a 2.0 GPA. It took the remaining four years to build back some GPAs to respectability. Many freshmen didn't recover from the rough start and left the Corps after the first or second semester.

Fortunately, by the time our senior year came around, the rook program was somewhat modified to better focus on studies after the first day of classes.

Don Cooper:
Double Vision

For those who went through the Fourth-Class Program, I don't need to explain the hazing, the bracing, the white glove inspections, and, of course, the punishment tours. However, I was always fascinated how we survived those critical first few days.

My situation was not unique. My parents and I were so impressed when we arrived on that first day. The senior cadets were dressed superbly, and we were treated with the utmost courtesy and respect. It reaffirmed our conviction that selecting PMC was the right choice. The day was September 6, 1966, and it was not going to end well.

My parents and I were escorted by a cadre member to Cann Hall where I was assigned to HQ Company. After saying goodbye to my parents, it did not take long before my tranquil world turned into a dystopian nightmare. Yes, the yelling and harassing was shocking enough, but the actions of a particular cadre member named Corporal Wren were quite disconcerting to me. While attempting to master the art of spit shining my shoes, he would enter my room, inspect the shoes, and quietly make a seemingly slight nod of approval. Five minutes later, he would blast open the door and screamed that the shoes looked like they were brushed with sandpaper! Another time, Corporal Wren would enter my room and check out my folded t-shirts and shorts and berate me because they did not comply with official room arrangement guidelines, then abruptly leave. Even before I had a chance to refold the clothes, he would again barge into the room in a rampage, vilifying me for making a sloppy bed.

Is this a case of multiple personality disorders or have I just entered one of Dante's Nine Circles of Hell? I'm no psychiatrist, but I was slowly reaching a conclusion that this is not a military institution, rather an insane asylum run by the inmates.

After a couple of days, I was transferred to a line company. (I was neither interested nor talented enough to play in a marching band.) I was glad to get out of that nut house, but I quickly discovered that Echo Company had cadres just as rough and tough as in HQ.

It was several weeks later that I found out that there were two Corporal Wrens in HQ. No, not the two fragmented dissociative identities of one corporal, but identical twins with two distinct personalities. As cadre, the Wrens proved in my eyes to be the best in "bore-assing." This finally put my mind to rest that PMC was not so psychotic after all. But as a Rook, being a little crazy sure helped one to survive the Fourth Class Program

Gerald Ferguson:
Senior Porch

An interesting tool that was used to ensure high standards across companies and to provide competitive rankings that would feed into the honor company competition was something called…"Senior Porch."

If you were to look at the Old Main Building from 14th Street you would see a patio or porch area protruding from the second floor and accessible by stairways on either side. Ordinarily only 1st Class cadets were permitted on the Senior Porch. Every Mess 1 morning formation during the week there would be an announcement made after companies were formed up that one cadet from each company must report to the Senior Porch for evaluation. The typical command from brigade staff would identify the unfortunate candidate as "best Rook" or third man 2nd squad, or squad leader 3rd squad, etc. Rarely would a senior be called forward and then usually as a joke.

Typically, after the call to report, there would be a scramble within the company leaders to check the uniform of the unfortunate victim for completeness. The company designate would climb the steps to be evaluated by 1st class members of the staff. In addition to inspecting the uniform, the representative would be asked questions on a variety of subjects from general orders to school history and Army information. Each rep would be graded, and a winner identified. Woe be the rook who did poorly at Senior Porch!

Abraham J. Gale:
A Combat Boot

My roommate and I were Rooks (1966-1967) in Hotel Turrell, 2nd Floor. Early on we used to set an alarm clock we had to sound off at Zero-Dark-Thirty to get the room and both of us ready for Mess I formation and daily inspections. Shortly after starting to set the alarm clock, we woke up in our room as The Corps was called to attention around the Horseshoe.

While waiting for the inevitable consequences certain to follow this (and they did), we decided to adopt a new strategy to avoid the "religious" experience cadre put us through for missing Mess I. The next evening, I set the alarm clock at the usual time, and racked out in the top bunk at light's out after placing the alarm clock in a combat boot that was laced up. The thinking was that no one could possibly not wake up to the alarm in the future while the clock was secured inside a laced combat boot.

The system worked fine for a couple of days until we, once again, woke up as Mess I formation on the Horseshoe as the Corps was called to attention by the First Captain. My roommate (who left PMC not long after this FUBAR) had apparently heard the alarm go off and, while still in sleep mode, sprung out of the bottom rack, seized the offending combat boot, opened the window, and threw the boot with the alarm clock sounding out the window, returning to the rack where he joined me in resumed sound sleep.

When we couldn't find the missing combat boot in the room, we opened the window and looked outside. Sure enough, the combat boot was laying outside our window on the pavement alongside Turrell. I switched to the bottom rack after this. I will leave it up to your imagination how creative, determined, long lasting and exhaustive cadre was on their second attempt to persuade us to join our Classmates for Mess I formation in the future.

James H. VanSciver:
My Path to the Chester Campus

If there is a traditional path taken to college, mine was anything but. My family was poor, very poor. My father graduated from high school and quickly entered the Army to serve in WW II. My mother dropped out of high school to be a plane spotter during that conflict. We grew up in a boat house floating down the Delaware River from Philadelphia, through the Lewes-Rehoboth Canal to Rehoboth Bay, and up Love Creek. It was so badly constructed that, during the winter, it was not unusual to find snow caressing the corners of the bedrooms under the windows. My dad was a dairyman and my mother worked in a small electronics shop to support me, my two brothers, and sister. Not one person in my family had ever been to college. It was made clear to me that, if that was the route I was to take, it would be up to me to find a way to pay for it.

Early in my junior year at Lewes High School, my counselor and I worked on a plan for continuing my education. Motivating me was not the pursuit of academics but the urge to continue my sports career in football, basketball, and baseball. Initially, he fleshed out a strategy for me to enroll at Lafayette College in Easton, Pennsylvania where the football coach was a young fella named Bill Manlove. That plan fell through as we were not able to secure sufficient financial support to make it work.

Next was the Coast Guard Academy in New London, Connecticut, where I dreamed of sailing the world on the Eagle, a 245-foot three-masted baroque used for training. It is still the largest tall ship flying the Stars and Strips and the only active square-rigger in the U.S. government service. I had spent most of my early years working on the water on Rehoboth Bay and saw this as a dream opportunity. In addition, attending the Academy would be at no cost to me.

I had amassed a strong academic background in high school, with perfect attendance for four years, while playing the three sports and captaining them all. It looked like my desire was going to come true. A high school friend of mine participated in a training exercise on the Delaware River near the Tacony-Palmyra Bridge in Philadelphia that was successful so all that was left was for me to undergo a perfunctory physical in that same city to seal the deal.

After the usual probes and inspections, I was confronted with a color-blind test, then another, and another. So bewildered was I by the end of the third that, by its conclusion, I was guessing. Unbeknownst to me, that experience killed any chance I had of moving to New London for the next four years. It was explained to me that all wiring in ships was color coded and that handicap on my part would compromise my ability to fulfil my responsibilities in the Coast Guard. It was back to my counselor for Plan B.

As a result of my academic acumen and athletic prowess, he worked with the staff at Pennsylvania Military College to create a financial aid package that included scholarships, loans, and work study plans that would reduce my financial hardship in attending the school. This was agreeable with my parents so, in the late summer of 1968, after my getting the buzz cut, my father took me to the Chester campus to enroll. You can imagine our shock when the staff at the registration desk asked my father to write out a check for a thousand dollars on the spot! He looked at me, motioned to get back in the car, and we drove the three-hour trip to Salisbury, Maryland where it was his intent to enlist me in the Navy as was the case with my older brother. Not a word was spoken. I could tell how downtrodden he was, not being able to help his son go to college. That experience has stuck with me for my entire life as I worked to ensure that my own children would never have to undergo that experience. I pledged to take care of the college expenses for each of the five of them.

We entered the post office and waited for the recruiter and waited some more. Apparently, that individual had taken an extended lunch break that day. My father, needing to get back to work, loaded me back in the car and we headed home. Upon arrival, my mother told us that PMC Athletic Director George Hansell had called and revealed that there had been some confusion in my financial aid package that had been cleared up and I was supposed to report the next day. Imagine my jubilation and my father's joy!

The circuitous route for me to Pennsylvania Military College was heavily impacted by my handicap and some incredible and unforeseen luck. For me, it turned out very well as I learned, not only the academic knowledge but the lessons of life that enabled me, a poor boy from a non-college family, to have each of my children earn a college degree absent having to endure the financial pressure of so doing.

Bob Schneider:
WHY Did I Choose PMC

After 50 years I still look back and think about why I chose PMC in 1968. As with all of us at PMC — this was a tough time in America — the military was not looked at very fondly. When I taught at Penn State (Behrend College) in the ROTC department (1979 — 1981) I came across some serious anti-military attitudes — many of my fellow faculty members at Penn State had been conscientious objectors during the war and had chosen the academic field to stay out of the draft. We had many "interesting discussions." This amid my responsibility to recruit future officers.

My guidance counselor at my HS in New Jersey thought that I should apply to as many schools as I could since I was an average student with average SAT scores. My councilor thought I would have trouble getting into the college of my choice. I applied to eight schools and he was shocked when I was accepted to seven of them — my first choice was Muhlenberg College but they were the only ones to turn me down (so I guess he was kind of right when he stated I wouldn't get into my first choice. He was a Tusculum College grad (Tennessee) and tried to recruit everyone to Tusculum. My sister fell for it for his recruiting efforts and spent one year there and hated it). My Dad and I were serious boaters so I thought I might want to be a Coast Guard Officer until I went to visit the Coast Guard Academy and they informed me, during my visit, that summer training cruises included climbing the masts of their training ship the USCGC EAGLE. My immediate reaction was "no way' (my dad was really disappointed) because heights do not sit well with me, especially hanging from a mast, in stormy weather, in the middle of the ocean. When I visited PMC, I felt during my visit that I belonged there, and I have never regretted the decision.

I had always wanted to be an officer (my mom and Dad had lots of influence) but couldn't get into my dream school (West Point) and after I visited PMC, I decided that it was the place I needed to attend.

James H. VanSciver:
And So it Begins

It was nearly a month since my roommate, George Weissgerber, from Pittsburgh, and I had an opportunity for an off campus leave at the beginning of the school year in 1968. Having endured and survived an intense Rook training experience, we felt we could easily pass the necessary white glove room inspection needed to unlock the door to the outside world. Attending to the tightness of the bunk blankets, using a toothbrush to clean between the tiles on the floor, folding our underwear perfectly with the rectangular cardboard inserts, and polishing every piece of brass in the room with the dreaded Brasso, we eagerly awaited the knock on the door signaling the entrance of the inspection team.

The door opened and we immediately resorted to the customary military protocols with a straight stand at attention and a firm salute. The inspection began. Bounce a quarter on the bunk cover, check. Check for folded underwear, check. Attend to the brass, check. Run a white glove over the desk, behind the door, over the windows, check. Next, something happened that we had never counted on. The white-gloved inspector moved to our desk, lifted one of our lamps, took out the lightbulb, and pounded the upside-down lamp on the desk. To our dismay, a tiny crumb of some sort tumbled out of the bulb case and rolled across the desk. "Inspection failed!" bellowed the upperclassman and we were doomed. After the door closed and the inspectors had exited, George and I looked at each other with a downtrodden glance and said, nearly in unison, "Holy crap! We are never getting out of here." Nearly 55 years later, I still vividly remember that experience.

William Troy:
Cadet Leadership

Incoming Cadets were called Rooks! Sometimes that was the nicest thing we were called by the Upperclassmen who served as our Cadre. Cadet Corporals, Sergeants, Lieutenants and Captains ruled our lives 24 hours a day as members of the Cadet Corps. Some were excellent leaders, and some were martinets. All were just learning their role. Their initial role was to break us Rooks down. This really began with "Step Out." At the initial step out we were made to stand outside our rooms and brace, which is a rigid form of attention but to we Rooks it was more like prepare yourself physically or mentally for something unpleasant! We were yelled and screamed at and made to do pushups and what was called the green chair.

The green chair was made when we squatted down into a sitting position with our back against the wall and arms outstretched resembling a chair. It was green because we were sometimes in our fatigue uniforms. When the Cadre called Step Out, we had to emerge however we were dressed. In the initial step out we were told that we had to square around the hall with the right shoulder to the wall. For example, to get to the latrine I had to exit my room, turn right, walk along the corridor until it intersected with the adjoining corridor, make a left face, cross to the other side, make a left face, then proceed to the latrine. Exiting the latrine, I had to keep my right shoulder against the wall and walk down the corridor until I reached the connecting corridor, make a left face, then cross making a left face. Keeping my shoulder against the wall, walk back to my room. All the time bracing! The same happened when exiting the building or entering the building. Once out of the building we had to run, not walk, to our destination, be it to formation, class, the library, etc. We had morning formation and marched to breakfast. We had an evening formation and marched to supper.

Our Cadre leaders, especially the Sergeants, made sure we followed the rules and learned our Rook Knowledge. They would ask us to recite the answer to the Question, How's the Cow? "Sir the Cow is fine. She walks, She talks, She is full of Chalk. The lacteal fluid extracted from the female of the bovine species is highly prolific to the Nth Degree, Sir!" Another favorite was What time is it? "Sir, I am deeply embarrassed and greatly humiliated that due to unforeseen circumstances over which I have no control, the inner workings and hidden mechanisms of my chronometer are in such accord with the sidereal movement of the sun by which time is generally reckoned, that I cannot with any degree of accuracy state the exact time, Sir! But, without fear of being too greatly in error, I will state that it is X minutes, X seconds and X ticks after the X hour!" We were asked other questions about school history or significant campus items, like how tall the flagpole is, and military questions. It made for doing many pushups.

My real purpose is to talk about what I learned from Cadet leaders. It was through them that I learned how best to spit shine my low quarters (shoes), how best to polish my brass, how to make sure my uniform was correct, and much more. We first learned how to march as Rooks. We spent many hours during our "Beast Barracks," the time before the upperclassmen returned and classes began, learning Drill and Ceremonies. We marched as squads and platoons. Our Squad Leaders, Platoon Sergeants, and Platoon Leaders correcting us. Those who had real issues often had individual instruction by a Cadet Corporal or Sergeant, usually accompanied by pushups.

Even as a Junior Sergeant, Squad Leader I remember practicing with the three other Squad Leaders, Ken Robinson, Glen Dower, and John Collins and our Platoon Leader, Robert Weidner, our column movements to make sure we stayed aligned. Once we Rooks mastered the basics of marching, we learned the manual of arms. We originally had M-1 Rifles—11 pounds to carry. Our Corporals and Sergeants taught us each movement and taught us everything about the weapon. We were taught how to disassemble and assemble it. How to avoid M-1 Thumb—most of us didn't avoid it! M-1 Thumb is caused by depressing the ammunition clip feed spring below the firing pin so the breach will close, but failing to remove one's thumb before the breach closes! The result is a bruised thumb. We fired the M-1 at Fort Dix, New Jersey and even then the upper class leaders were coaching us as to how to adjust our sights and how better to get into the firing position.

Our Cadet leaders taught us tactics. Our Squad Leaders taught us the elements of the squad, tactical formations, fire and maneuver, and the Five Paragraph Field Order. The platoon leader would brief the platoon sergeant on our orders and in turn the platoon sergeant would pass the order to the squad leaders who would brief the members of the squad. Squad leaders usually taught us how to dig a foxhole and establish a defensive position, individual and site camouflage, set up an ambush, and navigate using a compass and map. Even members of the Brigade Staff had roles. They helped plan, coordinate, and execute field training and functions on campus like parades. The S-1 Adjutant, S-2 Intelligence and Discipline, S-3 Operations and S-4 Supply all were important pieces of our leadership puzzle. As we progressed from Rook to First Classman, we honed our leadership skills by practicing them daily. I can say from personal experience of 28 years in the Army, both active and reserve, that what I learned from my cadet leaders and from being a cadet leader made my military life a whole lot easier and more effective. It also helped me in the corporate world to manage people and projects for an Aerospace Corporation.

James H. VanSciver:
It's a Rook Life for Me

For those of us attending Pennsylvania Military College in the late summer of 1968, few if any had any idea of what awaited us. For me, from Love Creek Bridge, Delaware, where, when we turned out the lights, it got dark, the difference in my life could not have been starker. Notwithstanding the intensity of the military training and the trials and tribulations of being a Rook, there was the matter of my room. Located on the third floor, I-95 ran next to my residence. Between that interstate and me was the railroad, and overhead was the flight pattern for Philadelphia International Airport. That, along with the constant police and fire sirens, caused me to not enjoy a night's sleep for the first two weeks I was there!

And there was the matter of being a Rook. Upon reflection, few of the protocols made any sense until one realized that the entire point was to relieve you of your background and identity and transform you into an important and working part of something bigger, better, and more productive. When the door to my restroom was immediately to my left, yet I had to walk around the entire hallway to my right to access it, when my shoulders had to caress the wall when I encountered an upperclassman, when I had to sit on the front six inches on my seat and recite some lengthy and untenable narrative in order to retrieve a scrap of food, when I had one set of underwear for display and a second to wear, and when a bugle awakened me very early each morning, not for breakfast but for formation, it was easy to ask oneself, "What the hell have I gotten myself into?"

In truth, there was attrition. While I'm not sure of the rate, I am sure that those of us who did survive were able to thrive for the remaining three years and in careers thereafter. That we endured this experience in addition to going to classes, participating in extracurricular programs, and maintained our sanity is a credit to each of us.

Virtue, liberty, and independence. Hail the Class of 1972 of Pennsylvania Military College!

Bob Schneider:
How's the Cow?

After 54 years I may be getting older and forgetful, but I know how the COW (I live in cow country) is doing. "She walks, she talks, she's full of chalk, the lacteal fluid extracted from the female of the bovine species is highly prolific to the Nth degree." Oh I forgot the "SIR!"

PS: A few others were: from Frederick Scheffler "Sir! I am deeply embarrassed and greatly humiliated that I am unable to state the time with any degree of accuracy. However, the sidereal movements of the earth around the sun are in such accord that I can state that it is 28 minutes and 47 seconds past the 10 o'clock hour. SIR!" Another version from Ted Howland: "I am deeply embarrassed and greatly humiliated that I am unable to give you the exact time, but according to my chronometer, I can say, to the best of my ability that the time is 0759 hours, 10 ticks and 25 tocks. SIR!!"

James H. VanSciver:
Digging at Dix

To say that there was a deep and concentrated military influence on the education the members of the Class of 1972 were getting at Pennsylvania Military College would be an understatement. The experiences included formations, drills, inspections, class lectures, and practical events that were held on Thursday morning and on some weekends. Of course, the formations, inspections, and drills were a daily occurrence. The content included military history, military protocols, weaponry, tactics, vision, purpose, and more.

While much of this training took place on campus, at times it was shared at other places such as Delaware Water Gap and Fort Dix. The agenda for the Fort Dix training was particularly exhilarating as it included a two-day composite of the happenings one would experience in combat. It was nothing like a Weekend at Bernie's. Upon arrival, we were treated to a meal, composed of what we were told were edibles slapped on our mess trays by individuals who seemed to have their emotions sucked out of their bodies. After choking down the provender, we joined a line in order to plunge our trays in a vat of boiling water. If there was ever a situation which included not a shred of care of cleanliness and germs, I thought, this was it. Obediently, in turn, each of us dunked and shook off the water from our trays and prepared for the Saturday events.

We were led to a desolate location of the fort and told to begin digging. For what? Gold, oil, treasure? Nope, we were digging for our lives. With three or four to a hole, this would be our comfortable bedding for the evening while we were on constant lookout for the inevitable attack from the Rangers. Early on, I noted that roots, rock, and rust were not friends of the excavator. An unattended backpack spade was of little use against the brittle earth it sought to pierce. In addition, we dug in the heat; we dug through blisters; we dug for each other. It takes persistence to open a wound in Mother Earth five feet wide and nearly as deep. Next came nightfall. The temperature dropped and we were spending our time in the cold damp dankness of our own creation. I was convinced that, to win a battle, just force your enemy to spend one evening like we did, and he would awake too stiff to do anything to protect himself.

Fortuitously, sunrise came. We were hustled out of our holes and moved to the target range for a full day of shooting and marking shots. I was caught by two surprises as my first role was firing. First, the rifles we used were remarkably accurate. Also, I had no idea of the extensive conventions one had to complete before pulling the trigger. Back home, at the creek, when we were shooting snakes with a 22, we just aimed and squeezed. And we were pretty good at it. I surmised that some of my classmates had never caressed the smooth steel in their hands and were appreciative of the thoughtfulness of our trainers.

Next, it was off to the targets to show our colleagues how well they were doing. The setup was interesting. We entered a deep trench protected in the front by a large bank of sand. The frames for the targets were made of grooved wood which provided for rapid sliding up and down. We were given long poles on the end of which were circular red plates to show the shooters where their shells had penetrated the targets. Behind the targets was a very large hill of sand into which the spent bullets made their way. The sound of them so doing made me think of what being hit by one would do to a human being. I was shocked from this lapse of attention to my responsibilities by the order to fire. It quickly became obvious that a number of the members of the Class of 1972 were unlike Gary Cooper playing Sgt. York in the 1941 film about the World War I hero. Bullets were flying everywhere! Never was I so thankful for wearing a helmet!

After untold hours firing and marking, we were marched to our transportation for the ride back to Chester. Few experiences have left such an indelible mark on me as did this one. We had begun to learn about the reality of killing.

Slipping into the comfort of my bunk on campus, I had one final thought. Regardless of the softness of the mattress, I will never fret about my bed again.

Paul S. Lewis:
Fire

Certain events from my Cadet days, mostly in the Rook and Senior years, loom larger than others in my memory. These are stories from those years. Some of them...are true!

First Days before coming to PMC, I had seen a documentary on the initiation process for new plebes at West Point. They call it "Beast Barracks" for good reason! I was expecting similar treatment for rooks in the first few weeks at PMC. To add to the dread, there was a song* that played every morning on some upperclassman's clock radio just as we were being roused from sleep. With open windows, you could hear it all around the quadrangle. The opening lines went like this: "I am the god of hell fire and I bring you...fire!" Those words always made me wonder what the Cadre was going to do to us that day. * "Fire" by Arthur Brown, 1968.

James H. VanSciver:
Discipline

There I was standing in formation, on the circle in the shadow of Old Main in Echo Company as a Rook in the Class of 1972 at Pennsylvania Military College in early September of 1968. A mosquito proboscis had just penetrated my cheek, to the right and just under my right eye. A company officer, performing an inspection, was blaring in my face while standing on the very front of my left shoe, creating the sensation that his shoe had all but wiped all the polish off mine.

Yet I was not able to even flinch.

What madness is this, thought I. If this goes on much longer, I'll be left lifeless, prostrate on the macadam, devoid of any blood, with nothing but smudges on what used to be my perfectly polished foot covers.

It was all about concentration and focus; it was about discipline. Is it possible for one to block out all distractions to become a critical piece of a body of men working in unison? That was my lesson for the day.

As days turned into weeks and weeks into months, the tutorials increased. Be on time. Be supportive. Be dependable. Do the right thing in the right way for the right reason. How to show this? Polished shoes, pleated shirts, folded underwear, tight bed covers, clean rooms, shiny brass. Everything we were told to do and did was about knowing discipline, appreciating discipline, and showing discipline.

Those who erred were swiftly and effectively corrected. Sometimes lengthy tours were assigned for the parking lot behind MacMoreland Center. These walks to nowhere were designed to have the perpetrator consider his transgressions and formulate a plan for avoiding recidivism lest the castigation be increased and intensified.

Pushups, running while holding a heavy rifle over your head, or sleeping on a box spring sans mattress did the trick. The message was clear. Discipline was expected and discipline would be delivered.

These expectations are fundamental if a military is to be successful. They are also important if one is to live a prosperous, successful, and happy life. Not abandoning your post until relieved is more than a soldierly value. So, too, are dependability, teamwork, dedication, focus, and hard work. This list could go on and on.

These are the attributes instilled into the graduates of Pennsylvania Military College and, in particular, the Class of 1972. As a result, the world is a better place in which to live.

Paul S. Lewis:
Oh Christmas Tree

Christmas Tree Escapade Remember the Honor Code—Do not lie, cheat, or steal, or words to that effect? For a short while, the Rooks of Charlie Company tarnished the code just a wee bit. After all, we had been ordered to decorate the barracks for Christmas and had to be resourceful. A tree was what our barren hall needed; the problem was how to get one at no cost. Someone had noticed a row of suitable trees in the neighborhood east of campus. A raiding party was quickly formed and under cover of darkness we slipped out the back door and shortly arrived at our objective. Not equipped with the proper tool for the job, the ringleader made do with a sharp implement and proceeded to cut away at the trunk which was maybe three inches in diameter. So as not to draw unwanted attention, he hacked at the trunk whenever a jet plane flew overhead to mask the noise. Whack-whack-whack followed by silence until the next plane approached, then more whacks. Eventually the tree was freed from its roots. We grabbed it and ran back to the barracks as fast as we could. The next morning the cadre inquired how this tree magically appeared. We avoided any mention of the word steal, using purloined, procured, or acquired, but not stolen!

William Speer:
Eyes

Our Rook year was quite an experience, something I never want to do again but I would not give it up for the World. One of our cadre members was Sergeant Gordon King and he was, in many ways, what one would call a hard-ass. As luck would have it, he was head of my mess table. Now Rooks had to eat a certain way: sit on the front six inches of the chair, stomach touching the table, body erect, eyes to the front (you could also look down), one hand on the table at a time unless cutting something or passing items. Each table had people assigned to different tasks, mine was to tell the sick joke of the day at dinner. I bought a book of them and memorized a story for each day. Sergeant King seemed to enjoy them very much (or I would have suffered the consequences).

One dinner I had the temerity to actually move my eyes to the left to look at him. Well, that was a fatal mistake. After a sufficient amount of chewing out, I was ordered to be in Dress Alpha (full dress uniform) at 0400 outside his room in the barracks AND I was to be bracing (let's just say, an exaggerated position of attention for the uninitiated). This of course I did after I spent the evening shining everything and getting it squared away. Now bracing becomes a habit and it is easy enough to do for a few minutes. I was worried that if I slouched or moved in any way, which would be the time SGT King would come out and catch me not bracing. So, for the next hour and a half I was bracing, waiting for him to open the door. Which he did promptly at 0530, towel in hand, dressed in a bath robe. He took one look at me, sweat pouring from my brow, and said, "What are you doing here, Speer? Get back in your room and ready for formation!"

Joe Edwards:
Computer Programmer (As told by his Wife Chris)

One of my favorite memories was from freshman year, Rook year to you. Joe and I had been dating since juniors in high school and after a short break from each other reconnected Thanksgiving break. I was at home on the phone talking to my friend about Joe and how much I missed him. The doorbell rang and Joe was standing at the door. I was overcome with joy! Joe wasn't sure how I would react and brought Artie Haffner with him for support. What can I say? We stayed together and had many memories of PMC. These memories included meeting "Tink" aka Greg Haugens on campus who always helped find Joe since girls were not allowed in the barracks. Another happy memory was "Little Army /Navy" game in Atlantic City. There were many frat parties that I was introduced to the famous "Purple Jesus!" And, of course, that were some not so happy memories like going to memorial services for fallen PMC graduates while serving in Vietnam. Although I did not go to PMC, I felt the brotherhood that you all bonded and felt included as that membership. Initially we made some plans to get married on the steps of Old Main on graduation day. We realized that was impractical and made plans for July. It was to be a small wedding of family; however our PMC brothers had other plans for our special day and informed us they would see us at the wedding. Well, our small plans just doubled. I have such wonderful memories of my wedding day, thanks mostly to my brothers from PMC. Today would have been our 50th wedding anniversary.

Regards,
Chris Edwards
From heaven Joe Edwards #107

William Speer:
How Cool are We?

My roommate Rook year was Doug Shepherd. He attended Valley Forge Military Academy high school so was a great help to me getting to know the ropes of the military routine. He helped me learn to properly spit-shine my shoes (and keep a spare set for show) and how to properly make my rack for inspection, among other things. He saved my butt more than once. We watched while the Rangers rappelled out of my window and while, I think, Jim VanSciver and other others used brooms to knock the snow off the roof to fall on the ROTC staff as they went into their offices.

One day he suggested we go to VFMA so he could see some friends and we could show off our unis. Well, of course I jumped at the idea and off we went one Spring weekend. Once we parked and started walking about, VFMA cadets saluted us, which was shocking for a Rook to experience but, of course, we just returned the salute and drove on (our company motto). In the barracks it was a whole new, yet familiar world. Doug enjoyed bore-assing the younger cadets and they gave us respect as was justifiably deserved. After a few hours, we tired of the routine and visited a few of his classmates now at the Junior College there. Afterwards, we came back to campus with a new appreciation of our plight. I have often wondered what happened to Doug, I don't think any of my classmates have been able to find him either.

Scott McGinnis:
A Rook's First Day

In early August 1968, my parents and I piled into the family 1966

Pontiac LeMans, and we headed off to Chester, Pennsylvania, home of Pennsylvania Military College. As a freshman, we had to arrive three weeks in advance of the start of classes, so the upperclassmen, selected as Cadre, would be able to train and counsel us in cadet ways before the remainder of the Corps returned.

At lunch that day, all of the freshmen and their parents were assigned tables hosted by a member of the cadre. Ours was hosted by Cadet Lieutenant Darryl Warchel, a senior. Such a personable guy. Witty, intelligent, and always smiling, he held the table spellbound as he talked about how wonderful life at PMC was for him. At one point he asked me why I had selected PMC. I gushingly replied, "It's always been a dream for me." I'm sure, internally, he thought, "What a dork."

Dinner completed; the new "Rooks" went back out to our parents' cars to unload our luggage. Since Rooks were not permitted to wear civilian clothes, my luggage was one suitcase containing underwear, black socks, black military shoes, and toiletries. The clothing we wore today would be shipped back home after we were issued uniforms the next day.

As my parents drove off with my mom crying and waving out of the window, I don't think I ever felt so alone or sad. I knew that the next time I saw them would be Thanksgiving, nearly four months away. A very long time indeed for someone who had never been away from home.

I had been assigned to Company A or Alpha Company. I picked up my suitcase and joined all the other lonely Rooks sadly trudging in the direction of our dorm rooms. Not sure that I knew exactly where my company area was, I spotted one of the cadre and asked directions. "MAGGOT, DON'T YOU EVER ADDRESS AN UPPERCLASSMAN UNLESS YOU STAND AT ATTENTION AND USE SIR, YOU WORTHLESS PIECE OF COWSH*T!!", he congenially responded, while his face was about an inch from mine. My knees nearly buckled. I thought, "What in the Hell was this?" I was paying to be screamed at? But I gave my best shot at standing at attention and meekly squeaked, "Yes Sir." "IT'S ON THE THIRD FLOOR OF THAT BUILDING ON THE LEFT!! NOW PICK UP YOUR GEAR AND MOVE!!" I prayed that this guy was not assigned to Alpha Company cadre. And heaven gave me the finger in response, I just had the pleasure of meeting my new Platoon Sergeant, Cadet Sergeant Morris.

Moving down the corridor as fast as I could, I found my room and sat down at my desk for a few minutes to calm down when in a few moments, the door flew open and a red headed guy ran in and slammed the door shut, while yelling "HOLY SHIT, THESE GUYS ARE NUTS!!" I had just met my new roommate, Greg Wall, later nicknamed Grungie, who was just as confused and nervous as me.

It was impossible to calm down as through our closed door, we could hear all kinds of yelling and screaming. Then we both jumped when someone began pounding on our door. Neither of us wanted to open it, but we knew it would be worse if we didn't. As I opened the door, who should come barging in but Cadet Lieutenant Warchel, our charming, affable dinner host. "YOU TWO DOUCHBAGS ARE REQUIRED TO KEEP A DOOR KEY IN THE OUTSIDE LOCK AT ALL TIMES. WE DO NOT KNOCK TO ENTER AND WE DO NOT RESPECT YOUR PRIVACY. WE COME IN ANY TIME WE FEEL LIKE IT. AND AS FOR YOU, MC-GINNIS, LOOKS LIKE YOUR DREAM HAS TURNED INTO A NIGHTMARE!! He then grabbed our key and jammed it into the outside doorknob and slammed the door shut. So much for my idea of sitting down and getting to know him better. I was wondering if I could catch my parents' car.

For the next few hours, Greg and I sat in our desk chairs and stared vacantly out of our windows, wondering what fresh hell awaited us on the coming days and months. Again, our door slammed open and two more of our cadre strode into the room. "Well, it looks like we have two little lost sheep," Cadet Corporal Wayne Smeigh sarcastically remarked. "DIDN'T YOU TWO SCUMBAGS HEAR US CALL YOU OUT!!" Cadet Sergeant Dan Murphy yelled. "BOTH OF YOU TWO IDIOTS BETTER GET DOWN TO BED MAKING INSTRUCTION IN ROOM 309 NOW!!!" We both ran down to room 309, where all the other Alpha Company Rooks were already gathered, being shown how to make hospital corners on our beds. A little embarrassed to be making a late, grand entrance in front of a bunch of guys I didn't know, I sheepishly grinned at my fellow Rooks upon entering.

Stupid move since Cadet Sergeant Bobby Morris was the one giving the instruction and noticed the grin. He stared at me and yelled, "YOU WIPE THAT SIMPLE GRIN OFF YOUR FACE OR I'LL WIPE IT OFF FOR YOU!!" I was completely mortified that I just got my ass chewed out in front of everyone. About five minutes later, when Greg and I were struggling to try and make hospital corners on our own beds, the cadre started screaming again. "GET YOUR ASSES IN THE CORRIDOR, GIRLS, AND STAND AT ATTENTION WITH YOUR BACKS AGAINST THE WALL!!" We were then given more instructions.

In addition to the cadre screaming their names, ranks, and duties as an introduction, we were given our Rook rules and regulations.

First, we were taught the "brace," an exaggerated position of attention, where you forced your chin to touch your neck and you tried to touch your shoulder blades together. At the same time, you had to keep your stomach flat, and chest puffed up. We practiced this ridiculous posture for the next 30 minutes or so while the ever-helpful cadre blared corrective directions to individuals and continued to look upon us as something odious that you would scrape off the bottom of shoes. We finally stopped when the sweat on our foreheads would hold a dime in place.

Second, we were commanded to square the corridors. This meant the walls always had to brush our right shoulders while we walked in a bracing position. Furthermore, we were never to cross the center of our corridor. In short, if the corridor exit was halfway down on the left, we were to go to the very end of the corridor, make a "left face" at the first corner, make a second "left face" at the next corner, and then proceed to the exit. There were no exceptions. I gathered that in the event of a fire, we would be destined to die a screaming, agonizing death while making frantic "left faces".

Third, if a senior, or First Classman as they were known in cadet world, were to pass you, you were to immediately throw your back against the wall and scream at the top of your lungs, "SIR, ROOK (insert last name here), CADET NUMBER 278, WISHES TO GREET YOU GOOD MORNING (or afternoon or evening)." If not done with the proper level of enthusiasm, you could be ordered to drop and start doing pushups or be thrown against the wall to show the proper level of enthusiasm. One of the final dorm rules was to yell "Room attention" and leap to attention whenever an upperclassman entered your room.

Lieutenant Warchel was right, this was a nightmare, and one, for which I was incurring student loans to pay for. What was wrong with this picture? After all the instruction, we were ordered back to our rooms and go to bed. But the cadre had one more big surprise for us. During our little bracing party one of the cadre snuck into all of our rooms and tore them apart. Soon I was picking my underwear off the window blinds.

James H. VanSciver:
The Blood Drive

It was sometime in early November of my rook year in 1968 at Pennsylvania Military College that the company commander of Echo Company told me, "Eat a good breakfast on Thursday morning. You're going to give blood." I wasn't volunteering; it was a directive.

I've always felt I had sufficient orifices in my body, so it was with more than a bit of trepidation that I looked forward to this ordeal. Up to that point, I'd not had so much as a prick of my skin. Hell, even my polio vaccine came on top of a sugar cube! It wasn't that I was afraid of needles; I had never even seen one! Perspiration began to form on my brow for the next two days as the anticipation of this experience would come to fruition.

In order to give blood, one must be 17 years old, weigh at least 110 pounds, and be in good health. I checked all three boxes. It takes the normal individual about ten minutes to have one pint of blood sucked from his body. That one pint has the potential to save three lives. It is well known that there is no substitute for human blood. Each adult carries about ten pints of blood on his person, which is about seven percent of his body weight. One must wait 56 days before re-entering the line to provide this important service for mankind.

About this I was not thinking as I walked up the steps to the Armory that Thursday afternoon and opened the door. The place looked like the casualty clearing station for the Battle of the Bulge. There were columns and rows of tables neatly arranged with the necessary medical equipment at each one. Blood Bank staff were scurrying around like bees collecting honey. Donors were omnipresent.

My commanding officer, who must have doubted my ability to find the armory was right behind me and nudged me into the hall. "Wait here," he commanded, "until your name is called." There I was…trapped. No way out. Uncertain about what retribution would be assigned for my escape, I resigned myself to my fate.

"VanSciver!" It was my turn. Again, sensing that I was unable to find my way to the table assigned to leak this important liquid from my veins, my Echo leader was right by my side. "There you go, get up there." The nurse tried to make me comfortable, but she was not a psychologist. She could only raise the pillow on which my head would rest and ask me which arm I would use. She took my blood pressure.

"Left," I meekly responded. As this time, I heard a loud bump and realized that the cadet immediately behind me had fainted and rolled off his table onto the floor. My stress level was now on steroids. I hardly noticed her cleansing the spot near my vein with some large cue tip that had been reddened with some kind of juice. Next was the rubber strap which tightened around my muscle and finally, the needle. It looked like it was ten inches long!

She told me I would feel a little pinch; I closed my eyes and waited for the insertion. She untied the rubber band, gave me a soft rubber ball, and told me to squeeze. I saw my own blood running through a tube and into a bag. A short time later, she said I was finished, extricated the needle from my arm, taped a bandage on my wound, and told me to hold my arm straight up. She collected my blood and told me to move to the rest area.

Now for the great part. I was given free soda and cookies!

On the way there, my commander looked at me and smiled.

Upon reflection, I feel I owe him a debt of gratitude since I have, during my life, donated pints, and pints of blood, so much so that the Blood Bank personnel told me I had to stop because of the scar tissue build up on my vein.

But I will never forget those first few steps up to the door of the armory in November of 1968.

William Speer:
The CB Radio

Before entering PMC, I had been a very active CB radio operator. I had a nice set up in my room at home and could go "mobile" with a few adjustments. I met my first real girlfriend that way when I was about 16 years old. Well, at PMC I missed the chatter on the CB and after a few months, asked the cadre if I could put mine in my room as I could find no regulation preventing it. It was approved and when I had a chance to go home, I brought my radio and a small antenna.

My room overlooked the city of Chester and since the school was on a large ridge, I was sure it would transmit a good distance. Once set up, in my spare time I would, as the kids say today, "go online" and talk to folks. One day a teenage girl (I forget her name) and I started chatting. She lived in Chester and asked her dad if she could invite me to dinner one Saturday. Well, what cadet is going to pass that up? The day came and I walked the mile or so to her home. We met face to face, had a wonderful dinner and chatted with her family. When her father found out that Rooks could not have cars on campus, he volunteered the street in front of his house for a place to park my car. I readily accepted and started parking there as well as changing into civilian clothes, but paranoid I would get caught told almost no one I was doing that. I would just tell the guys I was heading to her house and that was it.

We had a nice time and shared some interesting experiences but FAR away from campus haunts where an upperclassman might see us. The relationship went on for the rest of my Rook year. The following year she was off to college, and I had to find a new place to park off campus, but I never felt comfortable leaving my old Pontiac Ventura anywhere else.

Scott McGinnis:
"RISE AND SHINE TURDS..."

Were the first words I heard at 5AM the next morning as our door once again slammed open. We threw on our clothes from the day before and hit the hallways in a brace. We then went outside for a little physical training...pushups, sit-ups, jumping jacks, and squat thrusts. After about an hour of this, when our clothes were both stinky and dirty, we were ordered inside to take a shower. After our shower, and re-donning our gross clothes, we were ordered back outside to get in formation. None of us had any idea of what a formation was, and the ever-helpful cadre shoved and pushed us until we did. They then marched us to breakfast. There we learned some more Rook rules. We were to sit on the first 6" of our chairs in a bracing position, keeping our eyes straight ahead. We brought food to our mouths by moving the utensils straight up from our plates to a position level with our mouths and then straight over to our mouths. Most of us wore our food for the first week or so.

Next stop, the barber, to cut off all of our hair. But I kept a lot of it, since most of it stuck to the food on my clothes. But then we got our first issue of uniforms, army olive drab fatigues, and black leather combat boots. We returned to our rooms, peeled our way out of our destroyed clothes, placed them in boxes to be shipped home, and put on our new outfits. I looked in the mirror and saw...Sgt Rock of Easy Company?.. nope...maybe Beetle Bailey?

Then for the next three weeks, all we did was get ready to be a functioning cadet. A typical day started with exercise in the quadrangle outside of our dorm, followed by a mile run in combat boots, followed by marching around the campus in formation, followed by manual of arms training with our M-1 rifles, followed by room inspections. After dinner we'd enjoy more bracing parties and constant harassment, or "bore-assing" as we called it, by the cadre. Then we'd have about an hour to ourselves before lights out. Plenty of time to make homesick collect calls home and to get to know our roommates better, because we weren't allowed to leave our rooms.

When the remainder of the Corps returned and classes began, things eased up a little bit. Sure, we still had bracing parties and room inspections, but for the most part our evenings after dinner went undisturbed, so we could study and do our class assignments. I suppose some guys did anyways. For the most part I continued my time-honored habit of tapping my pencil to the beat of whatever song happened to be on my radio and daydreaming about the first mixer (dance) coming up in the next few weeks. At last, I would be able to flaunt my new uniform for the girls busing in from a couple of neighboring colleges, like Westchester State, Brandywine, and Harcum Junior College.

The day of the mixer finally arrived, and I spent the better part of my day pressing my trousers, polishing my brass, and spit shining my shoes. I also practiced perfecting my best impression of a rakish smile.

My friends and I arrived at MacMorland Center, the student union, early and hung around outside to watch the buses arrive. And when they did, we tried our best to act nonchalant, and failed miserably. Giggling, whispering to each other, punching each other's shoulders, we were all 10 years old again, playing spin the bottle. For the first hour or so, most of us Rooks stood against the wall, while the girls stood against the opposite wall, while the upperclassmen, who had been to this rodeo before, pretty much had their pick of girls if they hadn't brought their own dates.

I decided I had to talk to a girl. Swallowing my fear of rejection, I asked a blonde girl to dance. Her name was Linda and she accepted. I was a college guy dancing with a college girl from Westchester College and I literally could not stop shaking with excitement. And then came that dreaded moment when that very first dance ended. The moment that is sometimes punctuated with a sweet "Thank you" from the girl as she rushes back to meet her girlfriends and tell them about the bozo she had just been unfortunate to meet. But she didn't and we kept dancing.

James H. VanSciver:
Homecoming 1968

To say that high school homecomings are different from those in college would be an understatement. This I learned as a rook cadet attending Pennsylvania Military College in the fall of 1968.

My fellow freshmen football players and I waited with positive anticipation for the big game on Saturday when we could see our upperclassmen win one for the home fans. Friday evening was abuzz with the traditional bonfire, get-togethers, and strategizing.

A pudgy fullback named Jerry Borga sloshed through the rain and mud on Saturday to gain enough yardage for Western Maryland to send the Cadets and their followers home in disappointment as the Terriers eked out a victory. If that dampened the celebratory spirits of the Chester crowd, it wasn't obvious Saturday evening as parties sprang up all over campus. The revelry lasted well into the morning hours.

But that wasn't the end of it. Somehow the brothers of TKE fraternity discovered a remote hideout nestled in the foothills between Chester and West Chester and decided to make a day of it on Sunday.

A couple of my friends and I were invited to the party only if we agreed to be a date for some of the TKE brothers' girlfriends' girlfriends who projected nasty dispositions and were aesthetically displeasing to the eye. This type of dating was foreign to me but, wanting badly to attend the party, I agreed to the deal. So did several of my friends.

How we and our dates found our way to the Grist Mill escapes my memory, but what a place it was. A couple of half-torn down rock buildings were surrounded by what looked like an old stone fence. Truly, it was picturesque and belied the activity which was soon to unfold there.

Keg after keg of beer was unleashed on the gathered throng. A live band had somehow been assembled to promote a stimulating background. Fraternity brothers greeted everyone like they were best friends as the partying ensued.

For a while I worked at conversation with my accompanying female who I did not like and with whom I did not want to be seen. It was a struggle.

I soon found myself sitting at a picnic table and was given a beverage container filled with beer. As my female companion watched, I was drawn into a game of whale's tails, a novel drinking game to me. Apparently, one of the goals is to prey upon the neophyte drinkers, of whom I was one, and get them into a state of delirium.

This I discovered as I found that the finger was frequently pointed at me at which time I was to take a large gulp of the contents of my cup. I could see that the same was happening to my freshmen classmates who had joined in on the fun.

My final memory is responding to one last directive to consume some of my beverage, tilting my head back, and looking at the bottom of my Baskin-Robbins milkshake cup as beer ran down my face.

Some homecoming!

William Speer:
On Patrol

As Rooks, there was a lot of work done by the upperclassmen and ROTC staff to introduce us to the rigors of military life and routine. We drilled every day it seemed, and Saturdays were always devoted to inspections and training. One day it was announced that the following weekend we would be heading to Ridley Creek Park (where we did a good bit of training) for a two-day exercise. I am sure my classmates were as excited as I was to break the routine, practice our newly learned military skills, and just get off campus!

When the day came, we drew our weapons and blank rounds. Once we arrived, each company of Rooks was given a section of the perimeter to "defend" against a possible attack by the Ranger Platoon. We also had a 30cal machine gun, if I recall correctly. I was informed that in the evening I would be leading a patrol to scout the location of an "enemy" mortar position and report back. ME? Why me? Did I exhibit some leadership qualities they wanted to test?

If I recall correctly, at about 2300 we organized the patrol with an observer and began our movement to the suspected mortar position. We were in a deep valley and moved along the left side of Ridley Creek towards our objective without issue. We climbed about three-quarters of the way to the top of the ridge where I sent out two scouts to recon for the emplacement. Once they reported back it as there and how many tubes and men, we started back down the steep ridge. It was pitch dark, but I saw a light spot on the ground and decided to jump there. I hit the ground, falling backwards, and the metal butt of my M-1 scraped down a large rock, throwing sparks everywhere!

At that point the mortar position was alerted due to my foolishness, and we could hear them above us. Making a critical error, I ordered the patrol to return the same way we had approached (never do that!). Down on the opposite side of the creek bed was the enemy in perfect ambush position. When we got into the "kill zone" they opened up and we all ran for our "lives." Once back, breathing heavily, I was chewed out by our observer in a smart military manner, lesson learned!

BTW, later, late that night the Ranger Platoon did attack us up the hill. We fired our M-1s with blanks, as did the 30cal team, or so they thought. Suddenly above the heads of the Rangers were red tracers cutting into the trees (good thing they were firing high!). The Rangers hit the dirt and started yelling to cease fire. The Rooks on the gun had no idea what had happened. It turns out the ROTC staff member who was responsible for checking the ammo before the exercise did not do his duty properly. I believe that was the last we saw of him.

James H. VanSciver:
The Rook Haircut:

When it comes to hair styles, fellas have a vast array of options, ranging from flat top, to mullet, to mop, to swish back, and everything in between. Typically, gentlemen prefer a design that accentuates their facial characteristics in the most positive way. When getting groomed, they may choose scissors or sheers; they may amplify their hair with gels or other ointments. Who can ever forget Brylcreem?

All that went out the window when we were summoned for our turn in the "barber's chair" in the late summer of 1968 at Pennsylvania Military College. To call what we got a haircut was a misnomer...a canard. The experience wasn't measured in minutes; it was reduced to seconds. Little was the conversation between the one holding the sheers and the one getting sheered. No quick looks in the mirror to determine if the back "looked right". No attention to making sure the follicles were all taken care of in an orderly fashion. No time to create that little curl in the back or attend to the sideburns under each ear. It was gone, all gone. If there would have been a sign promoting this establishment, it would have read, "Hair today; gone tomorrow." The "barber" simply pressed the sheers against the head and began shaving, not unlike a woodworker using a lathe to fashion wood. Only, the woodworker treats his wood in a much kinder fashion than did those handling our heads.

Cleanliness was not a major part of the encounter either. It was not possible to know if there existed any residue on the cutting apparatus from the previous rook, or the rook who sat there five persons ago. The pile of hair on the floor began to resemble a bird's nest as more and more strands drifted their way down.

An immediate and unmistakable result of this development was that the facial and head parts that the hair style was designed to accentuate in a positive manner were now all exposed for everyone to see. Typically, the chin looked longer, the nose protruded further, and the ears stuck out wider. A real babe magnet! Everyone quickly grabbed their piss cutters and pulled them down as far as they would go.

Another feature of hair is that it serves as camouflage to conceal the otherwise unpleasant abnormalities of one's cranium such as unsightly lumps, extended curves, an exceptionally large skull, or ears that are not lined up perfectly. Now, with the hair gone, all that was uncovered for any and all disgusted onlookers.

There was an upside to being sheered. No need for money in the budget for shampoo. Showers should have taken less time, leaving more time for studying. Like that happened. We didn't have to worry about the wind wreaking havoc on the top of our head; there was nothing there to distort. And sleeping did nothing to change how we looked. It should have been wonderful.

Most of us, after our first cut, had a tingling sensation; it itched. We scratched. I'm not sure if that was good or bad. Thankfully, this first cut took place in the late summer, so we didn't have to worry about sunburn on our fat bald pate. Some worried if it would grow back, or if it did, would it look different. Like a cowlick that moved to a different place.

One thing for sure, we didn't spend a lot of time taking pictures of ourselves during those first couple of months of our Rook year in 1968. No selfies! We'd rather those images not be rekindled.

Paul S. Lewis:
Rocks and Sky Earth & Space Exam

Earth Science Final Exam ... our first semester at PMC was wrapping up with the week of final exams. My favorite class was Earth Science with Professor Richard P. "Rocky" Boekenkamp. A large class, the final was held in the old armory. When the allotted time ran out, the Professor said, "Time's up, pencils down please!" I still had one more question to answer so I blurted out, "Professor, we're talking billions of years of earth history here—what's one more minute?!" He did not relent. As we all learned at some point in our education, exams are not so much to show how much you know, rather, how efficiently you convey what you know. As it turned out, that one unanswered question didn't matter, I passed the exam with plenty of points.

James H. VanSciver:
Marching to God:

During our orientation prior to our rook year at Pennsylvania Military College in 1968, we were asked to identify our religious affiliation. It seemed not so uncommon a query. It led to a most interesting development.

During our second week of school, after reveille awakened us on an early Sunday morning, we were assembled in the quadrangle and formed into companies as per our responses to that question. Next, we marched down the streets of Chester to our respective churches. In turn, we stopped and those whose persuasion was espoused in a particular faith were peeled from the formation to enter their desired house of worship. In retrospect, it was a marvel of organization, timing the beginning of our trek with the beginning of services at each stop. Credit given where credit is due.

However, I often wondered what the citizens of Chester thought as they viewed this highly organized group of young men donning their military regalia, making its way down the middle of the street in their respective communities. Also, somehow, cars were not an issue impeding our advance. Perhaps it was divine intervention.

I do remember that with each forward step the wool pants I was wearing shaved more and more hair off the back of my calf to the point where my wife now laughs at my bare lower limbs. I am still without hair there. Such were the sacrifices of a Rook at Pennsylvania Military College.

Zechariah 10:5 reads, "Together they will be like soldiers marching to battle through muddy streets. The Lord is with them, so they will fight and defeat the horsemen." We were preparing to be soldiers; our streets weren't muddy; the Lord was with us, and we did not have to fight any horsemen. However, our experience was not far from that biblical interpretation.

My selection was Lutheran. I remember it being at the very end of our march. There weren't many of us left at that point. During our services, there is a lot of litanies read and we get up and down a lot.

A couple of weeks later, some of my friends persuaded me to go with them to the Catholic church. What I remember most is that the collection basket was passed around two times. I thought the second time was for those of us less fortunate to take out what we needed. A swift rebuke from one of my classmates erased that thought permanently from my mind.

As services ended, we made our own way back to campus. I figured it was just too much of a challenge to coordinate the pickup of rooks from churches whose timing was significantly different from each other.

Another peculiar aspect of this practice was that, as quickly as it was begun, and as effective as it was, it didn't last long. It was just a couple of weeks until we were left to our own devices to get to those places where our transgressions would be forgiven, and our souls saved.

Still, like many of the routines at Pennsylvania Military College, this experience had a profound impact on me and my future.

Steve Kenevich:
Night Maneuvers

Jeff Fasset and I, along with the rest of us, were on night maneuvers in some park behind a fallen tree when some idiot who thought he was John Wayne came running up the road firing his weapon. We returned fire but he kept coming, so I bayoneted him over the tree. As I did, he fired his weapon which went off next to Jeff's face. That left a blood line in his eye that never went away, even many years after. Then we heard everyone cease fire because they found live rounds in the 50-cal…what a nightmare!

Stories and Vignettes from PMC

William Speer:
Step OUT!

"ECHO COMPANY STEP OUT!" These few words were heard throughout the barracks corridor at 1030 every night except Saturday and we Rooks had but a few seconds to get outside our doors, bracing. Then the next thirty or so minutes were a lesson in discipline and physical endurance. The upper-class cadre had many different "games" they wanted us to play, with them yelling at us all the while.

One favorite position was the "green-chair." We had placed our back firmly against the wall and slid down so we were in a seated position: without a chair! Then we raised our arms parallel to the ground like the arms of a chair. How long were we in this painful position? Time moves slowly when enduring such "torture," so it is hard to say.

One night we had a competition against another Rook company. They were all jammed into one end of a long corridor, we the other. The object was to have someone from our company get to the other end of the hall and slap the wall. Winners rejoiced while the loser suffered. BUT there was a catch, we had to do this on the floor in a low crawl position. That meant crawling over, under, around, and through, my company mates and the "enemy." Not sure there were really any winners in "games" such as this! That thirty minutes every night until we were recognized is something we all can never forget.

Paul S. Lewis:
Blowing Up the PMC Mascot

I don't mean blow up using explosives, I mean enlarge. The school was going to celebrate a milestone, 125 or 150 years since its founding, or something like that. All Rook companies were tasked with creating a decoration to put on the walls of MacMorland Center. I came up with the idea for Charlie Co. We would create a larger-than-life size version of the PMC Cadet Mascot! How? By taking the decal of the mascot (about six inches tall) and using the opaque projector in the ROTC classroom, "blow it up" (i.e., project it) onto a white bedsheet and trace the now six-foot-tall image with colored chalk. We hung the bedsheet over the projector screen and went about creating our masterpiece. When it was finished, we took it down, but the chalk dust had penetrated through the sheet, leaving an identical and clearly visible image on the screen! In spite of our best efforts to clean the screen, a faint image of the PMC Cadet remained in that ROTC classroom, much like a ghost, even after the disbanding of the Corps.

William Speer:
Pick a Pushup

I was in Echo Company "the Best Company, The Honor Company" as a Rook and squaring around the barracks corridor was a real chore. You had to run the gauntlet of upperclassmen walking, or should I say prowling the hall. They could ask you various Rook Knowledge questions and on and on. Get it wrong and you paid the price. One particularly devious way the cadre developed was a game called pick-a-pushup. In a cap, they would have little slips of paper with numbers from 0 to 100, you picked one and did that number of pushups. Well, some guys got the bright idea to palm a slip of paper with a 0 on it as they braced around the corridors. One unlucky fellow was caught, if I recall correctly, it was Jim VanSciver. You see, the cadre had gotten wise and taken the zeros out and he still "pulled" one! I remember having to witness him pulling numerous times as a punishment and he had to do the total number of pushups. If I recall correctly, he did 100!

Paul S. Lewis:
Mother's Day Parade

Towards the end of the spring semester, the Corps conducted a special ceremony to honor the mothers of PMC cadets. Other honors and recognitions were conferred as part of the Mothers' Day Parade, including promotion to corporal of one 4th classman from each Company. I was selected to be the Mothers' Day Corporal for Charlie Company. Unfortunately, my parents weren't able to come to Chester to see their son honored in this way. Not a problem, said my roommate Ed Rogers. He'll ask his older sister Jo to stand in for my mother. Jo played her part well and received some special recognition too. A significant part of the parade involved honoring all mothers in attendance. The 1st Classmen went into the stands and presented each mother with a flower, a long-stemmed carnation (or was it a rose?) Jo, being the youngest and prettiest "Mother" there, caught the attention of several 1st Classmen and received a veritable bouquet of flowers!

James H. VanSciver:
I Died a Soldier

It was the late 1960's; the Vietnam War was ongoing and had become unpopular; and I had enrolled in Pennsylvania Military College to begin my Rook year in 1968. I was brought up in a very patriotic environment so there was no problem with my entering a military school at that time. Just two years before, my older brother had enlisted in the navy.

I remember the Corps experience doing a good job of teaching us military bearing and the protocols of being a soldier. The staff of the military science classes in which I was enrolled were astute at sharing content about military history, military strategy, weaponry, and the impact of geopolitics on the decisions our military leaders had to make.

The training exercises in which we participated were helpful in putting the book work to practical use, especially our time spent at Fort Dix in the foxholes, on the firing line, and marking targets. The transition from class work to experience was smooth.

So absorbed was I with this combination of delivery styles that I bought in entirely to becoming a leader in the army. I remember placing a poem on one page of my scrapbook and encircling it with pictures of servicemen in various acts of combat.

The poem was, "I Died a Soldier." A 20-year-old soldier killed in action in Vietnam on February 1 of 1965 was honored posthumously with the top 1966 Freedom's Foundation Award. It was presented to Mr. and Mrs. Donald A. Strickland of Graham, North Carolina in the name of their son, Pfc. Hiram D. Strickland, whose final letter to his parents was found among his personal effects after his death. The letter expressed "Butch's" strong patriotic spirit, his pride in serving in our army, and his willingness to die to protect our freedoms if necessary. So taken by the tone, voice, and content of this letter was I that I was willing to follow in his footsteps.

Upon reflection, I do not question that decision at that time, particularly when many in our country were protesting the conflict. However, now over fifty years later, my perspective is a bit different.

Young and naïve, I knew not of the horror of war or the atrocities of combat. Never, in any of the military science classes, were we shown graphic images of the consequences of conflict. We were told about the damage a slug fired from an M-60 could do to a person and the destructive potential of hollow bullets, but that was it.

I remember, while marking the targets at Fort Dix, and hearing the shells pound in the sand bank behind me, thinking of what that missile would have done to a human body. We did not encounter content of this nature.

The reality of war is much different than talking about it in a classroom. Seeing a fellow soldier's leg being blown off when he steps on a mine, looking at the charred face of a soldier who was burned in a fire in his tank, or smelling the stench of decaying bodies lying on the battlefield (as was shown in the beginning of the movie Patton) tells the "rest of the story." Watching a friend's intestines falling out of his stomach which was gutted by shrapnel tells the full story.

Perhaps it would have been a good idea to assign, as homework reading, Erich Maria Remarque's "All Quiet on the Western Front" for one of the military science classes. He wrote in full detail about the revulsion of battle.

That may not have made a difference in my thinking at the time. I feel I would have still reacted the same way…but with a much greater understanding of that in which I was getting myself into.

War is hell. As someone once wrote, the aftermath is when the living envy the dead.

Dave Neimeyer:
Days of Innocence

My mother was very sullen that day in the fall of 1969. She seemed annoyed at everything and happy at nothing. I attributed it to the fact that her oldest son was leaving to enter college, and let it go at that.

My father, on the other hand, seemed calm and relaxed, although he was far quieter than usual as we drove the eighty miles south to Chester and Pennsylvania Military College.

I looked out the window and watched as the trees and houses passed by under the cloudless blue sky. Did I really want to go to college? I thought I did, but now I wasn't so sure. Did I really want to leave home like this? We passed through a series of small towns, each slightly larger than the one before. The scenery took on more and more an atmosphere of concrete and steel, in contrast to the woods and rolling fields of my home.

Why had I chosen a military college? There were several good colleges with ROTC in our area; I could have commuted to one of those. Why ROTC at all? I wasn't quite sure. Did I really want to be a Cadet, or was it just a thrilling overreaction to John Wayne movies and stories of West Point? I was still uncertain, but now the decision had been made. My tuition for one year at Pennsylvania Military College had already been paid; I was obligated to go. Besides, once I started something, I hated to back out. This characteristic had gotten me into trouble more often than I cared to remember. Would this be just another example of that? We drove south in silence.

At last we pulled into the PMC parking lot. My father relaxed and turned off the engine. "Well, we're here," he said cheerfully. We got out of the car and stretched at cramped muscles. Yes, but where is "here"? The buildings and walkways glared back at my contemptible ignorance of their names and functions. "Where do we go now?" my father asked.

"The papers the school sent me said I should go to the lobby of MacMorland Center, so I guess we should try to find that first," I replied.

It was easier to find than we had expected; all we had to do was locate a crowd of confused-looking people and join them. I merged with a group of confused looking young men while my parents milled around with an equally confused looking group of adults.

The confusion was ended as several Cadets arrived on the scene. Within minutes a sense of organization ensued. We were formed into lines and our processing began to run smoothly. I looked at one of the Cadets. His dark grey trousers were neatly pressed and spotlessly clean. Below the cuff-less trouser legs glowed a pair of incredibly glossed shoes. They seemed to be twin black mirrors, reflecting any light that struck their gleaming surfaces.

The black mirror of the shoes was contrasted by the golden mirror of his brass belt buckle. Above that was a short sleeved white shirt, its heavily starched creases standing out like knife edges. On the collar, shoulders, and pockets were fastened various insignia whose purposes were meaningless to me at that time.

I looked on in wonder. Would I look like that soon? Wow, wait till the guys saw me…better yet, wait till the girls saw me! Our parents were looking at the Cadets much as we were. Will my son look like that? Wait till my mother sees him! Better yet, wait till my mother-in-law sees him! The Cadets worked methodically, apparently unaware of the effect they were producing.

My 140 classmates and I were divided into four companies, plus a fifth group for the band detachment. I was assigned to Charlie Company. The name sounded strange to me. I received my room assignment: room 200, second floor, Cann Hall.

"Well, let's get your gear unloaded" my father said. I agreed and we spent the next half hour lugging boxes, bags, and suitcases up several flights of stairs. Someone else had their luggage in the room already, but no one was around. I read the lettering on a footlocker. "Orazio Nastace: Snowshoe, PA." I barely had time to wonder who Orazio Nastace might be when a young man walked into the room. "Hi…I'm Raz Nastace."

"Oh, uh... hi. I'm Dave Neimeyer. I guess we're roommates."

"Yeah, uh, I guess so."

I introduced my father and the three of us made small talk for a while. As we talked, I sized up my new roommate. Hmmm, couple of inches taller than me... I'd say about 5' 10". Also, about 20-25 pounds heavier; probably about 170-180. Seems friendly enough. Looks like we'll get along fine.

Raz suddenly stood up. "Hey, I've got to go find my parents. Hope you'll excuse me."

We agreed readily, realizing that my mother was waiting for us, too. We left the dorm and soon found her talking with a group of similarly misplaced and forgotten mothers. A quick glance at the clock tower revealed it was almost time for supper and my first experience with PMC food.

We made our way to the cafeteria, where we found preparations for a formal meal underway. We found a table, sat down, and waited. There was an opening prayer, and then food was brought to us, family style. As I ate, I surveyed my surroundings. Quite a few tables set up, most of them filled. A lot of young men in civilian clothes. Even more parents and other adults. Here and there were a few scattered Cadets. Looked like a nice sized crowd.

We had almost finished our desserts when a man stood up at the front table. He stepped to a microphone and made a short speech welcoming us to the college. Several other gentlemen made several other speeches, all saying much the same thing. Eventually the program came to an end. It was time for handshakes and good-byes. My parents jammed our last few minutes with words of advice. At the same time, I jammed them with words of reassurance, insisting I'd be fine, study hard, and write often. Then it was over, and those last few minutes were gone. I watched my parents drive away, and then I walked back to my room. Raz was already there.

"Your parents leave yet?" he asked.

"Yeah. How about yours?"

"Uh-huh. They left right after dinner. What are we supposed to do now?"

"I don't know." I replied. "I guess just start getting our stuff put away."

We began arranging things in our lockers and drawers and proceeded that way for several minutes. Suddenly we heard a shout from the hallway. "Charlie Company, Step out!"

Step out? What the heck was a "step out"?

"Come on, get out here!"

We got. All along the corridor, curious heads thrust out of rooms, joining the few brave souls already standing in the hall. Four uniformed Cadets stood along the hallway.

"All right, people," one of them bellowed. "When we call a step out, we want you out of your rooms, standing at attention next to your doors. Now get back in there and we'll try it again... Charlie Company, STEP OUT."

The bellowing Cadet looked up and down the corridor at our rigid bodies. "That's much better. OK. Let's get down to business. I'm Sergeant Howald. I'll be your Cadre Sergeant. With me are Sergeant Peterson and Corporals Hollander and Yiaski." The Cadets nodded and raised their hands as their names were called. Sergeant Howald went on with his monologue. "We're gonna be running a rough program here... probably rougher than anything you've been used to. If you put out, you'll get through just fine. If not, there's the door. Leave."

He continued to harangue us for several minutes. Regulations books were passed out; we were told to read and obey. We were told that from then on, we were to be known as "Rooks", and were given a book of "Rook knowledge" which we were required to know. It included the history of Pennsylvania Military College, important dates, a list of Cadet Staff, and a few other odds and ends.

We were instructed on the proper manner in which to greet upperclassmen, namely to yell out something along the lines of "Good morning, Sir: there are three days until we beat Upsala!" (or whatever the next team we played in football happened to be), or, if the upperclassman was a senior, to sound off with "Sir, Rook so-and-so requests permission to greet you good morning!" The emphasis was on the decibels: the louder they were, the better they liked it.

Sergeant Howald paused in his lecture to light a huge cigar, and then continued to enlighten us. Now we were informed that from then on we must "square" all corners inside the dorms. This meant that from the time we stepped outside our rooms until the time we left the building we must walk as close as possible to the wall on our right. At corners we were to stop, make a military facing movement to turn, and then proceed on. It was a very time-consuming process. Also, we weren't allowed to cut across the corridor. If we wanted something across the hall, we had to walk completely around, keeping the wall on our right, as before.

We were told of several other things we'd be responsible for, such as keeping ourselves informed of current events, and being prepared for daily room and personnel inspections. Finally, Sergeant Howald was through with us...for the time being. "Remember, gentlemen; PMC is the only place in the world where your rights are taken away and given back as privileges. Step in."

We tottered back into our rooms, staggering under the weight of a new way of life. Raz and I stared at each other. "Wow, this sounds like it's going to be tough!" Raz said, and I quickly agreed. A few minutes later we went to take showers before going to bed and had our first taste of the new system. Along with several other Rooks we squared and greeted our way around the corridor and past several upperclassmen to the bathroom, took our showers, then repeated the process back to our rooms.

It was a hot night. Although it was September seventh, the summer had lingered on. Barely a breath of air passed through our room, so Raz and I opened the windows all the way, then opened the door in hopes of encouraging a breeze. We got into our beds and settled down for the night. About ten minutes later one of the Corporals walked by, reached in, and closed the door. Probably thought we had forgotten to close it ourselves. I leaned out of bed and opened it again. A few minutes later the Corporal walked by again, saw it was open, and closed it once more. For the second time I leaned over and opened it. I was just dozing off when he saw it was open again and came back and shut it. I drowsily leaned over and reopened it. This time he was waiting for me.

"You're supposed to leave your door closed at night," he said.

"Oh, uhh, okay," I sleepily replied.

He closed the door and walked off. A few minutes later I reached over and opened it an inch or two. It was going to be a long year.

The next thing I knew, it was morning...or almost so. A few grayish streaks modified the blackness inside the room. From the hallway came an ungodly racket.

"All right, Rooks! Let's get on the ball! You were issued fatigues yesterday, now get them on and get out here. MOVE!"

We moved. A short time later we stepped out and joined the growing group, yawning and blinking in the hall. Here and there a few people were struggling with the laces of their combat boots, and then finally they too stood up at attention. Twenty-nine pairs of sleepy, confused eyes stared at the Cadre. Four pairs of eyes stared back at us.

"Okay, Rooks, down these stairs. Form up under that tree by the sidewalk."

We plodded downstairs and under the tree. Wonder what he meant by "form up"? We soon found out.

"Let's get in some straight lines! Come on; don't just stand there, MOVE!"

After a few minutes of moving, we had finally managed to form three reasonably straight lines. In this platoon order we were marched over to the football field for calisthenics. Several other companies of Rooks were already there, and the rest joined us within minutes.

We formed up in one huge formation and waited for further instructions. We were learning. A tall, skinny, black Cadet stepped forward. "Good morning, gentlemen. I'm Corporal Lewis." His voice was reasonably resonant. "We're now going to do some PT: physical training; but first, let's hear you growl…GRRRAAARRRW-WLLLLL!"

We tried to mimic him, unsuccessfully. "Oh, come on, gentlemen. I know you can do better than that. GGGRRRRAAAAWW-WWLLLLL!" We tried again, with better luck. "Much better, men. Now then, our first exercise will be pushups. On your stomachs!"

After an apparently endless series of pushups, sit-ups, jumping jacks, and other exercise on the dew-soaked grass, we were marched back and sent into the dorms for showers. As I walked into the dorm, I glanced up at the clock tower on Howell Hall. Five after six. I yawned deeply, then trudged up the stairs.

We had barely gotten cleaned up when it was time for another formation. This time we were marched over for breakfast. At last, I could relax again. I moved through the line and sat down at a table with several of my classmates. We had just started to eat when a corporal walked over and informed us that this was not how things were done in the Corps of Cadets. From then on we learned to remain standing at attention until an upperclassman had seated himself at the head of the table.

To our dismay, we discovered that breakfast and the other meals had just as many restrictions as walking and talking. We couldn't speak unless addressed by an upperclassman, we had to request permission to take seconds or to leave the table, and even our table manners were scrutinized and corrected. Could Rooks do nothing right?

Breakfast was soon over. We were dismissed and sent back to our rooms. Raz and I sat down to contemplate our new mode of existence. Suddenly the door flew open, and Sgt. Howald stomped in.

"Room Tenn-hutt!" he growled. "From now on, when anyone walks into this room, you don't look, you just snap to attention. You understand?"

"Yes, Sir."

"Who has the top rack?"

"I do, Sir." Raz said.

"Sgt. Howald looked annoyed. "When I ask a question, I want your name and number. Now then, who has the top bunk?"

"Rook Nastace. Sir: number three-forty-nine."

"That's better. Is this bed made correctly? Look at this: does that look straight to you?"

"No, Sir."

"This should be tucked in better...like this. Understand?"

"Yes, Sir."

"What's that in the corner? Is that dust? You're supposed to keep this room clean!"

"Yes, Sir."

"And whose shoes are those?"

"Mine, Sir...uhhh...Rook Neimeyer, Sir. Number two-oh-one."

"They don't belong there. Put them in the shoe rack where they belong." Sgt. Howald opened our cabinet drawers. "I want all this stuff folded better, and make sure it's in there correctly. Check your

Rook Knowledge book to see where it all goes. There are diagrams in there that tell you everything."

"Yes, Sir."

Sgt. Howald closed the cabinet doors and surveyed the room once more, then turned to leave. "This room has a lot of…you're still at attention, Mr. Neimeyer. Look straight ahead."

"Yes, Sir." I snapped back to a rigid pose.

"This room has a lot of improving to go. You fail inspection."

He closed the door behind him and walked off to the next room. Raz and I sank back down in our chairs for a second and looked at one another, then Raz got up and began to remake his bed. I grabbed a rag and began dusting the room. Our Rook year had begun.

Douglas P. Cervi:
First Time Experience

The parents were leaving after dropping off all the new cadets to begin what we thought was your typical college experience, or so we thought. I hear all this screaming out in the hall, so I ask my new roommate, Glen Dower, what is going on with all the noise as I had just asked him when is dinner!!! Glen said to me you have no idea what this place is all about and my response was, look I came here since my parents thought that it would be a good idea to come to PMC for the structure and I could play college football. My father was a B-17 radio operator in the 6th Army Air Corps during WWII and he said nothing about the military. One does not appreciate an experience until one is older. Would not trade those four years for anything, the X has served me well.

Douglas Cervi:
Fred

During homecoming in 1969, Fred Chiaventone was an amazing artist and drew some amazing art for football games, one of which I donated to the PMC Museum that he had done on a white sheet. Well, Fred did not restrict himself to art, but the making of bombs to send over to the opposite dorm from his dorm window using a sling shot made from surgical rubber. Things did not go as planned and Fred blew himself up and he looked like the mad scientist with his glasses tilted and his eyebrows singed and smoke bellowing out of his room. Laughing out loud just remembering this event.

David Neimeyer:
A Special Kind of Crazy

We were mostly teenagers living away from home for the first time, in most cases. Add to that the fact that we were Cadets in a military college dominated by three times the number of civilian students at the same college. Then throw in the special stresses of being underclass "Rooks" under constant review by upperclassmen, and it's no wonder that we often found special kinds of crazy ways to express and amuse ourselves.

Charlie Company's Rook corridor was on the second floor of Cann Hall. With the slope of the ground on which the dorm was built, that meant about a seven or eight foot drop to the ground from the base of the window sill of most rooms. That increased a bit at the end of the dorm. As rooks we couldn't just saunter out of our rooms and out the doors. We had to "square" the corridor. Leave your room, come to full attention, and perform a smart "right face," then march to the end of the corridor. At the end, do a "left face," then another left face to position yourself by the exit door. Then you would execute a right face, enter the stairwell, and exit the building. If you were going to the bathroom, instead of entering the stairwell you'd continue to march down the hall to the bathroom door. At this point, another right face would get you through the bathroom doors. Upon completion of your time in the bathroom you'd exit the bathroom and repeat the process until you reached the door to your room, at which time you'd complete another facing movement and enter your room.

Adding to the challenge, if at any time during your circumnavigation of the corridor you happened to come across an upperclassman, you'd have to come to complete attention while slamming your back against the wall and shouting as loudly as possible "CHARLIE ALL THE WAY, SIR!!" During football season, we had to add an equally enthusiastic "FOUR DAYS UNTIL WE BEAT UPSALA," filling in the correct number of days and our next opponent. Most upperclassmen would grunt a response and let us go on our way. However, there were some who delighted in extending the experience. "How many eagles on the PMC ring?" the upperclassman might ask. "When was PMC founded?" "Who is the current Secretary of Defense?" Almost any question was fair game, usually taken from our detailed "Rook Book" of facts, trivia, and other required knowledge. Lord help the Rook who stumbled at providing the proper answer in sufficiently enthusiastic (i.e. LOUD) manner.

With all that needed just to exit the building, it was natural to wonder if there was an easier way. I don't recall who it was (probably Jim McKelvey or Bill Znidarsic) who first considered using the windows to avoid all those facing movements. From there, it was a natural progression to wonder who could hit the ground first. After a series of competitions, the powers-that-were discovered the competition. The result was a formal order prohibiting jumping out of windows.

Ok, we couldn't jump out of windows. There was still plenty of entertainment to be had. Although we couldn't jump, the windows still could be used as a sort of mountaineering challenge to get to someone else's room. Charlie Kortlang was especially adept at this. He'd go out one window, then use the window ledge and frame as handholds to cross to the next window. It was not uncommon to be sitting in your room and suddenly hear a knock at your window, only to see Charlie grinning at you from outside, insisting that you open the window to let him in.

In addition to using the windows as an exit or for mountaineering practice, we also made paper airplanes and tossed them out to see whose could go the furthest. That soon got boring. As military cadets we had a number of training exercises where we were issued blank ammunition. It was easy to pocket a number of rounds when we turned in our M-1 rifles. We'd easily pop the wadding off each blank cartridge and pour out a teaspoon or so of black powder. We would then take a small rectangle of paper, pour the gunpowder onto it, and fold it like a teabag. We'd then staple the teabag to our paper airplane and attach a fuse of scotch tape sprinkled with gunpowder. As one person got ready to launch the paper airplane, a buddy would light the fuse. With luck, the plane would soar until the fuse hit the teabag and ignited with a small "poof." The flaming remnants of the paper airplane would crash to the ground below in often impressive fashion. It wasn't long before the ground outside our windows was marked with a number of small, burned areas.

Our pyromania was not limited to paper airplanes. On at least one occasion, someone set fire to Fred "Pony Soldier" Gerber's horse blanket that he had hung out his window to air out after a session with the PMC Mounted Troop, the Marauders. Cursing and stomping ensued as Fred quicky dragged the burning blanket back inside and stomped out the flames. More common, however, was what we referred to as "the ordeal of fire and water." Our floors were tile, and there was usually a gap of about ¼ to ½ inch between the bottom of the door and the tile. Several conspirators would gather outside the room of the victim. One would pour a generous cup of water on the tile by the closed door, so that it would start to flow into the room. A second conspirator would then squirt a healthy dose of lighter fluid on the water, which was then carried along with the tide flowing under the door. A third conspirator would then toss a match onto the mix of lighter fluid and water. The result was a flaming deluge crossing into the victim's room. Usually, the flames quickly went out as the water dispersed.

If we were especially devious, we'd heat the doorknob with a "right guard torch" created by a constant spray of deodorant ignited by holding a lighter under the spray. When the victim saw the flaming flood coming into his room, the first response, after ensuring the fire was out, was to grab the inside doorknob, intending to charge into the hall to confront his attackers. The heat transfer from the heated doorknob was not enough to seriously burn the victim, but it did provide a noticeable jolt of heat. A variation on the theme was to "penny" a person in his room before starting the deluge. By quietly forcing pennies between the door and the frame, it would build up enough pressure that the door would stick closed. Only by vigorous jerking of the door knob (or an assist from outside) would the door finally open. We'd usually stop with the lighter fluid after the first burst, but a bit more water to add to the flood was often appreciated by all concerned (except for those in the room).

It remains a mystery to this day how we somehow managed not to burn down the dorm or end up in the emergency room with sundry burns or broken bones.

Scott McGinnis:
The Cadet Hypnotist

Sometime after Christmas vacation in early January 1969, I decided I wanted to learn to hypnotize people and bought a book on how to do it. I have no earthly idea now why, but it wouldn't surprise me if it had something to do with girls. And I actually think I learned it a little, of course I couldn't do it with a swinging watch or "Look into my eyes" schtick, but I found I could do it by having someone stare at an immobile burning end of a cigarette in a darkened room without blinking. And for it to work, there was one other requirement, the subject had to be very dim. And there was one guy in our company who fit that bill, Dennis Berte. Dennis was really a sweet, shy, even-tempered guy who had biceps as big as my thigh. So one night I had a bunch of guys in my room, Greg Wall, Steve Adam, Bobby Gerling, and a few others, including Dennis, and I said I was going to try and hypnotize one. I asked Dennis if he'd let me try. He agreed.

I lit the cigarette, placed it on the desk, turned off the lights and told everyone to be quiet. Then I started in a very quiet voice, "You are getting very sleepy, you cannot hold your eyes open, blah, blah, blah" and after about 15 minutes of this, he actually did appear to be asleep. I then gave him a post hypnotic suggestion, something very mature, "Every time I say the word, man, you will pick your nose." I then brought him out of his slumber while everyone watched. I said something, included the word man, and he jammed his finger in his nose. I did it several more times and each time he responded. I was pretty damn impressed with myself, and I put him back to sleep and subsequently woke him up, reminding him he wouldn't remember anything.

When he woke up, he groggily asked what happened, and I said, "Oh man, you ..." And his finger went back up his nose. I thought he was kidding and asked him what he was doing. He insisted he wasn't doing anything and when I said, "C'mon man," his finger was in his nose again. He also didn't look or act right. He sounded very loopy and couldn't keep his eyes focused, then he just fell back asleep again. This time, I couldn't wake him. We all started to panic and then the rats started abandoning my very leaky ship, until it was Greg, Dennis, and me.

I didn't know how I was going to explain this fiasco, but I ran to the bathroom to get a glass of water and started to sprinkle it on his face. He started to wake a little and when he did, Greg and I sat there and stared at him, scared shitless until he woke up again and sort of staggered back to his room. The next day he seemed sort of normal, but oddly quiet. He never came back after Spring Break and for weeks I scanned newspapers for reports of ritual killings where the only clue was a smeared booger on the bodies of the victims.

Paul Lewis:
Hair

In the spring of 1969, all Rooks were looking forward to the "Old Man" recognition ceremony. Not only would we be fully accepted into the Corps and would no longer have to do Rook sorts of things, such as bracing in the halls, we could grow our hair and look normal again! In anticipation of that day, my roommate Ed Rogers would turn up the volume of his radio whenever the popular song from the musical Hair was playing and he'd start mouthing the lyrics karaoke-style. We became Old Men on April 10, 1969 and immediately began growing hair again! More than 50 years later, how many of us "Old Men" wish we could still grow hair as we did back then!

Dave Neimeyer:
Nicknames and Other Animals

It soon became obvious that we were going to have difficulty identifying people and describing them to others. After all, we all wore our hair the same way (trimmed neatly to within 1/8 inch of the scalp), and we all dressed alike: namely in grey trousers, grey shirts, grey hats, and black ties, belts, and shoes. A military school such as Pennsylvania Military College leaves little leeway for individuality. In fact, it became so bad that it was a standard joke to describe someone by saying "Oh, you know who I mean...he stands this tall, has short hair, and wears grey all the time." Of course, everyone had a real name, but it was too easy to confuse which name went with which Cadet.

Our solution was simple: we began to use nicknames when talking about someone. The plan worked perfectly; too much so, in fact. Soon we were solidly in the habit of using nicknames, and somehow that habit was never broken.

Some nicknames were easy to explain. "Crazy Charlie", for example. Charles Kortlang arrived at PMC with thoughts other than getting a college education...considerably other thoughts. He was not given the name Crazy Charlie: he earned it. One of Charlie's favorite tricks was to low crawl out of the cafeteria on his stomach, slither down the stairs, and slide under one of the benches on the lower level of the building. From this vantage point he'd wait until an unsuspecting civilian student (preferably female) walked by, then he'd spring out and bite his hapless victim on the ankle.

Charlie also had a deep-rooted fondness for things that went boom. If it was any kind of exploding device, you could be sure that Charlie would be on hand to cradle it, caress it, take it apart, and make it tick.

In the field of explosives, though, there was someone even more devoted than Crazy Charlie. Fred "Mad Bomber" Chiaventone took top honors in this category. Fred earned his nickname near the end of our freshman year. In order to properly celebrate the recognition of the freshmen as upperclassmen, Fred was preparing a little device with which to surprise his supervising Cadre of upperclassmen. He fastidiously saved several dozen rounds of blank ammunition, gathering them a few at a time from various field training exercises. From these he carefully salvaged a modest amount of black powder. To this he planned to attach a triggering device fashioned from flashlight batteries, wire, and a flash bulb.

Unfortunately, Fred accidentally triggered the device prematurely as he was assembling it. In true IRA manner, it blew up in his face. With burned hands and face, his sight saved only because his glasses kept the flames from his eyes, Fred ran screaming down the corridor. Screams of agony? Hardly. No, what Fred was yelling was: "It works! It works! It has its drawbacks, but it works!"

Bill Znidarsic was also highly enthusiastic about bombs and blew up his own room at least once a week, primarily to annoy his overly fastidious roommate. Bill received his nickname in another manner, however. It was right before the Christmas furlough, and our Cadre decided they'd be nice to us and let us have a party. Once people were full of holiday spirits, things really began to get wild. As so often happens, cross words were exchanged, and Bill snapped out. As Bill's antagonist raced down the hall for the safety of his room, Bill picked up one of the cinder blocks that supported our attempt at a Christmas tree and bounded down the hall after him. Taking long, bounding leaps, Bill looked more like he was flying than walking. When it became obvious that the offender would escape, Bill hurled the cinder block at him, only to see it shatter against a rapidly closing door. Because of Bill's apparent flying ability and super strength, coupled with a slight physical resemblance to a commercial super-hero of the day, Bill was dubbed "Cookie Man". The name stuck, and his famous cinder-block recipe became a standard company joke.

Some people got nicknames because of difficult surnames. In this manner, Donald Kajioka became "Kaj" and Nickolas Tscheremischin became "Transmission" or simply "Mr. T." Others were awarded nicknames on the basis of physical appearance. Rick Parsons was short, with the pinched, squinty look reminiscent of a small burrowing animal. He became "The Mole". Doug Percz's stiff style of marching earned him the short-lived moniker of "Mr. Machine" until popular demand replaced it with "Lizard" because of his constant scowl, which was said to resemble that of a lizard waiting for its prey. And, of course, there was Jim "Happy Sperm" World. As one of our classmates put it when asked why Jim was given that nickname: "Because he looks like a happy sperm."

Even upperclassmen were not immune (although never addressed by nickname to their face). Thus, Perry Silver became "The Penguin" or "The Gay Blade". A tall, lanky senior became "Birdman" Esto. Others received even more unattractive monikers based on their zeal for enforcing discipline or harassing us freshman.

Some of the nicknames had unpleasant connotations. For example, when Dave Morge developed a case of terminal athlete's foot, he scratched his way into posterity as "Cheesefeet" Morge. There was Arthur Jackson Newell, who was elected president of the Freshman class by more votes than there were freshmen. A cry arose that ballot-stuffing had occurred. Art loudly and sincerely proclaimed his innocence. A second election was held, and Art pulled in even more votes. An investigation was begun, and Art quickly resigned his title as Mr. President and assumed a new name as "Honest Abe" Newell.

My own nickname is a little harder to explain. For a while I was referred to as "Ratman," then as "General Neimeyer," and also by several other appellations, but none of them seemed to fit. One day, however, Cookie Man and I were sitting in the cafeteria talking about a book we had just read: "The Lord of the Rings." I casually remarked that one of our classmates fit Tolkien's description of a Dwarf perfectly. We spent the next several minutes fitting other classmates into the various categories of Dwarves, Elves, Orcs, and Hobbits that Tolkien used to populate the lands of "Lord of the Rings." After a while, Cookie Man asked "Dave, what would I be?" I considered the question for a moment or two, then replied "You'd probably be a Hobbit." Like Tolkien's Hobbits, Cookie Man was chubby, good natured, and loved to eat and make things with his hands (usually bombs, in Bill's case).

Bill then asked, "What would you be, Dave?" I thought about it for a moment, then realized that the description fit me as well. "Probably a Hobbit too." Bill laughed gleefully, then spread the tale that we were both Hobbits. Bill already had a nickname as Cookie Man, but I had none, so from that day on I was invariably addressed as "Hobbit."

In these and dozens of other ways, we gradually found nicknames for nearly everyone we came in contact with. A person could go for months, defying all efforts to have a nickname tacked on himself, then a careless phrase or gesture would create a name that stuck. We seemed to sense immediately and instinctively when the correct name had been found. It would just sound right, somehow, and within a day or so the recipient would be addressed more and more frequently by his new name. Often in a month or so his true name would have been forgotten and only "Mr. Eyebrows," "Connecticut Yankee," or "Pony Soldier" would remain. (Years later, when I was a Junior, there were freshmen who addressed me as "Sergeant Hobbit," thinking that Hobbit was my real surname.) Despite the restrictions of a military lifestyle, we were gradually discovering a way to regain our individuality through nicknames.

Dave Neimeyer:
Interior Decorating

Our rooms in the Cadet dorms at Pennsylvania Military College were bland. The cinder block walls were a pale sort of yellowish green. The floor tiles were a sort of muddy maroon color, with streaks of grey and brown. The cabinets were cream colored, as were the bunkbed poles hanging from the ceiling, supporting two modest sized beds, affectionately known as "racks". Adding to the bland was the requirement that our beds be crisply made, topped with our scratchy red wool PMC blanket. The scrawny pillow was centered above a crisp six-inch border created by folding the sheet and red wool blanket just so. Of course, all corners of the bed were tucked in crisp and tight.

The lockers were precisely arranged. Underwear on the top shelf of the main cabinet, folded around a piece of cardboard so that identical rectangles of stacked white cotton greeted the observer who opened the cabinet door. Most cadets meticulously folded and arranged several sets of underwear to meet the standard, then threw the rest in a bag in a drawer which was not usually inspected. The open hanging wardrobe held the shirts, pants, jackets, and coats of the two roommates. Each roommate had a specific side. Items faced inward, fully buttoned, and in a precise order. The free world would definitely collapse if, for example, a jacket preceded the starched and buttoned shirts, instead of holding its place towards the outer edges of the closet. Shoes were precisely lined up below, fully shined.

The plain metal desks were topped with faux wood, with a standard lamp placed exactly where regulations demanded. The desktop was to be kept clear, except when actually doing homework or similar activity, in which case a textbook, notebook, pen, or related items could be exposed.

As freshman Rooks, our rooms were subjected to impromptu

inspections at any time. Deviations from the standards were to be avoided at all costs, and corrected immediately when brought to our attention, which was usually done at extreme volume with cascading comments on our habits, heritage, and general (lack of) potential. Formal inspections were done at roughly one or two week intervals by the military staff.

We quickly learned a few tricks to help survive the regimentation and inspections. If there was a particularly demanding upper-class cadet, bribes such as candy or cookies from home often helped reduce the vitriol. To deflect the military staff, if was best to find out their military branch (for example, armor, cavalry, etc.) and then build a model of something related to that branch and display it (per regulation position, of course) on one of the shelves. As the inspector entered the room and began to inspect the premises, their eyes would fall on the model.

"Whose model is that?" they might ask. "Is that an Abrams?"

"Mine, Sir" a cadet would respond, in appropriate volume.

"Nice job. I see you've included a tool bag on the railing. When I was serving on one, that's just where we'd hang it."

"Yes, sir," we'd respond.

"Whoops, I'm running behind. Your room passes. Nice job on the tank."

If one lacked the skill or resources to create a distinctive model, there was always "pledging the floor." Floors needed to be spotless for inspections, of course. When dusting the room, we often resorted to using the dust rag to get dust nurdles off the floor. The danger was that the furniture polish/dusting spray (usually "Pledge" brand) would make the floors slippery. A little applied near the door would become a trap for the inspector. The inspector usually stepped briskly into the room. If they encountered a slight slip, it would often leave them a bit off balance and disconcerted for the inspection. They'd subconsciously want to finish the room quickly and be done with it. However, a bit too much Pledge, and the accompanying broader slip by the inspector would usually evoke a chewing out by the inspector, who realized what had been done, and who would then conduct a very thorough inspection to see what the duplicitous Cadets in that room were trying to hide.

In late spring of our freshman year, we were finally "recognized" as full cadets, no longer lowly Rooks. That opened up a bit more leeway in personalizing our rooms. Posters and photos could be hung on the walls, and more items were allowed on the shelves. Bill Znidarsic managed to take the leeway to its furthest extreme.

Bill had been a Charlie Company rook for most of the year, but eventually decided to drop out of the Cadet Corp and college and join the Army. After finishing boot camp he returned to PMC in our sophomore year to visit his former fellow rooks. Inspired by his Army training, he used magic markers to fill one wall of my room with a mural "The Spirit of the Bayonet." A life size GI was blasting an enemy soldier under the legend "The Spirit of the Bayonet — to kill, to kill without mercy." During a subsequent inspection, Staff Sergeant Behney quietly observed the mural, then said simply, "You'll need to paint over that at the end of the year." Of course, we decided it would be unfair to deprive future residents of that room the pleasure of enjoying the mural.

Sometimes our efforts were focused on specific friends. Doug Percz was known for his somewhat prickly personality, with a bit of paranoia thrown in. If he caught you glancing in his direction, he'd usually accost the gazer with something like "what are you looking at?" accompanied by a scowl and piercing gaze of his own. Sometime during our sophomore year, he went home for a weekend. That's when the conspirators struck. Several of his classmates had been cutting eyes out of magazines for some time and had amassed an impressive collection. They now set about to distribute the eyes throughout Doug's room. The eyes were taped inside lampshades, on his desk and walls, on closet doors, or light switches...anywhere that could hold a pair of eyes or two. They even randomly inserted eyes within the pages of his books.

When Doug returned to campus and entered his room, his shouts of dismay could be heard up and down the corridor, continuing as he discovered and removed more and more of the offending eyes. On the positive side, after his initial shock, Doug took it very well. Months later he jovially remarked "Hey, look what I found!" as he displayed a set of eyes that he had discovered in one of his textbooks.

Less obtrusive were our efforts during junior and senior year to bring some life to our rooms, while preserving the heritage of the corps. We'd remove the closet doors, turn them around, and leave our artwork on the reverse side of the doors. Among other efforts were a map of J. R. R. Tolkien's Middle Earth, a drawing of the Hulk, and various other quotes and offerings. As we were expanding our art gallery, we came across proof that other Cadets before us had similar ideas. Inside a locker door in room 210 Turrell Hall, we found the following: "To whom it may concern: I wish you good luck throughout your years at Pennsylvania Military College. These will be years of trials, and there will be many pressures placed upon you. Above all else, maintain your personal dignity and honor. They are irreplaceable. Have no fear; meet events squarely. Remember the Golden Rule and practice it often. Otherwise, you will be a hollow man with nothing more than a stained record. You will make mistakes but learn from them by not repeating them. Face your shortcomings and strive to correct them. May God bless and keep you safely." That ended our artistic efforts. No way could we top that.

Stories and Vignettes from PMC

Dave Neimeyer:
The Great Dead Rat Trick

To us, as freshman Cadets, the year seemed endless. We had already undergone a long indoctrination period, and, from the looks of things, it was going to drag on even longer. For Freshmen, or "Rooks" as we were called, the only break in the monotony of classes and military training came on weekends, when we were granted the dubious honor of being allowed to go into the city of Chester on twelve-hour furloughs. We were thrilled. A whole twelve hours in one of the dirtiest, most crime ridden cities on the eastern seaboard. It was not without reason that Cadets referred to Chester as "the Armpit of the East."

It was during one of these weekend interludes that two of my classmates and I struck upon a true prize, one that was to have reverberations throughout the Cadet Corps. For as Kaj, Cookie Man, and I walked along, we discovered a group of Chester Urchins playing with a dead rat. Now the sight of a dead rat was nothing new to me. However, the crushed, cardboard stiff corpse which was presently serving as a football for a handful of kids bore little resemblance to the well-rounded rodents proudly displayed at home by my cats after a night of successful hunting.

"Hey, do I ever have a great idea!" said Cookie Man. "Let's take that rat and send it to the Corps Executive Officer! Oh Wow!"

"Send it to the XO? Are you crazy? He's a Senior!" said Kaj, ever mindful of the strict class system within the Cadet Corps; a class system that made Freshmen into dirt and Seniors higher than gods.

"Why not? After all, he's the one responsible for our long Rook period. We'll put it in a box and mail it to him. He'll never know who sent it!"

I was starting to get caught up in the project. "Why don't we put some insignia on it, too?"

"Yeah," said Kaj, as he too warmed up to the idea. "Or maybe a regulations book or something."

"Oh, wow, this does sound good!" Cookie Man laughed. "It will be the best trick ever! Hobbit, go get the rat!"

"Me? Why me?" I protested. "Why should I be the one to have to go get that thing?"

"Why not?" said Kaj. "It's dead. It won't bite."

"Yeah, but it's got all kinds of germs and stuff on it. Besides, I hate to take it away from those kids." I quickly started to walk away.

"Aw, come on," said Cookie Man, dragging me back. "You can pick it up with a stick or something."

"Yeah," Kaj chimed in. "It didn't hurt those kids any."

I stood and watched as the Urchins disappeared around a corner, leaving the rat lying in the gutter. I wavered for a moment. "Well, you guys gotta help."

Kaj and Cookie Man grunted their approval, and soon we were back in my room, showing off our prize to our admiring buddies. We closed the paper bag which we had used to carry the rat back from Chester, then set about with our plans.

"Let's wait until tonight, then take it over to his room." someone suggested.

"What are we gonna do with it till then?" someone else asked.

"Let's leave it in Hobbit's room."

"My room! You're not leaving that rank thing in my room! I don't want to get caught with it!"

"Aw, it will be all right" said Kaj. "Just put it in a plastic bag. It'll be ok till tonight."

"Yeah, Hobbit, come on. We're depending on you."

Under their arguments, I finally relented. It really was much better after we interred the carcass in a plastic bag and threw it into the storage space of our locker. In fact, with that taken care of so easily, we felt free to head off to the student center for supper and a hearty bull session there.

Several hours later I returned to the dorm. As soon as I entered the stairwell I knew that the plastic bag wasn't strong enough. The faint but unmistakable scent of something dead was beginning to permeate the building. I ran to my room, closed the door behind me and opened the windows as wide as possible. Then I ran to find my co-conspirators. "Hey, we gotta get rid of that thing right now. It's stinking up the whole dorm." The last sentence was superfluous. Adding credence to my words, once free of my room the smell had followed me down the hall and settled into the bull session I had interrupted.

"Jesus Christ, Hobbit! Close the door! You're letting that stench get in here. Lord, what a rank smell!"

"Come and help me get rid of the rat!" I insisted.

"It's your room; you get rid of it!"

After some fruitless pleading I realized that no one was going to help me. I trudged back to my room to prepare our little present to the XO. I gathered together my supplies: an extra cadet Private insignia, a regulation book, a half used can of shoe polish, and a broken collar stay. I emptied some odds and ends out of an old shoe box and prepared it to receive its new contents. Finally I retrieved the plastic bag and began to open it.

As soon as the bag was unwrapped, out came a stench of such magnitude that it seemed to take the paint right off the walls and turn the ceiling brown. I choked. I gagged for air. I staggered back and stuck my head out the window. Air! Good fresh air! I drew several deep breaths. Ah, to be able to keep my head out the window all night, breathing the cool air. Yet I knew the job must be done. I held my breath and drew back into the room.

I ran to my locker and armed myself with a can of antiseptic foot spray in one hand and a can of Right Guard deodorant in the other, then turned and let loose with both barrels. The rat lay indifferent as the spray slowly soaked into its matted fur and puddled up in the bag. After a few minutes, the spray began to take effect. My room smelled like a deodorant factory, but at least the air was a little more breathable.

After another few minutes of leaning out the window, I threw the reg book into the shoe box, then dumped the rat in on top of it. I picked up the private's pip and crunched it into the rat's shoulder. Into the box went the shoe polish and the other paraphernalia, topped off with several more minutes of spray, just for good measure. The lid was quickly taped on, and a note added: "For Dave Esto, Corps Executive Officer." The deed was nearly done. Only the delivery remained.

Picking up the box, I headed out of the building. However, just as I got to the door I saw that the weekly dance in the dining hall was breaking up, and the quadrangle between my dorm and the XO's dorm was covered with young couples walking about. By this time, the smell of the decaying rat was starting to defeat the Right Guard, and my lungs were begging for relief. I wavered, and my resolve broke. "The heck with it" I mumbled, as I shoved the box into a nearby trash can and retreated back into the dorm.

As I wandered around, waiting for the air in my room to become breathable again, I bumped into Crazy Charlie Kortlang and told him of the rat's final resting place.

"Aw Hobbit, what did you do that for? Let's go see if it's still there."

It was.

As soon as we saw that, Kortlang began to cajole me into completing the mission, but this time I stood firm. "Oh no" I insisted. "I ain't touching it any more. I've had it with that thing. It is over. Kaput. Finished."

"How about if I carry it and you cover me?" asked Crazy Charlie.

"Well, I don't know..." I hesitated.

"Come on, Hobbit!"

"All right," I reluctantly agreed. "Let's get it over with."

So, with me walking next to Crazy Charlie to hide the box from view, we took our gift to the upper-class dorm. Crazy Charlie zipped inside while I loitered near the entrance and waited for him to emerge. Within moments he was back outside. "I set it in the hallway next to his door," Crazy Charlie triumphantly announced.

The next morning Cookie Man came bursting into my room. "Hey, guess what! They found the rat!" he cried.

Crazy Charlie and I jumped up in excitement. "Yeah? What did they do?"

Cookie Man was exuberant. "Oh Wow! They're going nuts! It was something else!! From what I hear, Esto really blew his top! He's over there now screaming for the guy that did it."

When the XO of a unit screams, the noise usually travels for quite a distance, and makes some waves in the process. Throughout the Corps, freshmen were grilled and quizzed to no end. Thorough checks were made for missing reg books and insignia. Luckily, we had prepared well and had already replaced the materials we had used. Classmates who had earlier left the Corps had unknowingly donated their discarded reg books and insignia for our plot. Our trail was covered well. Only a few people knew who the culprits were, and those few were trusted friends.

The XO never quite got over it. The ruckus calmed down in a week or so, but his curiosity was working full time. Who had sent him the rat? Who? It looked as though he would never find out. However, a joke is never really complete until everyone can laugh at it, so we made plans for a little epilogue to smooth things over.

Our opportunity came several weeks later, on the night we were "recognized" as upperclassmen. Our Rook period was officially over, and the XO had mellowed considerably as far as our pranks were concerned. We stood in the hallway of our dorm as he congratulated us for making it through our Rook year. A holiday atmosphere blanketed us all. Now was the time for the proper punch line. I walked over to where the XO stood. "Uh, Captain Esto..." I said, "If you're done with my private's pip, can I have it back now, Sir?"

He looked at me confusedly for a moment. It did not hurt that I had a reputation as one of the least rambunctious freshmen in the Corps. Then his eyes widened, and his mouth dropped open. "You! You're the one! You sent the rat!" A grin erupted on his face, then he broke into hearty laughter. We all joined in. The Great Dead Rat Trick had reached its climax and had ended up as one of the best practical jokes of the year. Final score: Freshman 1, Seniors 0.

Dave Neimeyer:
Seeing Double

Although I only lived an hour or two from PMC, some of my classmates lived considerably further away. I often took friends home with me on holidays, or for a weekend escape when we became upperclassmen. For Thanksgiving of my freshman year, I took Jim McKelvey home with me. Jim was from California and would otherwise have been stuck on a nearly deserted campus. Besides, things were a lot more fun with a friend around.

Because we were still freshman "Rooks", we were required to be in our Cadet uniforms, even when we were off campus. We weren't quite sure who would see us and report us that far from PMC, but we weren't about to take any chances. Uniforms it was, as we headed off to see a high school football game between my alma mater and a neighboring rival. Jim and I were both suitably impressed when we arrived at the stadium and the ticket taker just waved us in without having to pay.

Nice! Later that evening we went on a double date with Debbie and Donna Speer, friends of mine who were identical twins. When we got to the movie theatre, the ticket taker again waved us in without having to pay. I guess the "Doublemint" effect of identical twin girls with two similar looking guys in identical Cadet uniforms was a winner. We had a hard time paying for anything while wearing our uniforms.

Later that spring I again asked the Speer twins out on a double date when I took another friend, Fred Butler, home with me. Fred's dad served in Europe in World War II and had married a German war bride. Her father, Fred's grandfather, and her brothers had served in the German army. Fred's grandfather had been in charge of one of the prisoner of war camps for Allied prisoners. He and at least one of Fred's uncles were killed during the war.

When we arrived at the Speer house, one of the twins answered the door. I cheerfully introduced her to Fred.

"This is one of the Speer twins," I said.

"Which one," she quickly demanded, with a grim look.

"Debbie," I quickly responded.

She smiled and welcomed us inside. Thank goodness I had guessed correctly, or that evening could have been over quickly.

As we waited for the girls to get ready, we made small talk with their mother. Their mom mentioned that the girl's father had served in the Air Force. I jokingly said "Oh, that's the service where they can retreat at 600 miles per hour." Mrs. Speer responded, "He spent several months 'retreating' in a prisoner of war camp after he was shot down in World War II."

Fred immediately chimed in, "Which one? Maybe he knew my grandfather."

Luckily Debbie and Donna appeared about then, so I quickly stifled Fred and we headed off to the car, leaving Mrs. Speer standing there with a puzzled look on her face.

Dave Neimeyer:
The Sage of Jim McKelvey

Jim McKelvey was our friend. We were worried about him. Jim had gained fame as a wrestler at his high school in Fresno, California, but had always had trouble finding a girl to share his thoughts with. Even after he won an Army scholarship and crossed a continent to come to Pennsylvania Military College, he still could not win the hearts of fair young maidens and gain the love he needed.

We worried about him with the zeal and concern of friends everywhere. Long hours were spent in bull sessions devoted to the problem of finding him a girlfriend. Jim gave his tentative approval to our efforts, then went on to pursue his own line of attack.

The bull sessions struck pay dirt first. "Mole" Parsons remarked that there was a cute girl that went to his church near campus. McKelvey went with Mole the next Sunday and gave the girl the once over. He approved of what he saw and made the proper overtures. The girl responded, and before long they were dating regularly. We all breathed a sigh of relief and went back to our normal daily tasks, convinced of our omnipotent powers as matchmakers. McKelvey was happy at last, with a girlfriend of his own.

Then disaster struck. As it turned out, the girl's father was the minister of the church, and just as his daughter and Jim were basking in the enjoyment of each other's company, Daddy felt the spirit move him. He soon determined that his duty was to fulfill himself as a missionary. Within a matter of weeks, he had carted his entire family off to New Zealand to spread the Gospel, leaving Jim McKelvey lonely and despondent once more.

Jim began to go off the deep end. He neglected his studies and his grades dropped alarmingly. He stopped caring about his appearance and thus incurred the wrath of innumerable Cadet Corporals,

Sergeants, and Officers. As a pastime, Jim took to organizing races in which he and someone else would jump out of second floor windows to see who would hit the ground first. Clearly, we had to find him a girlfriend again soon.

This time it was Jerry Amadei who came up with the best suggestion. Seems he had this cousin at home...She was unattached, not too ugly, and just the right age for Jim (namely, old enough to know better and young enough not to care). She'd be perfect!

Jim and Sandy Amadei were introduced and spent an evening double dating with Jerry and his girl. There were mixed reactions to the evening: Jim was in love, convinced that this was the only girl for him. Sandy decided she'd rather not see him again. Definitely a conflict of opinion.

McKelvey settled down to solid effort. He put his whole being into winning this girl. He wrote letters, he called her home, he tried to see her. She turned a deaf ear to all his pleas.

McKelvey snapped. He walked around in a daze, something inside him broken. He bought a model of the sixteenth century warship "Indomitable" and busied himself with putting it together. He missed classes, meals, and military formations. His sole goal was to get the model together in time for Sandy's birthday a few days off.

He called us into his room a few days later. He pointed to the finished galleon. "It's done. Think she'll like it?" It was beautiful. Hand painted accurately and precisely, every sail in place and properly rigged. It was indeed an excellent job...a labor of love. "I'm going to take it to her tonight. Tomorrow's her birthday. It's kind of a dumb present, but it says what I feel. Do you think she'll like it?"

"She'll like it, Jim. She has to." Yes, she had to, in more ways than one. We could all sense how much was riding on this simple warship model, so painstakingly assembled. Yes, she had to like it.

It was nearly midnight when Jim came in. He walked quietly to his room and closed the door softly behind him. Jerry walked in a few minutes later and stomped off to his own room. We followed, eager for information. Jerry was fuming. He took off his coat and threw it on the bed, then sat next to it and started to untie his shoes. "That bitch! I don't care if she is my cousin, she's a bitch!" He threw one shoe against the wall and turned to untie the other one. "She wouldn't even listen to him. He stood on the porch and asked her to talk to him, and she closed the door in his face."

Jerry tossed the second shoe after the first and stood up. "My aunt let us in the house 'cause I was with him, but Sandy still wouldn't listen. She wouldn't even take his stupid ship model. After all that work he put into it! He finally just left it sitting on the porch, next to the door, in case she changed her mind. That bitch!" Jerry picked up his shoes and threw them at the opposite wall. "That damn bitch!" He glared at the shoes for a few seconds. Then he said "Let me go talk to Jim again. I'm worried about him."

Jerry stomped down to Jim's room and knocked on the door. From inside came a muffled "Come in" and Amadei disappeared inside. We drifted back to other tasks, but none of us put much heart into anything. Our minds were all on Jim. What would happen to him now?

Several days later my door slammed open and Cookie Man Znidarsic stuck his head in. "McKelvey's leaving the Corps!"

I jumped up from my desk. "What!"

"Yeah, he dropped his scholarship and enlisted. He'll be leaving in a couple of days."

I sat down in amazement. McKelvey leaving? It couldn't be...he was my buddy! He couldn't leave. We had lost people before, but never like this...never so suddenly. He couldn't go, not Jim. I sat for a while, numbly, then got up and walked to Jim's room. I knocked softly. "Jim, can I come in?"

"Yeah, come on in...I wanted to see you before I left anyway." Jim looked up from the pile of belongings he was sorting through. "Grab a seat and sit down, Hobbit."

I walked in slowly and sat on the bed. McKelvey prattled on. "Hope you'll excuse me... I've got to sort this stuff out. Hey, if you see anything you want, just let me know. I'm going to throw out whatever I can't get rid of. I won't need much where I'm going. The Army will give me all I need." He looked up at me with a grin.

I looked back at him. "Jim... why?"

Jim seemed not to hear. "Hey, Hobbit, wait a minute. I want you to listen to this new record." He fumbled through a stack of records, pulled one out and stuck it on his stereo. The needle dropped into place and the music began. I recognized it as the opening bars to "Your Song" by Elton John.

"Jim..."

McKelvey cut me off. "Shhh, Hobbit, listen... it's a great song."

The instrumental was past, and Elton John had started singing. "It's a little bit funny, this feeling inside..." The words went on and on. I barely listened. A few feet away McKelvey was smiling and humming along with the record. The song drew to a close. Elton John sang out the last few words. "I hope you don't mind; I hope you don't mind, that I put down in woooords, how wonderful life is with you in the world."

McKelvey smiled and flicked off the stereo. "I wish I could say things like that. Maybe if I could, Sandy would have listened to me." McKelvey's grin flickered and fled, but just for a second, then it was back again full force. "Need any uniform parts, Hobbit? I'm just throwing them out anyway."

"Why, Jim? Why did you do it?"

Jim sat down on a pile of white dress gloves and looked at me. His face was serious now. "I'm not sure, Dave. I guess a lot of it is Sandy, but she's not the only one. I loved her, but she wouldn't listen... none of them ever listen. Seems like every time I like a girl she just tunes me out, or gets taken away, or something. I hoped it would be different once I got to college, but it's not. I've decided now that it's me that has to change. It would be great to stay here with all the guys, but it's not doing me any good. I need a total change, and the Army's going to provide it. Does that make sense to you?"

I nodded. "Yeah. I understand. I think I know how you feel."

Jim smiled again and slapped my shoulder. "Good...I don't want you guys to worry about me. Now, are you sure you don't want any of this stuff?"

Several days later we got up early to take Jim to the train station. It was Halloween morning, but none of us cared for the trick fate had played on us. I squeezed into Kaj's car, along with Jerry, Crazy Charlie Kortlang, Cookie Man, and Jim. Kaj drove in silence to the Chester train station. None of us felt much like talking.

We arrived, Kaj parked the car, and we filed inside the train station. Jim walked over and bought a ticket to Philadelphia for the first leg of his journey to Fort Dix Training Center in New Jersey. The cashier counted out his change and slid it across the counter to Jim, along with his ticket. The six of us walked upstairs and through the waiting room. We stood on the platform and waited silently in the chill morning air. Finally, we saw the train approaching from the south. Suddenly it seemed as though we would need hours to say everything we wanted to say, but only minutes remained.

The train slid into immobility and hissed a greeting at us. We said goodbye and we each shook hands heartily with Jim, then said our goodbyes again. The conductor looked at us knowingly. He must have seen such scenes before, but despite his sympathy he had a schedule to keep. "All abooooard." He smiled kindly at us, and we stepped back to let Jim go. Jim smiled and waved, then disappeared into the car, to appear seconds later at a window. He waved again and we all waved back. The train huffed its way out of the station and picked up speed down the tracks. We waved after it, then slowly stopped and let our hands drop to our sides.

The others turned to go. I watched as the train grew smaller and smaller in the distance.

"Come on, Hobbit, we're ready to leave now." Kaj said softly.

"Yeah, I'm coming," I replied, and turned to follow them down the stairs. "Looks like we'll just get back in time for formation."

Dave Neimeyer:
Rook Peer Reviews

Jim World was a strange one. I first met him when I arrived at Pennsylvania Military College in the fall of 1969, and we were thrown together as freshmen rooks in Charlie Company. Jim was short and stocky, with the kind of blunt looks that made you think of a Brooklyn enforcer. The turtleneck sweater he was wearing heightened the impression that he had no neck and added to the bulk of his frame. He definitely looked like a guy you didn't want to mess with. Then he spoke. His voice was on the high side and a bit squeaky, and immediately dispelled any "tough guy" image.

It turns out he was raised by Salvation Army missionaries and had spent most of his life in (I believe) China. As a result, he was out of step with most of the cultural norms of the other cadets. For example, he had never picked up the habit of cursing, although we quickly filled in that lack of education. That's when I realized that there is a grammar to cursing. Jim was using all the proper words, although a few times they were a bit out of place, such as following instead of preceding the noun or verb being modified. However, his inflection and cadence were off. When he cursed, it just sounded wrong. His actions were often as out of step as his cursing. He was unique.

At some point during our first semester, some higher-up thought it would be a good idea for each rook to submit peer reviews of our fellow rooks. How to describe Jim World? I think it was Greg Lamphier who came up with the idea of creating new words to describe our otherwise indescribable classmate. While most classmates were described as "friendly", "laid-back", "brown-noser", "studies a lot", and so forth, Jim World was described as "a platitudinous estophosy," "warbly," and "fribulous," among others.

We knew we had hit the mark and knew true joy as we "squared" around the corridor, past Cadre Sergeant Russ Howald's room. Our crusty, gung-ho cadre sergeant sat there with a pile of peer reviews in front of him, frustratingly paging through a stack of dictionaries, cursing as he went. Jim World could definitely have picked up some pointers on proper cursing if he spent just a few minutes listening to that stream of invectives spewing from Sergeant Howald.

Dave Neimeyer:
What the Heck's a 'Pulaski"?

"Listen up, rooks" the Cadre Sergeant intoned to two dozen freshman rooks bracing in the corridor of second floor Cann Hall. "Next Saturday the Corps will be marching in the Pulaski Day Parade in Chester. You will be the sharpest looking company of cadets in that parade, or I promise you there will be hell to pay." Ok. We're going to be marching in a parade. What the heck is a "Pulaski", and why is there a parade for it?

"Uniform will be dress Delta with Keefer box" the Cadre Sergeant continued. Oh crap! Not with Keefer box! The dreaded cartridge box was a holdover from the Napoleonic Wars. Although only about eight inches wide and six inches high, and about two inches deep, it needed to be centered in the small of our backs, supported by two straps. The straps were each about six or seven feet long and two inches wide. They rigged through buckles on the back of the Keefer box. It was darn near impossible to rig them so that the box hung evenly at its proper location, and so that any extra strap did not hang loosely from under the box like a wriggling bait designed to catch the wrath of any passing upperclassman.

"Ok, Rooks," the Sergeant began wrapping up the bracing session, "now get in there and start polishing your shoes, your Keefer box, your belt buckles, and anything else that needs shining. I swear to you that if I can't see my reflection in your stuff you are going to be polishing your floor tiles with a toothbrush until you figure out the system! STEP IN." We didn't have to be told twice. A cacophony of slamming doors sounded throughout the corridor.

On the appointed day we formed up in company formation and assembled in the holding area in Chester while waiting for the parade to start. At the front of our formation the platoon leader started chatting up a majorette from one of the other organizations. She stood between him and the platoon, about five feet in front of the first rank, with her back towards us. While they chatted, the platoon sergeant slowly lifted his sword and nudged it under the hem of her short majorette skirt. Then, ever so slowly, he began raising his sword to a horizontal position, raising her skirt as he raised the sword. Hmm; nice thighs. He finally stopped with the tip of his sword a few inches above her waistband, exposing the very nicely filled out bottoms of her majorette uniform. For once I was glad that I was short. I was in one of the first ranks of the platoon, with an unobstructed view. After a minute or two, a stirring in the groups let us know that the parade was about to start. The sergeant slowly lowered his sword, letting her skirt slowly resume its normal position. A few minutes later we marched through the streets of Chester as one of the highlights of the parade.

So, what had I learned? I learned that Casimir Pulaski was a Polish nobleman who fought in the American Revolution, although we remained unclear as to his relationship with Chester, PA, and why they had a Pulaski Day. I also learned that cheap thrills are better than no thrills at all.

Ed Albertson:
Believe it or Not

In the early days, literally, of our Rook year, my Roommate was Tom Williams, from Pittsburgh, PA. Tom and I, as had our fellow HQ Company Rooks, had been drilled in one of the critical Rules of "Rookdom," that rule being, when in your room, your room key was left in the door; conversely, when outside your room, your key was to be removed. Violating either condition was an infraction inviting a variety of undesirable physical repercussions sufficient to warrant their avoidance. One evening, as we were "invited" to "Step Out," Tom left his key in our door. As soon as he realized what he had done, and concurrent with its notice by one of the Cadre Sergeants, Tom grabbed at the key, and it broke off in the door. Our vigorous "Step Out" began and throughout, I silently wondered to myself, how are we gonna get back in there when this is over. At our "Step Out" conclusion, Tom as sneeringly queried, "Whatcha gonna do now, Williams?"

Now our room was on the Third Floor of Hotel Turrell and beneath our two windows was a concrete stairway descending into the basement of Turrell, so our room and its associated windows were essentially four stories above the nearest hard stop of ground, the concrete floor at the end of those basement stairs.

Without pause, Tom opened the door of the room next to ours, crossed the floor to the window, and to the amazement of an incredulous Marty Bailey, climbed out the window, onto that window's ledge, stretched to the window ledge of one of our two windows (mine, actually) which happened to be open, climbed back in through that window, crossed our floor, and casually unlocked and opened our door from the inside! Four stories above the ground zero of that basement!

After that, I never doubted the lengths Tom would expend in any endeavor, nor did our Cadre ... any of them!

Paul Lewis:
Hairline with LTC Frey

The Commandant of Cadets, LTC Frey, will always be remembered as a stickler for haircuts. Probably every cadet at one time or another was told "Get a haircut!" I had my encounter with him some time in my senior year. LTC Frey observed what appeared to be too much hair covering my forehead. After he issued his usual command, I responded that I had a low hairline. His comeback was, "Nonsense! Only apes have low hairlines." A few days later, I had a banana with me when I came back from breakfast. I saw LTC Frey approaching in the corridor, so I thought I'd have some fun. I grabbed onto a chin-up bar in the doorway and hung with one arm while eating the banana with the other and pulling my feet up, primate style. LTC Frey said, "Alright, Mr. Lewis, you made your point. Now get a haircut!"

Jim Hulitt:
Inspections

We all know how much we loved inspections, especially "White Collar" inspections. Well, my roommate, Chuck Hasbrouck and I would always turn these events into a challenge for the inspector. Several examples were: Freshman year, Chuck returned from Thanksgiving break with alcohol! OMG! He brought back two bottles of Sake and a bottle of gin. The sake went pretty quickly, and we turned one into our water bottle to sprinkle our shirts when ironing (we were too cheap to have them professionally done). The other we filled with gin. A side note...after band practice, we would have "cocktail hour" before Mess III formation. The cadre and our classmates were none the wiser. Anyway, during inspections, we purposely put the sake bottle in "hidden" view so that the inspector would see the "water bottle" sake and have a fit! That is until they investigated and found that it was water. They never would check for other bottles (the gin).

Another time, we somehow found a payphone somewhere and hung it on the bed post. Major Lynch came in to inspect our room and as he inspected, Chuck did his imitation of a phone ringing, turned to the payphone, and answered it. "Good morning, Cadet Hasbrouck speaking, how may I help you? Major, it's for you." Major Lynch actually went over to the phone and then realized that we got him! Score one for the Rooks!

A second incident was another white collar, again with Major Lynch. This time we didn't have the "heart" to tell him what was going on. Since I was a biology major at the time, I brought back a beating frog's heart from lab on a Friday in a Petri dish. Major Lynch came in to inspect, saw the frogs' heart and was totally fascinated. He spent about five minutes looking at the heart and talking to me about it. Never inspected the room. We passed.

Stories and Vignettes from PMC

A third incident was when Chuck and I assembled two remote control model tanks. We figured that since Major Lynch was Armor, we could have fun! Major Lynch came in, we stood at attention, and the Major started his inspection. Suddenly out of nowhere, a Panzer tank appeared! Then a Sherman tank! OMG we have a recreation of the Battle of the Bulge right there in Turrell Hall. Major Lynch was totally fascinated and wanted to play too. So we gave him one of the remotes and he ended up playing with us, never completing his inspection. We passed again!

As God as my witness, these are true stories. "A cadet shall not lie, cheat or steal..."

SOPHOMORE (THIRD CLASS) YEAR

David Fiedler:
The Holidays

Just before Christmas 1965, with the informal approval of the cadet chain of command, the 4th class was told to decorate the barracks in keeping with a long-standing PMC tradition. What was unspoken was that the tradition meant that the cadets were to fan out in the local area and steal the decorations off local homes and businesses! After dark on the appointed day, the 4th class, suitably attired in BDU's and with faces and hands blackened with shoe polish, were set loose. The effort was fairly successful in that a very large number of Christmas decorations, including some really expensive lighted and motorized ones were "acquired".

Unfortunately, two of the troops did not return because they had been caught by the local cops and arrested!! The next morning the Commandant and the administration called out the entire Corps and ordered that ALL Christmas decorations in the barracks be deposited in the Howell Hall guard room. I saw the pile of decorations and it filled the front of the guard room and overflowed onto the front steps. This was then followed by a large parade of local citizens there to reclaim their property. The results, the school was greatly embarrassed, the two arrested cadets spent the night in jail, but thanks to MSG Cloud's influence with the local cops, they were not charged and were released into his custody. The cadet chain of command dummied up and denied sending out the "raiders". NO ONE WAS PUNISHED! Ironically, both cadets caught stealing CHRISTMAS decorations were JEWISH!!!

David Fiedler:
Christmas

The day before the Great Christmas Tree Raid detailed above, I was working in the original/first PMC Museum (not the one we have now) along with Wade Hall who was a year ahead of me. While there, two of his classmates showed up and asked if the museum still has the German engineer bayonet that we had on display. The bayonet was unique in that the back of the blade was a saw about 18 inches long. The bayonet was outlawed for use as a weapon because the saw would inflict terrible wounds if it was used to stab anyone. Of course we had the thing, so they asked to borrow it since they stated that they were "on a mission" which was cadet speak for you don't want to know!

As it turns out, the cadets went out on the night of the raid down to the Chester (Carnegie) Library Arboretum and used the saw to cut down two very rare evergreen trees and then bring them back to the campus where they were decorated with ornaments stolen during the raid and placed on both sides of the Howell Hall main entrance. As a result of the raid and the arrest of the two cadets, it didn't take much police work to associate the vandalism at the library, the two missing trees, and the Corps of Cadets.

The police detectives came on the campus and headed straight for the Commandant's office. Guess where they parked their police cars, right on the street in front of Howell Hall and what do you think they spotted by the front door! Later that day, the arborist from the library identified the trees but the strange saw marks on their trunks could not be identified. The tree cutters were never identified, nor was the tool used to cut them. PMC agreed to pay the library $600.00 to replace the very rare evergreens.

David Fiedler:
Cadet Chemist

In 1965, one of the budding young chemists in CHEM-101 decided to impress his fellow cadets with something he learned in chemistry class. He mixed together Nitric acid, ammonia, and iodine. The reaction formed a red crystal-like compound called nitrogen-tri-Iodide. These crystals were stable as long as they were kept wet on top of some filter paper. When dry, they became highly EXPLOSIVE!

Initially, he made a very small amount and exploded it in the chemistry lab to impress his fellow cadets. It went off like a small firecracker. Then the jokers of the Corps took over! They had him make more, which they kept wet by wrapping it in the filter paper. They then went into the barracks and pushed some of the compound into the keyhole on some victim's room door where it dried out. When the victim inserted his key into the keyhole the crystals exploded, blowing the key out with considerable force. The victim's hand was not hurt, and the door lock continued to function, so all concerned had a good laugh.

Since this worked out so well, the jokers now had the chemist make more Nitrogen-TriIodide crystals. These they painted wet onto the heels of their next victim's shoes. After he had unknowingly put them on, as he walked, small explosions and a slight "hot foot" resulted. Another good laugh from the jokers.

At the next lab session, the jokers told their chemist who was now a co-conspirator to make an even bigger quantity of the Nitrogen-triIodide. Which he did. As it was sitting wet on the filter paper, the lab assistant asked what it was. When he was told, he said that is very dangerous in such a large quantity. You flush that down the trough that ran down the center of the lab table and get rid of it, which he did.

Unfortunately, the flush job was not very good and some of the crystals remained overnight in the trough where they dried out. When the professor (Professor Gotlieb) came in the next day, he was greeted by a series of good size explosions down the lab table trough! Gotlieb got really excited and feared that the building was going to blow up in a repeat of the 1880 fire that destroyed half of Old Main and caused the creation of the chemistry wing (the building they were still using) to be joined to Old Main via the iron bridge (still there) so it would not happen again! He then spent a good bit of time flushing the remnants of the crystals down the trough.

Gotlieb then informed the Academic Dean of what had happened and the two of them suspended the cadet chemist from chemistry class. He had to make up his chemistry course the next summer at a local college near his home, which he did. Interestingly, this all apparently was never reported to the Commandant at all. Aside from the suspension from chemistry class, the cadet chemist never walked a tour, was never awarded any demerits, and was never restricted in any way.

This showed me that my suspicions were correct and that the faculty and the Commandant's staff were so disconnected that the faculty had almost no clue the Corps existed. I believe they thought they were building the Harvard of Pennsylvania and the cadets were incidental, if not an impediment.

The cadet chemist later became a cadet lieutenant, graduated with an engineering degree, was commissioned in the Signal Corps, and later became a member of the technical staff at IBM working on the space program at the Kennedy Space Flight Center at Cape Canaveral.

David Fiedler:
Military Officer in Charge

In 1965, the "new dorms" were still being constructed and there were plenty of construction materials in the area near the Howell Hall Quadrangle. Also in Howell Hall was the orderly room where the cadets who were on guard duty stayed during duty hours. In addition, located in the orderly room was a small apartment containing a bedroom, a toilet, and an office with telephones, a desk, and chairs. These quarters are where the Military Officer In Charge (MOIC) lived and slept during his evening tour of duty. MOIC duties were shared among the junior officers on the Commandant's staff and the senior NCO's on the ROTC staff. When performing that duty, the MOIC was responsible for keeping order on the campus, controlling cadet life, conducting evening formation, responding to emergencies, inspecting the cadet quarters, and generally representing the Commandant and administration during his tour of duty.

Out of respect, when the MOIC was one of the ROTC senior NCOs, things in the cadet areas were generally very quiet and under control, but it was always "open season" when the MOIC was a captain or lieutenant from the Commandant's staff, who were generally not respected much at all.

One cold night in the Winter of 1965, the MOIC was a captain on the Commandant's staff who really was not respected at all. He was mostly a nit-picking dictator that carried a "swagger stick" and thought a lot of himself. Despite the fact he was a PMC graduate, he was universally disliked by the Corps. This being the case, after this officer retired for the night, a group of "the boys" went to work.

Without making a sound and with many willing helpers, they constructed a large wall across the doorway into the MOIC quarters from bricks being used to construct the new dorms. Those in charge were upperclassmen engineering majors that knew how to build a very thick reinforced wall that was very hard to knock down, even though no mortar was used to hold the bricks together.

The door to the MOIC rooms, like all others in the dorms opened inwardly. So, after a good night of undisturbed sleep, a shave, a shower, and a fresh uniform, when first-call sounded the captain opened the door and was greeted by a solid brick wall that he could not penetrate, even though he tried. His calls for help were ignored by the guard detail who later claimed they had spent the night in their own rooms and went directly to their positions for morning formation.

Fortunately for the captain, there was a back window in the room he was trapped in that overlooked the parking lot behind Howell

Hall. He could not exit the room by jumping from the window since the drop was more than 20 feet, so he just yelled for help…that, of course, no cadet heard.

Lucky for the captain, the parking lot was the way that both the ROTC and Commandant's staff entered their offices under the building. After an hour or so, Colonel Fuller, the PMS, drove into the parking lot and heard the calls for help. Fuller then formed a rescue party consisting of his staff, some of the Commandant's staff, and some of the construction workers. They managed to break down the wall and free the prisoner.

The Corps got a great laugh out of all this activity and the officer concerned became a little less of a pain in the ass to the cadets after he was embarrassed. No cadets ever were punished for this action because we were all smart enough to have "cover stories" to account for our whereabouts during the previous evening. Everyone swore that we were all snug in our beds when questioned by those investigating this caper!! So tight were our stories that we all had "plausible deniability," and no one ever cracked. So, the Commandant could not pin this action on anyone. I don't think they tried very hard anyway because the victim was so disliked!!!!

After the "bricking in" incident, this officer did tone down his act a bit, but he still remained a pain in the ass so "the boys" just waited for any opportunity to continue harassing him. It came again on another night when he was MOIC. The cadets on the guard detail noted that when he retired for some unknown reason, he placed his nicely spit shined shoes outside the door to the MOIC quarters in the Howell Hall orderly room. Since this individual was obviously OCD (hence the swagger stick and the shiny shoes and brass) maybe it makes sense, I don't know. Anyway, some observant cadets reported this to the cadet grapevine. That night some of "the boys," probably science/chemistry/ engineering majors, mixed up some super strong epoxy cement and then snuck down unobserved to the orderly room where they glued the spit shines to the floor.

The next morning, the victim had quite a time trying to free his shoes from the floor. In fact, bits of the shoes (mostly the black rubber heels) remained stuck to the floor. When I was told the story, I did not believe it so I was taken by one of the cadets involved and shown the remains of the heels and a clearly visible outline of the shoes still stuck to the floor. It must have taken quite an effort to free them. This became a sight to see for a while and those who saw the shoe remains and were told the story were quite amused. The evidence of the crime remained until the cleanup crew came and buffed the floor. The Captain still remained quite a pain and "the boys" remained watchful for more opportunities to strike another blow for freedom.

David Fiedler:
Lock In

In the so-called "New Dorms" (Turrell, Howell, Cann, etc.), all of the cadet room doors opened inwardly. A few of the jokers one day discovered that the doors all had a tiny bit of space between the door and the lip of the door frame that it contacted when the door was closed.

A certain group of cadet jokers (known as "the boys" or sometimes "the lads") discovered that if you jammed an ordinary pencil in the space between the door and its resting place on the lip of the frame, the bolt in the door latch was pushed against the door frame latch receptacle so tightly that it was impossible to turn the doorknob and open the door. If the room was occupied when the pencil was jammed between the doorframe and the door, it effectively imprisoned the occupant or occupants. The jam was so tight and the doorknob so small and hard to grip that not even the strongest of us could turn the doorknob. If more than one cadet was locked in, it was impossible for two people to get a grip on the doorknob and turn it. Pounding on the door frame, if thought of, did not help because it would not release the pencil. In a very few instances, the prisoner was so strong, and his grip was so tight that the knob finally was forced to turn, freeing the occupants, but this was very rare. In effect until someone in the hallway pried out the pencil, the door could not be opened from the inside.

Rumor had it that one of "the boys" had gone to a private military high school and he had learned the trick there. In 1966, armed with this knowledge, "the boys" got even with a Senior cadet officer by locking him in his room just before evening formation. He could not turn the doorknob to get out of his room. He just barely made it to formation and dinner by jumping out his window and didn't realize what had happened until he returned and found the pencil in the door jamb. Prior to that he had thought the door lock had failed.

To my recollection, over my four years at PMC, this trick was repeated at least five times, mostly as a joke and the jokers released the victim themselves after a short time. At least twice, however, it was done as an act of revenge for being awarded punishment due to some infraction. In these instances, the prisoner had to be rescued by his classmates or fellow members of the cadet chain of command. I saw one rescue where a cadet officer's saber had to be used to pry the pencil out of the door jam.

David Fiedler:
Rangers Lead the Way!

In 1966, the Ranger Platoon decided to do a field exercise where they defended a night defensive position. Captain Ralph Kennedy, the Ranger ROTC advisor, selected a small hill parallel to a stream and a dirt road behind what was then called Washington Park, but now holds the Widener Stadium and field house. The ranger platoon was small but well-armed. They all had M-1 Garand rifles plus grenade simulators and a model 1919A6 Browning light machine gun, all with hundreds of rounds of blank ammunition.

The night selected for the exercise was not dark because of a full moon. Actually, you could see very well due to the moonlight. The terrain was wooded, but not heavily, with many clear spots. The Rangers did not have enough personnel to man both a defense and an attacking force, so Captain (later major) Kennedy asked for volunteers to form an attack force. The exercise was on a Friday night and all participants were relieved from Saturday morning inspection. With this as an incentive, I volunteered.

After dark, the Rangers deployed to their defensive position and we, the OPFOR, infiltrated Washington Park from the North, armed with our own M-1's and plenty of blanks. By around 2100 hours both forces were in position, quiet, under cover, and waiting for Captain Kennedy to unleash the OPFOR. When he did, we were supposed to Bonzi across the stream, cross the road, and come up the hill into the Rangers position. Later, Major Kennedy told us that he picked this terrain and this form of attack because it was similar to the terrain on Guadalcanal where the Japanese attacked the Marines on Edson's Bloody Ridge.

Then, when both sides were quiet, to our amazement a car came down the road and stopped dead center at the point where the attack was coming and turned off the lights and the engine. We could see quite clearly that the car contained a young couple, maybe of high school age, and that they were seriously engaged in romantic activities in the back seat of the car! We stayed quiet. Just when these activities really got going up went Major Kennedy's flare, starting the attack.

Then, out of the woods and into the stream came about 100 cadets firing their M-1's. The occupants of the car clearly freaked and dove into the front seat and attempted to restart the car, but it stalled. At the same time, the Rangers rallied, and counter attacked the OPFOR, led by the M-1919A6 gunner who charged down the hill just in front of the stalled car firing from the hip as fast as the gun would shoot! The two forces were having a great time firing blanks at each other all along the road when the car finally got started. We did not believe how fast the driver was able to drive in reverse back up to the main park then do a 180 degree turn and burn rubber up Melrose avenue.

Boy, did we get a laugh out of that incident. We concluded 1—that the kid driving was a hell of a good driver, 2—that had it been a year or two sooner it could have been one of us, and 3—that the girl probably never wanted to see the guy again! Somewhere in Chester is a guy with a great and tragic story to tell!!!

Bob Kukich:
The Band—Headquarters Company

Many friendships were developed at PMC, but friendships among HQ Company cadets (the band) were quite different. All Freshmen cadets, called Rooks (rookies), were treated much the same by upperclassmen regarding discipline and training. It was expected that over time Rooks would develop a sense of pride as a PMC Cadet and assimilate and become undistinguishable in all aspects as members of PMC's Corps of Cadets. However, this was not the case for HQ Company/PMC Band Rooks who were not afforded the luxury of time to assimilate. This was for good reason!

In 1965-66, the 1965 class year the PMC Band won the prestigious National ROTC Band Association's competition (marching phase) at the '64-'65 New York World's Fair. They had also marched in the NYC St. Patrick's Day Parade, the Philadelphia Loyalty Day Parade, as well as performed at a formal Retreat Ceremony at the US Army War College at the personal invitation of the commanding general. That same year, they also cut a 12-track PMC Band record album.

The 1966 class year Band was equally busy on and off campus, including a performance at the '66 Mardi Gras Rex Parade and cutting another record album titled "The PMC Band in Old New Orleans."

So, in the 1966-1967 class year there were great expectations, and many scheduled off-campus performances for HQ Company. In addition to campus parades and concerts, HQ Company had a heavy schedule of significant Public Relations performances for PMC, to include the nationally televised November 1966 Eagles-Cowboys NFL Pre-game AND Half-time "trick marching" shows, lead band for the 1966 1967 Mardi Gras Rex Parade, New Orleans, LA., Azalea Festival Parade, Norfolk, VA, etc.

The 1967-year Band was made up of 64 members (8 ranks and 8 files). HQ Company Rooks were expected to replace recently graduated bandsmen with no degradation in sound and appearance—there was no room for slackers. All HQ Company cadets, including Rooks, were expected to set the standard in appearance, and be proficient in marching ability and musicianship from day one. To add to the stress, all Band members were required to memorize the music they played for the trick marching shows! That meant committing about six tunes to memory. This was necessary to prevent the embarrassment of dropped music during fast trick maneuvers, such as the trick performance at the Eagles-Cowboys game at Franklin Field in Philadelphia.

Fortunately, HQ Company was comprised of cadre and upperclassmen who took pride in the unit and seriously accepted their responsibility to train and educate Rooks in the HQ Company way of doing things. Yes, HQ Company Rooks received a similar amount of, dare I say, "hazing" and "good-natured abuse" at the hands of upperclassmen and cadre, but it was tempered by a pride and desire to assimilate Rooks immediately into this prestigious unit, not only as cadets but as excellent bandsmen into this prestigious unit.

As such, HQ Company Rooks received what I can best describe as "responsible mentorship," not only from cadre and cadet leaders but from all HQ Company upperclassmen, to include those beloved Senior Privates, all of whom took pride in the unit, accepted their responsibility seriously, and pulled their weight respectively. HQ Company Rooks were mentored not only in cadet life but were encouraged to enhance their musicianship. It was this "responsible mentorship" on the part of the cadre, leaders, and all upperclassmen that resulted in Rooks being assimilated quickly into this close-knit organization, which resulted in the development of many life-long relationships and friendships.

David Fiedler:
Band Box Parade and John L Geohagan

The normal procedure for a "band box" parade was for the band to form up at the end of 14th street by the barracks. The Corps would form up by companies around the "Old Main" horseshoe. The band would then play a march and march down to just past MacMorland Center (NOT WHAT WIDENER CALLS IT NOW), reverse, and march back to their original position and reverse again. The full band would then play colors, the French 75mm gun on the lawn would fire a round, and the full band would then sound retreat. After this, the Corps would march past the command group as the band played another march and into MacMorland Center for dinner, followed by the band. In November 1965, we were quite surprised to see the band in position for an unannounced full band box parade.

Instead of their usual performance, the band sounded the Star-Spangled Banner and did not march, which struck us as strange. Colors and retreat were sounded as usual. The march the band played as the Corps rounded the horseshoe was very slow. When we got into the dining room, the adjutant announced that John L Geohagan, past 1st Captain of the Corps of Cadets, had been killed while serving with 1st Battalion, 7th Cavalry, 1st Cavalry Division in Vietnam (in the Battle of the Ia Drang Valley). Not much dinner got consumed after that and the room was very quiet! Corps morale hit a new low and it may have caused a few cadets to rethink the military as a career and why they were at PMC.

Thomas J Dougherty III:
Sophomore Year

Fast forward (or is that fast backup?) to my year as a 3rd classman. Paul Porcino and I were selected as Color Corporals 1966-1967. We were housed on the 1st floor of Howell Hall—everyone else on the corridor was also Brigade Staff—but all 1st classmen.

Paul and I would regularly spar with the upperclassmen, albeit in a most friendly manner—i.e., major hand to hand combat in the corridor—all in fun, regardless of any bruises or blood involved. Across the hall from us was Jack Spriggs and Tony Torcassio—Tony was an easy-going laid-back senior—Jack was a no-nonsense mountain of a guy who would regularly appear in our doorway, reminding us of any noise etc.

Down the hall was Dave Housch, along with a number of other

seniors. Invariably on inspection Saturdays, Paul and I were about the only ones who had their room inspected. We found out if we moved quickly and found a good reason, we could be absent during the time of the inspection. We also found out that if you propped a stick against the door lock from the inside, you couldn't enter our room with a key—it just wouldn't turn the lock.

We would exit out our window to the parking lot behind Howell Hall—it put us above the basement level, so we had to use a couple of tied sheets to shimmy down the back. Prior to inspection, we usually had little to zero wax etc. so we would just wax the area directly in front of our door but on both sides, so it looked like we had done the entire floor. The inspection team would not be able to enter our room but would see the waxed floor and assume we did a proper job—right.

Coming back to the room, we had figured out that if we slid a coat hanger under the door, we could knock the stick down and then use our keys to enter accordingly—this went on for most of the year we were in Howell Hall—good times for sure. The seniors definitely took us under their wings and gave us the benefit of their experience as upperclassmen—especially during exam time—it was greatly appreciated.

That's the story and we're sticking to it. It was a most interesting time to be a cadet—many memories—fond and otherwise.

David Fiedler:
Expelled Cadets

In the Spring of 1966, the army got serious about ROTC and who was going to really get a commission. As a result, MS-III became a very important course and if you failed it, you could lose your ROTC paycheck and your Senior ROTC contract. In addition, it was also announced all MS-IV cadets would have to take the army basic training intelligence test that was never required of ROTC cadets before. The basic idea was to weed out cadets hiding in ROTC in order to avoid the Vietnam era draft. If you failed either one, not only were you dropped from ROTC, but your draft board was informed and told to change your classification from 1D (member of reserve component) to 2S (student) or even 1A (available for military service) if you left school completely.

Under this kind of pressure, one of our cadet goof-offs decided that he really needed to get a good grade in MS-III. At this time, the ROTC offices were located on the ground floor under "new dorms 4, 5, and 6". They are still there today. Since we lived above the ROTC detachment offices, it was easy to just walk down the stairs and you were there. Each officer in the ROTC detachment had a private office with a door that locked. Normal army security mandated that this door be locked, along with the desks and file cabinets in the office after duty hours. The weak spot in the system was that over each door was a tilting transom that could be opened to allow better ventilation. The transom was the width of the door and about 18 inches high and supported on each end by sliding arms that could be disconnected from the window part of the transom, allowing the window to come down on its hinge. This left a space the width of the door and 18 inches high that could be used to gain entrance to the office. The transoms were usually kept open, so disconnection of the arms and entrance through the space was pretty easy.

Upon hearing that the MS-III exams were printed and ready to go, the cadet in question went down to the ROTC offices at night, climbed through the transom of one of the Assistant Professors of Military Science that was teaching MS-III, and did manage to come up with a copy of the exam. Unfortunately for him, the door had some sort of security lock on it so he couldn't just exit via the door but had to go out the way he came in. Sadly, for him just as he was coming back through the transom he was nabbed by some member of the ROTC detachment. He left PMC the next day.

Right after all this, the rumor mill got going full speed. First rumor was that he was going to be charged with breaking into a federal government office and theft of federal property. Later we heard the school hushed it up and he was not. Next everyone was trying to determine just how he got caught. One conjecture was that he showed a light or turned on a light and someone came to investigate. Another was that one of the detachment NCO's was sleeping down there because he had some early morning duty and caught him. This was never confirmed. The one I thought was most likely was that due to the political situation with the Vietnam war protests etc., motion detectors and security locks were installed in the area to protect federal property. The school and the ROTC detachment never revealed what tipped them off.

David Fiedler:
Engineering Week

In March 1966, during Engineers Week, the College (s) invited C. P. Snow, a famous English scientist and author, to speak to the student body. A formal academic conclave was set up in MacMorland Center with all the formality and elegance one would expect at a primo academic event. Chairs were arranged on both sides of the Center with a speaker's podium at the front. The Corps of Cadets was on one side of the aisle and the Penn-Morton student body was on the other side.

As the party of dignitaries, including Snow, Dr. Moll and senior members of the faculty, proceeded in formal procession down the center isle past the cadets, Dr. Moll who by that time was at the height of his unpopularity and was nicknamed by the cadets as "the snake" was greeted with loud and clear hissing sounds. Members of the Commandant's staff and the cadet chain of command tried half-heartedly to stop the hissing, to no avail. Moll was very embarrassed, Snow looked confused until he realized that the hissing was not for him. He then delivered an interesting but boring speech and the party went on to a formal dinner in the faculty dining hall.

The war between Moll and the Corps of Cadets had already begun by March 1966 but this was open warfare and a great insult/put down to Dr. Moll since he was an academic lightweight to begin with. Moll was determined to avenge this, and he did. This was the tipping point. After this, Commandants of Cadets who showed any gumption were gone. General Biddle had already left, he was followed in subsequent years by Colonel Menard and Colonel Cleary and all that were left were empty uniforms. Biddle, Menard, and Cleary never even got a farewell dinner or a parade or a dinner. They were there one day and gone the next.

After this public insult, Moll moved quickly. In six short years, it was all gone and we all know the rest of the story. Had the cadets not hissed, maybe there would still be a PMC today. Who knows???

Don Cooper:
Keep Your Rifle Dry!

It was in the fall of 1967 when I as a 3rd Classman enrolled in the PMC Ranger Platoon program. I managed to keep up with the endless daily jogging encumbered by combat gear through the streets of Chester chanting, "I want to be an airborne ranger" and had gone through rappelling, bayonet, and self-defense training. But I'll never forget the next exercise under the category of KEEP YOUR RIFLE DRY!

A bunch of us trainees were to report to the basement of the Armory where the swimming pool was located. The sergeant indicated that during night patrol unexpected things could happen, and one must adapt quickly. When my name was called, I stood up with shined boots and starched fatigues. I was given a wet backpack to put on and before I could yell Geronimo, I was blind folded, escorted about, spun around multiple times, and then pushed into eight feet of water. I remember how exhausting it was to stay afloat and how difficult it was to take off the backpack.

After getting mouthfuls of pool water into my stomach, the cadre was finally yelling instructions on the techniques of how to get the backpack off. I finally succeeded and looking up, they all appeared to be having a good ole time. Next, they handed me a rifle and told me to do the side stroke with one hand while holding the rifle out of the water with the other. Again, exhaustion ensued, along with mouthfuls of water. The cadre did have a long pole for anyone needing help, so as I was reaching out for that pole, looking for a sympathetic helping hand, I could only hear the cadre shouting the encouraging words — "Keep that rifle dry, Cooper. Keep that rifle dry!"

Bob Schneider:
One Fraternity Pledge Night (Fall 1969)

Artie Hafner and a group of us (military and civilian friends) decided to pledge Phi Epsilon Pi fraternity (merged with ZBT unfortunately). Phi Ep was dominated by Seniors, so if the pledge class wasn't strong, then the frat would probably close on campus. One night during our pledge cycle, we were notified that we needed to get to the frat house immediately and to dress appropriately for the weather. As we gathered at the house, the brothers loaded us into their cars, blind folded us, and drove us to a dark wooded area. They then told us to get out of the cars.

As we all stood in the dark, they informed us that we had to find our way back to school and that they would be waiting when we got back, and when we returned, we could "enjoy some entertainment." They all left laughing, and we were left standing in this unused roadway strategizing on our next move. Our great "orienteering" training at PMC helped us climb the slope directly to our rear (about 1,000 feet) to some homes that had their lights on. Arte was well familiar with the area. We climbed the hill and entered a fenced yard and Arte knocked on the door which was answered by his dad. His dad served us some drinks and some food and then drove us back to school. We had been left off in Valley Forge right where Arte had grown up—we got back to school, thanked his dad, and went to the frat house and waited for the brothers for about two hours until they returned—needless to say, the rest of the evening was not very entertaining.

Side note: About five years ago, I was contacted by a ZBT national representative to see if I would be interested in helping with new fraternity starts near my home in Dayton. I told him I was interested; it had been 45 years since I had been involved in a fraternity, but the biggest reason was that I would have been embarrassed meeting him because I didn't remember the handshake or the secret greeting.

Bob Schneider:
MY NY METS and the 1969 World Series

Some background information first. All my friends at PMC and here in Dayton, Ohio know I am a diehard NY Mets fan. Since 1967, I have kept track of every game they have played. I tell people I am not a baseball fan—I am a NY Mets fan. My office at home is painted Met blue and orange, I wear my Met tie whenever I need to wear a tie, I have the appropriate hats and shirts, I head to Cincinnati when the Reds play the Mets, and I have a brick from Shea stadium in a glass case on my office bookshelf (I bow to the east every morning). My one dog was named Shea. My second daughter is married, and her name is Shea. My son, a surgeon in Dayton, listens to games through the operating room sound system when he is operating during the season and his son and daughter are also fans. ZACK DAY (former Montreal EXPO pitcher) was in my Indiana Wesley University class, and we discussed one evening his record against the Mets. He was shocked when he saw I had a record of the games he pitched against the Mets. The Mets have taught me much about perseverance.

Anyway, what has this to do with my PMC story. During a PMC home football game our sophomore year (1969 The Miracle Mets), Carol, my girlfriend/wife, were in the bleachers during the first game of the World Series. I was so excited because the Mets had come out of nowhere to win the pennant and they were playing the vaunted Baltimore Orioles (I met a Baltimore fan recently who was still mad that the Mets had won). The football game was being played during the first game of the series and over the loudspeaker a classmate announced for all to hear that the Baltimore Orioles had defeated the Mets 4-1 in the first game. "See, I told you Schneido, the Mets will not win the Series." he laughed. I spent the next week in the snack bar, missing classes to watch my beloved Mets win the final four games and the world championship. Of course, I had to wait another 17 years before they did it again, but who's counting? We are getting close now and maybe with this publication I can die knowing that they have won it again. If not, as we say as Met fans, "there is always

next year." As the Mets poet laureate Frank Messina says—Do you know what it's like
  To be chased by the ghost of failure
  While staring through victory, door?
  Of course, you do,
  You're a Mets fan. (That's me)

William Speer:
Blanket Party

My sophomore year was one of growth and development for me. Rook year was a blur but now I was an upperclassman! I was in a room with some other fraternity members getting ready for an intramural basketball game in the Armory. We were loud, probably obnoxious, definitely profane. A voice call from down the hallway, "Hey you guys, keep it down!" I responded with a typically profane response. It turns out the guy yelling was on the phone at the end of the hall and couldn't hear (yeah, we were really loud).

This senior officer stormed into my room and told me I was under room arrest. I told him to go to hell and left for the basketball game. Well, by the time I got back from the game to my room, my company commander came and said I was up for a non-judicial punishment (lots of tours) for disrespecting a superior officer. He left; I went to bed. Evidently that night in the middle of the night some seniors decided to take the matter into their own hands and organized a blanket party.

Now, if you have watched *Full Metal Jacket*, you have seen a blanket party. It's when a guy is held down by his blanket while others pound on him with a towel embedded with a bar of soap. It is quite painful, but the target of the "party" never really knows who did it. Turns out my company commander stood outside my door and stopped it from happening. Lucky for me he was a fraternity brother!

William Speer:
ATL City Party

Others have written about our experiences at the "Little Army-Navy" game at Atlantic City over Thanksgiving. It was something we looked forward to every year. Starting my sophomore year, I joined a fraternity and like all of them, we planned our post-game party. I was asked to be at the door as the party was for members and dates only. Sure, no problem. That is, until a group of football players wanted to enter. I told them they couldn't as there were not members of the fraternity. Well, that didn't sit well with them, and they started yelling, which attracted other frat brothers. I re-emphasized they weren't allowed in and the guy in the front cold-cocked me right in the jaw. I fell backwards and a few of the brothers caught me and held me. The player approached and hit be again while I was being held! Guess they were satisfied and left. I looked at my "brothers" and said, "Thanks a lot!"

William Speer:
PT

As Rooks we had physical training every day, running long distances (never fun in combat boots), various exercises, sits-up, squat thrusts, better known as "burpees," and, of course, pushups. Our sophomore year things changed, and PT was only on Saturday mornings. We were grouped by class and a classmate was chosen to lead us. One fine day, my roommate was chosen to lead us in pushups. I guess he decided to impress the upper-classmen and really put us through the ringer: long holds in the up or down positions and what seemed like hundreds of pushups.

Needless to say, the entire class was furious with him and began to discuss a plan for revenge. I warned them if it involved our room, not to mess with any of my stuff. My roommate caught wind of the plot and began to sleep with a machete under his pillow. Weeks later, we went on leave and the event was long forgotten, or so I thought! I came back to find every item in our room that belonged to him was epoxied to whatever it was on. Desk items to the desk, shoes to the floor, uniforms to the hangars and them to the rod. My stuff? Completely untouched. That day I requested a room transfer and moved to another interesting roommate, but that is another story.

David Neimeyer:
SÉANCE: The Haunting of Nickolas Tscheremischin

We were bored. Life at a military college begins with a flurry of activity: there are shoes to be shined, brass to be polished, books to be read, and numerous other things to attend to. After a while, however, Cadets become proficient at all of these and can keep things in order with a minimum expenditure of time. The result is long hours, especially on weekends, when there is nothing that needs doing, and nothing else to do.

We had reached that point, and we were bored. Even the usual bull session was lagging, plodding its way to a slow death. Then someone casually mentioned séances. The room went off like a rocket. Everyone was exploding with stories of ghosts that moaned and knocked on tables, and of Ouija boards that revealed mysterious warnings and prophecies.

Jerry Amedei jumped up. "It's all set. We're doing it! Now, who's going to be in on this?" His roommate Craig instantly volunteered, followed quickly by Crazy Charlie Kortlang and Cookie-Man Bill Znidarsic. A classmate of ours with the impossibly long name of Nickolas Gehrhart Tscheremischin became the fifth volunteer. It was felt that one more person was needed to fill out the circle. Somewhere they had to find a sucker to lure in. Needless to say, they soon talked me into participating.

We gathered in Jerry's room and set about the task of preparing it for our spirit rendezvous. The room had to be completely dark, so we put blankets over all the windows and taped the cracks. We turned out the lights and tested. Pinhole leaks and cracks were taped over, and the test repeated. After a number of tests, we had assured ourselves that no light at all was entering the room. The door was locked behind us and its cracks taped shut. Our last escape route was cut off.

We sat on the cold tiles of the floor and joined hands. Jerry snapped off the lights and stumbled over to join us. After several moments of silently preparing our minds, the intonations began.

"Oh spirits, we call you," Jerry moaned. "Come to us, spirits, we call you forth. Give us a sign, spirits, give us a sign." The moaning continued. My feet began to get cold. "Oh spirits, give us a sign. We call you forth. Come to us." Jerry was intoning louder now. My legs ached. "Give us a sign, spirits, give us a sign. We call you forth, give us a sign." Jerry was in a mild frenzy. My back was getting stiff. "Give us a sign."

A shattering scream tore through the room. The door slammed open and the scream dopplered down the hall, as Nick raced through the corridor to his own room, followed instantly by Jerry and the others. I remained sitting on the floor, trying to figure out what had happened. All at once I realized I was alone in the room and the door was slowly drifting closed. I quickly decided to go see what the others were doing. I found them in Nick's room.

Nick was in bed with the covers pulled up to his chin. He lay there and shivered; his fingers clutched tightly on the rough wool of the blanket. His eyes were wide open and darted swiftly about the room. A mangled story was coaxed from his lips; a story of a ghostly figure that had appeared during the intonations. Dressed in a gaudy, quasi-military uniform, it had drifted down from the ceiling to point an accusing finger at Nick. Nick, of course, was the only one to see the apparition, but all of us soon decided that we too had seen a strange glow at about the same time. Yeah, that was it; we only saw the glow, but Nick could see the ghost. He must be sensitive or something.

Things quieted down somewhat, and Jerry, Craig, and I gathered in my room to discuss our experience. We sat on my bed and whispered softly, so as not to disturb my roommate, who lay sleeping a few feet above us on the top bunk. As we talked, his sleep became restless. Finally, he rolled over and his arm dangled off the bunk to swing lazily a few inches above Jerry's head. Jerry glanced upward and saw the hand. He gasped and tore out of the room, convinced that the spirits were out to get him, too. Nick's hysteria seemed to be infectious. It is a documented fact that several people slept with their lights on that night.

In the days that followed, Nick seemed to be a changed man. He acquired a suspicious nature, glancing constantly around as he walked. He sometimes snickered to himself, as at some private joke. Worst of all, his roommate claimed that Nick spent hours chanting to himself and drawing weird occult figures on his floor and mirror. He was surely possessed. Something had to be done.

There was nothing else to do. We had to consult with "Warlock" Gleeson. Gleeson was a Cadet in the class ahead of us, and he claimed to possess the strange powers of the Black Arts. We all agreed that he was strange but weren't quite sure about his alleged powers. At any rate, he had a large collection of books on witchcraft and the occult, and we hoped to gain something from these.

Gleeson listened with interest to our story, then chuckled joyfully. He admitted that Tscheremischin was certainly possessed but felt that it was more a product of Nick's mind than of marauding spirits. The thing to do now was to play the situation for all it was worth. The Warlock's ultimate suggestion: "Let's convince him that we're a witches coven and get him to sell his soul to the Devil!"

We weren't sure if it would help Nick, but it sounded like fun, so we all joined in. By the next night, we were all set. Promptly at midnight, Nick was led blindfolded into Warlock Gleeson's room. A lone candle flickered on the table. Several figures in hoods and sheets stood solemnly about. The blindfold was removed from Nick's eyes, and he was pushed into a chair.

Gleeson gave an evil-sounding laugh. "You have been brought here for a reason. We possessed your mortal body last week, and now we want your immortal soul." Nick stared, mouth agape. Gleeson grimly explained the seriousness of the matter, then stressed the possible gains. Each of us told our story: bad times, an offer from Satan, a moment of weakness and acceptance, then good luck ever since. We pointed out various instances of unexpected good luck that had befallen us: a sudden promotion, an escape from injury, good grades, inexplicable popularity with females, and so on. In each case Nick was forced to admit that our fortune was undeserved, and certainly unearned.

He decided that he too wanted to get on this sleigh ride to Hell, so he agreed to turn over his soul. All he asked in return was the combined military genius of Napoleon, Bismarck, Alexander, and Caesar. Gleeson laughed in his face. "For your puny, rotten soul? Don't be ridiculous! We'll get your soul anyway in a few years. This deal is just a matter of convenience for us. At most, we'll give you a few spells of good luck, like the others. Military genius indeed!"

Nick was taken aback. He expected something more in exchange, and now he hesitated. We impressed upon him the force of the powers of darkness. He left the room shaken, asking for more time to make up his mind. Gleeson leaned out the door after him. "By tomorrow night your decision must be made. We shall not wait longer."

With Nick out of the room we gave way to laughter at his reaction, then we settled down to a council of action. We were starting to get to him. All we needed now was the grand finale. It was time to pull out all the stops, and what better way to do it than in another séance?

Cookie Man volunteered his room this time, and the following night we made the usual preparations, with one exception. This time we squeezed Jerry Amedei into the storage space of the upper locker. We were all set. Everything was running smoothly. Nick was led in, blindfolded as usual. He announced that he was prepared to sell his soul. We nodded grimly. "Let the ceremony begin!" Warlock Gleeson said solemnly.

We assumed our positions on the floor, hand joined, moaning softly. The blackened room was filled with an eerie sound. Gleeson led the incantations. "Oh spirits, we call you from the great beyond! Rise and join our circle; come to us, oh spirits of the depths. We bring you a soul, oh spirits." The incantations continued. Nick fidgeted nervously as the tempo increased. Gleeson maintained his chanting. "Come to us from the depths, oh spirits. Give us a sign that you are near. Give us a sign!"

KNOCK—KNOCK—KNOCK

Silence quickly engulfed the room. No one spoke.

KNOCK—KNOCK—KNOCK

Gleeson quietly said "The spirits have arrived. We may proceed."

The ceremony continued. "Spirits, if you can hear and understand me, knock once for 'yes', twice for 'no', oh spirits."

KNOCK

"Are you prepared to accept our sacrifice of a human soul?"

KNOCK

"Will you call forth your dark master for us?"

"Hey, what is this anyway?" interrupted Nick, who had apparently thought better of his offer to sell his soul. "That's just somebody knocking on the door."

Luckily Amedei had the situation well in hand. Before Nick could protest further, he was hit by a paperback novel. Guided by the sound of Nick's voice, Amadei threw several more paperbacks, just for effect.

Nick was frantic. "No, no, I believe in you! I believe in you!" The barrage of paperbacks ceased.

Gleeson proceeded, his voice harsh. "Are you, Nickolas Gehrhart Tscheremischin, prepared to give your immortal soul to the Dark Lord?"

A pause, then Nick whispered a meek "Yes".

"Are you prepared to serve him for all eternity?"

Another meek "Yes".

"And are you prepared to accept the gifts the Dark Lord gives his servants?"

"Yes." There was nothing meek about this reply. Nick knew what he had come for.

"Then take them!" Cookie Man jumped up and flicked on the light. Jerry threw open the locker door and tossed a pile of paperbacks at Nick. The rest of us were rolling on the floor, laughing till our sides hurt. Nick stood staring at the sight, dodging flying paperbacks as best he could.

"You bunch of fakes!" he cried. "I knew all the time it was just a trick! You didn't fool me for a minute!" He stepped over our helpless forms and stomped off down the corridor. We noted his departure, then went back to our laughing. The possession of Nickolas Tscheremischin was over.

Bob Schneider:
Navy Pilot Training (Spring 1970)

Sophomore year just prior to us signing our contracts with the Army, I decided that maybe I wanted to go in the Navy (that old boating itch came back) so I signed up to take the Navy flight school test. I didn't pass it the first time, so I decided to sign my Army contract. I got a call from the Navy recruiter a few days later and he informed me that they had lowered the flight school score requirements and wanted to know if I was still interested in flight training. I asked the obvious question — "Why did you lower the test scores"? His answer (I'm today still unsure if he was joking or serious) was, "We are losing lots of carrier pilots over Vietnam, so we need more." Needless to say, I turned him down, even after such a great recruiting pitch. I probably would have ended up in the backseat of an F-4 because of my eyes. After watching both Top Gun movies and realizing that I wasn't very fond of heights, it ended up being a great decision.

Ed Albertson:
Lucky

Sophomore year, Bob Castelli and I were roommates, and we kept a bottle of Seagram's in our (dirty-clothes, "laundry bag" for occasional sipping during our nightly games of Solitaire during study hours (after all, we were Upper Classmen now!). One evening, we had concurrent and extraordinary runs of good luck with our respective card games and imbibed more heavily than usual. By the time it was lights out, for us it was really "lights out."

Our third-floor room in Turrell Hall was a corner room and from our windows we could not only see and hear the I-95 traffic each night, but we could see "Lucky," the Sherman tank, which had been relocated from near the Armory to just outside our window, granted three stories below. The next morning, as we awoke in a haze of Seagram's and deep sleep, I looked out our window and exclaimed to roommate Bob that it had snowed and showed him how Lucky was covered in heavy snowfall.

We crossed the hall to the latrine to get ready for Mess I formation and whatever the day's adventures would bring. As we entered, joining our HQ classmates energetically engaged in preparing themselves for their day, we both proclaimed our discovery of the snow on Lucky.

Every one of them looked at, first in disbelief and then with a knowing suspicion. One of them asked, "Do you not know what happened last night?" We looked first at each other, then at our classmates and jointly replied, "Yeah: it snowed." Our classmates then proceeded to tell us that somebody had firebombed Lucky the previous night, about five Chester fire trucks had come around, sirens wailing, and foamed the "unluck" Lucky until the fire was extinguished. What Bob and I had seen that morning was the result, a foam-covered Lucky.

More startlingly, was the fact that we had "slept" through the entire incident in a Seagram's-induced fog, never hearing the sirens or commotion that night.

Stories and Vignettes from PMC

JUNIOR (SECOND CLASS) YEAR

Jack Kane:
Reminisces

Summer of 1956, Sam Lucasse (who did not return that fall) and I worked for PMC. We did many tasks, but the one I remember was taking the asbestos squares out of the attic of a band barracks. In those days, no one knew anything about asbestos and protective gear was a tee shirt and pants. Well, late the first afternoon, when we went to shower, we learned in a hurry. The first rub of the soap up the arm, painful. As the dirt came off, hundreds of tiny red spots appeared on us. It took a long time to shower.

I recently spoke with a respiratory MD. I related the story, and he told me that the glass particles are still in my lungs. Luckily, no "meso" so far.

Across the street from the barracks, a gentleman by the name of Clarence, had a very small cheese steak and hoagie shop. I think his main clientele was the Corps. He even let some run a tab. Anyhow, with the opening of the on-campus canteen he would lose his business. MG Mac Morland offered Clarence a job in the canteen. This was a win, win, win. Clarence had a job, the cadets had an on campus good steak and hoagie maker, and Gen Mac Morland showed leadership.

If I remember correctly, Sam and I convinced a few early arrivals that they needed haircuts. Don't think we charged any money but did have fun. I was a day cadet, so maybe some resident could add to the barracks/canteen story.

Harry Carlip, written by his wife Freddi:
Traditions

PMC had a tradition of having a casual fall parade through the surrounding neighborhood for Halloween and as a prelude to Homecoming. Cadets had permission to decorate instruments, dress in crazy clothes, and make a lot of noise. It was a lot of fun for the Cadets and the spectators who, of course, included some of the school's top brass.

In 1964, Cadet Harry Carlip (Class of '65) and I were dating. Harry had a lot of interesting ideas to have some fun and wreak a little havoc at PMC. Harry's hijinks plan unfolds…

For Halloween/Homecoming 1964, Harry's havoc included me. Harry, a PMC Band/Headquarters Company member (French Horn), thought it would be a great idea to shake things up. He asked me to be part of the parade. Was he insane...or a risk taker...or both? He said, "We'll dress you up as a Cadet, in Dress Alpha (full dress) uniform. Wearing a shako hat with pompom will hide your hair and some of your face." I was going to carry, and try to play, an instrument. Harry was very persuasive, and his good friends and band members, Max Gayer and Mark Barbieri, were in on it.

I lived in Northeast Philly and was attending Temple University. I had to make sure I arrived early enough to be TRANSFORMED! Was I crazy? Would going along with Harry's plan get him expelled (and me banned from ever setting foot on PMC's campus)? Actually, I thought it was a terrific plan. And if we got away with it...it would go down in the annals of PMC hi-jinks. The Halloween/Homecoming hi-jinks plan is executed...

When I got to Harry's dorm, in Hanna Hall, he had a complete Dress Alpha uniform ready, including white cross belts and ammunition case. In about 20 minutes, I changed from a 19-year-old Temple coed, into a Pennsylvania Military College Cadet. Since the parade was in the evening, the darkness would help conceal my true identity. For the line of march, Harry placed me in a middle row. I was ready to play my instrument—a ukulele. It was showtime!

I tried to keep a straight face as we began to march. I got more than a few double takes from the Cadets who weren't in on the prank. Kids and adults lined the streets as the Band played. I was in high spirits, although my marching skills were lacking. But my high spirits began to fade when I saw Major General William S. Biddle, the Commandant of Cadets, straight as a ramrod, among the closest spectators. I was trapped! And Harry's days as a Cadet could be coming to an end.

I shouldn't have worried. The dapper general looked at our line of Band Cadets, saw me, but said nothing. Perhaps he had been sipping spiked apple cider pre-parade. I just kept strumming the uke and marching. Was the notorious Lt. Michael J. Hubbard, aka Zeus, Assistant Adjutant, among the spectators? Probably. Did he notice me? I'll never know. But I'm sure he heard about it later.

After the parade, the word was out. One of the cadets in the Band who wasn't in on the plan, wondered why the new cadet's Dress Alpha blouse had bumps. Harry had pulled it off, with a little help from his friends. For me, the Halloween Parade is burned into my memory and into my heart. For one SPOOKTACULAR night, I was a PMC Cadet.

William R. Moller:
Our Third-Class Year

In our Third-Class year, my roommate, Max Gayer (RIP) and I enlisted in the Pennsylvania National Guard while we were also under contract as ROTC Cadets. We were assigned to the 28th Infantry Division (Bloody Bucket) of the PANG at the Chester, PA, National Guard Armory. Because of our PMC ROTC status, we were inducted as PFC E-3's. We joined because our PANG drills were always on Saturday Mornings. This permitted Max and me to don our BDU's, leave the PMC Campus, and totally miss standing for the routine PMC Saturday Morning Room Inspections!

Max and I went to the PANG drills on Saturday mornings where we performed small arms instruction. However, PANG drills were not conducted every Saturday. On Non-Drill Saturdays, Max and I would wear our BDU's, leave campus, and have a long breakfast in downtown Chester. In our First-Class year, the PANG demanded that, at PMC Graduation, we be commissioned in the PANG. LTC Phillips and PMC ROTC Detachment won out and Max and I were commissioned as Reserve and RA Officers, respectively. One thing that we were unaware of was that upon commissioning, we both enjoyed two years of prior service seniority—which advanced both of us for earlier Army Officer promotions. Thank you PMC for SMI!!!

William R. Moller:
Cadet William Bohan, PMC '67

The PMC Corps of Cadets, led by the Colors and HQ Company (PMC Marching Band) marched in downtown Chester in the 1964 Pulaski Day Parade. At some point in time during the parade, taking his camera, Cadet Bohan made his way to the North-bound NY Central Railroad Bridge. He was attempting to take photographs of the PMC Corps of Cadets for either "The Dome" or "Sabre and Sash" from his elevated vantage point. Apparently as he leaned forward against the edge of the bridge to take photographs, he must have extended his leg behind him. A North-bound train car clipped him and killed him instantly. I understand he was buried in his PMC Dress Delta Uniform in a private service. From the Fall of 1961 through the Spring of 1965, this was the only PMC Cadet Campus death that I was aware of. RIP Cadet Bohan.

David Fiedler:
Brigadier General Moll

In 1966 (approximately), word got out through the cadet spy ring that in the cadet tailor shop President Moll was having Willy Bell make him a Brigadier General uniform. The cadets immediately tried to determine what justification could possibly exist for Moll to wear a General's uniform. As it turned out, there was a Civil War era Pennsylvania Statute that said that the President of the Pennsylvania Military College was a General Officer on the staff of the Governor.

I also did some research at the time and as it turns out prior to the National Defense Act of 1907, each state actually had its own army. That is why George Washington wore his Virginia uniform as he lobbied the Continental Congress to become Commander in Chief. It is also the reason Abraham Lincoln, as his first act in office, was to ask the state Governors for troops to put down the rebellion. At that time, many states had armies (National Guard) much larger than the US Army. Under the 1907 act, the State Troops of the National Guard were brought under the control of the Federal Government for training and mobilization. Guard officers were/are still appointed by the states, but after 1907 had to meet federal standards and pass a federal board of review to be recognized as a federal officer, BUT the Governors could/can appoint State officers whenever they feel like it. State officers cannot wear the US brass on their uniform but do wear authorized state insignia. In Moll's case, it would replace the US with PA. To this day, National Guard orders for annual training read "by order of the President and with the APPROVAL of the Governor".

I believed at the time that the word was leaked out in order to see how the Corps of Cadets would react to a BG Moll. The reaction was not good for Moll. At first, many compared him to Colonel Hyatt who only used his federally recognized rank (COL) and never tried to use the PA law to get a general's star. Moll was first laughed at and then ridiculed severely by every cadet in the Corps, such was the hatred for him by that time. Bottom line, Moll got the message and never had the nerve to appear in State uniform at PMC. It remained on the shelf at Willy Bell's tailor shop.

David Fiedler:
Streaking

During my time at PMC, I was made aware of at least three streaking incidents:

Incident 1 — One cold winter night in 1966, a few of the cadets were sitting around in the hall in "New Dorm #4" and the subject of streaking came up since someone had just streaked an athletic event in Philadelphia. Some cadet said, "I'll streak all of Chester, even in this weather, if there is enough money in it." Out came the collection hat and the fun seekers came up with over $100.00 dollars. The deal was struck, rules were, as I remember, from campus down Edgemont Avenue, around the downtown traffic circle with the newsstand kind of near the train station, then up Providence Avenue back to Dorm 4. Time was set for about 2 AM so not many citizens were around (the bars closed at around 1AM). The streaker was to be followed by a car to witness the streak and recover the cadet in case of frostbite or being spotted by the cops. THE GUY ACTUALLY DID IT AND THOSE IN THE CAR SWORE HE DID. I was later told he took a shortcut over the I-95 foot bridge which was deemed okay, and he got the money. I only saw him leave and come back, so I must take the word of my fellow cadets.

Incident 2 — Some frat told a pledge that all he had to do was go with them down to Rittenhouse Square in Philadelphia, be let out naked from a car, streak the Square, and jump into another car on the far side and take off. Of course, when the time came, and he was halfway across the square, BOTH cars took off and he was left there NAKED!! The Philly cops came, threw an overcoat over him, and dropped him at a police building. PMC sent our van with his roommate and his uniform to go collect him. I knew the guy that drove the van. He was embarrassed, and the cops thought it was hysterical.

Incident 3—This incident was sad. I had a classmate who was always considered "a little nuts" by us. He lived in new Dorm #6 that ran parallel to Melrose Avenue on the second or third floor. In our senior year, with maybe three months to go before graduation, he decided to "Moon and also Sun" the traffic going up and down Melrose Avenue, including the city bus. Of course, the local cops came, as did the Commandant's Staff, and I think a crew from the Crosier-Chester Medical Center. They took him away peacefully, and we never saw him again. Some of my classmates who knew him way better than me said that he just cracked up, others were not so sure and claimed it was all an act to get him out of military service. It might have been a combination of both, but he was a cadet with us for well over three years.

David Fiedler:
Engineering at PMC

In the Fall of 1966, I was approached by a team of three cadet engineering majors from the class of 1967 that I knew very well. They said that they needed my help on their senior engineering project. The project was to create a low-cost NIMBUS weather satellite terminal for which the engineering department had funded the first $50.00 of their costs. I said, "Why me?"

The answer was because of my position as a student assistant in the physics department (working for Dr. John Prather) and because I was president of the student chapter of AFCEA. I had the keys to the penthouse atop Kirkbride Hall that was the location of the AFCEA funded and operated amateur (ham) radio station. I also had access/control of all the lab equipment in the physics department, including power supplies, vacuum tube test sets, oscilloscopes etc.

The penthouse and roof were a perfect location for a satellite receiving station. Of course, I immediately joined the team as an unofficial member.

The engineers broke the effort into three parts. The radio receiver that operated on a frequency just above the commercial US TV frequency band, the demodulator/processor that took the weather information off the signals received from the NIMBUS satellite, and a high gain/high efficiency receiving antenna array.

For the receiver, the cadets went to a yard sale and bought an old RCA TV set that looked like it was in good condition, but they could not get it to work. Finally, I said, "Let's check the vacuum tubes." I brought out the test set from the physics lab. After we replaced the three defective tubes in the set (courtesy of the physics department), it worked fine. The TV was then modified to receive on the NIMBUS frequency, and you could hear the broadcast in the TV speaker. With the help of the ham radio antenna book, we then constructed a good receiver antenna and connected it to the modified TV receiver. The NIMBUS signal got even stronger!!

The last part of the system required that a demodulator/processor be built, the output of which went to a display. This required some research into how the NIMBUS worked, but luckily for us, the information could be found in open-source literature. It was basically working like a FAX machine. Of course, we had no means to build a circuit board at PMC and chips were not even invented at that time, so we hand wired transistors and other components and built a demodulator processor.

After we put the whole system together, we realized we had no display, so I went down to the physics lab and came back with the largest TEKTRONIX oscilloscope we had and hooked it up. It had a hood so only one person could look at a time. The first guy looked in and said, "Holy s**t, it works!" When it was my turn, I looked in and I could clearly see the lower east coast from Florida to South Carolina with the locations of cloud cover etc. but all with a green glow because of the scope display. The image, however, was better than what we saw on nightly TV, which was slightly distorted. Ours was clear as a bell because we had a better demodulator/processor.

The project was presented on PMC Industry Day to local companies like Boeing and Sun Ship Building Inc, etc. and their reaction was, "Wow, and you did this for 50 bucks, an old TV set and, some odds and ends from the lab?" BUT that is NOT the end of the story!!

About a week later, all the members of the team plus the school got a large envelope from the General Electric Company who had the NIMBUS contract with the government. At this time, GE was selling NIMBUS terminals to every local radio and TV station so that they could show the weather conditions during their weather broadcasts. Some newspapers were also printing NIMBUS photos on their weather pages. The GE terminals were priced at better than $10,000 (in 1967) each and they were making lots of money! The "lawyer letter" claimed that the cadets had violated a long list of GE patents and proprietary information but since GE was a very magnanimous company and understood that the cadets were students, they would not sue them if they signed the attached non-disclosure agreement and returned to them within a week and never spoke about what they did or how they did it.

Fortunately, one of the cadets had a family lawyer who said "total BS" meant to shut you up because GE was making big bucks off NIMBUS!!

When the letter was not answered, all then got another letter with stronger language, threatening even harsher penalties unless we agreed never to disclose any details of how we built the system. By this time, the family lawyer had done his homework and we knew

GE was blowing smoke and there were no more restrictions on what we had done than there were on building a TV set. We didn't answer that letter either. We then got another letter offering to license back to us our own work. We didn't answer that one either. In those days, three broke cadets about to go on Active duty were not about to start a business.

These days we might have become Steve Jobs or one of those other guys that started in a garage, but not then. The next semester after the three had graduated, somehow, I got a call from a GE guy who asked me if any school grant money was used in the project. I told him I was originally from The Bronx and that was for me to know and him to find out. He said to me, "Well, that could make you an accessory to a criminal act."

I said, "I am so scared. This is what you can tell your big boss, I am going to document what we did, and then have it published in both the ham radio magazine (QST) and AFCEA's magazine (Signal). The people that read those publications make their own stuff as a hobby. They will take it to users, and you are going to lose a pile of money, plus your case will be thrown out of court, plus we will then sue you for filing a frivolous lawsuit. What do you think of that?" He hung up!!! Of course, I never did any of those, who had time?

I never heard from GE again, but I will bet that PMC never got a donation from them.

It's still better. Just before I graduated, I got a call from the USAF Air Weather Service (AWS) located at Scott AFB in the Midwest. They had somehow heard this story and asked for the demodulation details. I sent them a copy of the PMC Industry Day presentation.

Better still. Just before my graduation, the AWS guy sent me a copy of an ad from a trade magazine with a GE ad that announces a new ultra-low cost ($1500.00) NIMBUS receiver terminal with an improved low distortion display!!

Better than better—30 years go by, and Dave Fiedler is a Deputy Program Manager of the Army/USAF Joint Tactical Fusion Program (JTFP). His boss says that in the Army divisions, the AWS mans the new weather system, but the Army provides the equipment. You are in charge of the Integrated Meteorological System (IMETS). I have a meeting with the AWS and the Army project manager (PM) to talk about upgrading the current system and in the system is a NIMBUS terminal.

I told the above story and now I am the NIMBUS expert. Even better, the guy from AWS says, the call you got from Scott AFB about the demodulator, that was me!!! I asked if they ever made one. His answer was, "No, we bought the one from GE. It was cheaper and they are still being used."

How is that for a PMC story? No telling how much money we saved the taxpayers!!!

David Fiedler:
Fire in the Barracks

Upon returning from my job in the physics department one afternoon in the Spring of 1967, along with two of my friends, we entered what was then called New Dorm #4. As we entered, we smelled smoke and the odor of fish. Just a few days before, all of the room doors had been wiped down with a wood perseverative that must have contained fish oil or something like it.

If you recall, in those days cadets were required to tape their academic schedules to their room doors so that they could be located to assure that they were where they were supposed to be. One of the big pranks of those days was to set the taped-up schedule card on fire, pound on the door, and leave as a joke. The victim would then open his door and have to deal with the problem. In this instance, the jokers did not realize that the fish oil in the wood perseverative was highly flammable and the residents of the room were gone. This door was fiercely ablaze and the flames were getting close to the mattresses on the bunk beds and the laundry bags located not far from the door.

Upon discovering this, we quickly got the fire extinguisher from the hall and put out the fire. Everything in the room was fine but the door was pretty well gone on the hallway side. The next morning the buildings and grounds guys came and replaced the door. No one confessed to setting the schedule card / door on fire.

A day later, I was presented with a letter from the Commandant stating that the residents of the rooms surrounding the burned doors would be charged $20.00 to cover the door damage that totaled $250.00 because we must have been involved due to the location of our rooms. At that time, $20.00 was about all the money I had to my name. I became very irate and wrote a letter to Dr. Moll stating that when the fire started I was in the physics lab on the other side of the campus with Professor Prather and that when my two friends and I entered the building the door was already on fire AND that I was the person who put the fire out and I had witnesses to all of this.

I also told Moll that I acted so quickly that it was put out without the need to call the Chester Fire Department. Moll never answered my letter.

A few days later, I got a "report to the Commandant (Colonel O'Hara) after class" message. I reported to the Commandant, and he had Moll's letter. First thing he asked me was did I think it was appropriate for me to write a letter to his boss, the president of the college. I answered yes because the $20.00 charge was grossly unfair, and he was the individual who had the power to right this wrong. O'Hara (who I had had problems with before) and refused to look me in the eye even though I again stated that I was the one who put out the fire and probably saved a considerable amount of damage in excess of $20.00.

He then looked at me and said, "If you don't give me $20.00, I will not let you register for next semester." That semester was the first semester of my senior year. I then reached down into my wallet, pulled out my last $20.00 bill and threw it on his desk. I then said, "If it ever happens again, I will let it burn" and walked out of his office without being dismissed. We never spoke again.

At that time there was for the senior class what was called the "linear promotion list". The list was supposed to be used for cadet promotions to cadet officer and senior NCO rank as positions became available. Guess who ended up at the bottom of that list...which was okay by me because I never had to buy a saber or a sword!! When I told Dr. Prather the story, he said I'll talk to both of them. I said thanks but don't bother, they are already promoting people below.

David Fiedler:
Fire!

In early 1967, I returned to my room on the 2nd floor of "New Dorm #4" and found a bunch of my Company (D Co.) gathered around a room at the east end of the hall. The windows of the room faced a small patch of lawn. In the center of the lawn patch was a vertical pipe that was the fill pipe to the oil storage tank located under the patch of lawn. The pipe fed the oil burning heating and hot water equipment located in the basement of the building.

The oil delivery truck had just completed filling the oil tank and the careless delivery driver had overflowed the storage tank and left a large puddle of fuel oil around the fill pipe and spread over the lawn. The cadets in the room were amusing themselves by flicking lit cigarette butts out the window in an attempt to set the puddle of oil on fire. The lit butts were not doing the job.

This went on for a while until one of our more brilliant cadet science majors showed up and said, "That's fuel oil. It's not as volatile as stuff like gasoline or kerosene, so the butts won't light it up. What you need is this." "This" turned out to be a roll of toilet paper from the nearby latrine that he soaked in zippo lighter fluid. When lit, he tossed the flaming roll out the window and into the oil puddle! He was correct, the oil burst into flames that shot up almost to the second floor before dying down. Luckily, there was not that much oil in the puddle and the delivery driver had put the cap back on the fill pipe before he left. The fire and the oil spill did, however, wipe out a good size patch of lawn that took months to regrow!

This was typical of what cadets would do out of boredom or to relieve the stress of cadet life. As the flames roared up, everyone disappeared and not a cadet could be found on that end of the building for at least an hour as they went to establish plausible deniability as to their location that afternoon. No one cared (me included) that they could have under slightly different circumstances set the whole building ablaze. Amazingly, this prank brought down no heat from the Commandant or the cadet chain of command. No one seemed to notice the burned out patch of lawn near the oil fill pipe. Those in the know kept the oath of silence and thought that the whole thing was pretty funny!

Bob Kukich:
A Raid on the Moravian Campus

One evening in the fall of 1968, a number of HQ Company cadets decided to paint the Moravian Campus in Bethlehem, PA red prior to the Homecoming Football game. We split up into three cars with specific targets. In our car were the driver — Dana Wren, shotgun — Fred Sample, and back seat participants — Bill Feyk and myself.

Our target was the famous Comenius statue in the center of the campus. Unbeknownst to us, the Bethlehem Police and Moravian campus cops were waiting for us, having been tipped off by an observant gas station attendant. Stopping for gas near the Moravian campus, the cadets of one car were overheard talking about their plans by the gas station attendant. To make matters worse, the attendant saw them mixing the water-based paint in the gas station bathroom. When we arrived on campus, we discovered a campus cop guarding the statue.

Not to be thwarted, someone suggested Fred (a PMC and NCAA track star) lead the cop on a wild goose chase through the campus while we painted the statue, which is exactly what we did. Having successfully exhausted and eluded the campus cop, Fred rejoined us as we finished painting. We quickly departed the Moravian campus and Bethlehem using the back roads.

When we arrived back at PMC, we learned that the Bethlehem police had called the PMC Officer of the Day, informing him that two carloads of cadets had been detained at a police roadblock, arrested, booked, and jailed for destruction of property. The cadets were jailed for a few days, required to clean all the painted areas, perform some community service, and pay individual fines before being released. Those cadets made the front page of the Bethlehem News with a photo of them standing behind bars in the Bethlehem Police Station. We learned many valuable lessons that night, which served us well in our miliary careers.

Don Cooper:
The Junior Ring Dance or Lessons Learned from Operation Barbarossa

During four years as a PMC cadet, the Junior Ring Dance was one of those special events that create lasting memories. It ranks up there with graduation, commissioning, and even becoming an "Old Man." On this occasion, two of our cadets from the Class of 1970 became engaged and nine cadets pinned their steady girlfriends. The evening was to be filled with cadets in alpha blouses and girls in formal evening gowns dancing to a live orchestra and enjoying the after-dance parties.

The one person who was exceedingly excited about the ring dance was my classmate, Bill (The Duck) McDevitt. Every day since we returned to school in September, that's all he talked about. He had one problem though; he could not find a date. After hearing these incessant complaints and concerns day in and day out, I broke down and convinced my reluctant cousin to go with Bill to the ring dance. I assured her it would be a nice opportunity to meet other cadets and that I would be close by if she needed help. Bill was ecstatic. But now, he concentrated his efforts assessing all potential eventualities and developing contingency plans to ensure a successful operation. In case of rain, Plan A, in case of car problems, Plan B, and the lists went on and on. For Bill, every possibility was covered so he wouldn't screw up this night.

It was December 1968 and the highlighted weekend started on Friday the 13th. (That should have given me a hint.) The Martha and the Vandellas concert was great and everything seemed to be falling into place. On Saturday, the day of the dance, I was able to pick up my dad's old Chevy. My date was a student from Rosemont College (a small Catholic college for girls), my buddy John Perrelli's date was a local girl. The Duck had his own car and was picking up my cousin.

The dance ended well without a major incident other than The Duck hovering over my cousin like a monkey holding a banana. It was now time to go to the various parties outside of campus. I told my cousin I would see her at one of the parties.

As I was leaving MacMorland Center to pick up the car, unexpected flurries started to fall gently upon the campus grounds. Our dates were a bit concerned, but I reassured them that there was nothing to worry about and that everything was under control. Everything was under control, that is, until we approached one of the few hills that led to the party. By then, the streets had a thin layer of snow blanketing the surface. Undaunted, I downshifted and charged up the hill. We were about halfway up when the old Chevy could no longer advance, and it slowly began to drift backwards and sideways down to the bottom.

Despite the ice hidden beneath the snow, I accepted the challenge and tried again, this time with John upfront as my copilot while the two girls were placed in the back seat. After more unsuccessful attempts, the girls were screaming and wanted to go home.

We finally made it back to Rosemont College. My date arranged for John's girlfriend to stay in her dorm until the weather broke in the morning. Both were not happy campers. In the meantime, word must have gotten around their campus because a bunch of very attractive girls approached us. As John lowered the window to start a pleasant conversation and possibly find a new relationship, he got pummeled with snowballs. After losing our dignity, we retreated. With our alpha blouses wet and feet getting colder, I opened up the trunk to see if there were any blankets. To my surprise I found tire chains. Putting chains on in the snow without gloves was tenuous. Fortunately, I lost no fingers to frostbite. In these desperate hours, there was salvation. There was a light flickering from a large stone mansion on the campus grounds. We knocked on the door and a nun appeared. We told her about our story, and she invited us into the convent and gave us hot tea and crackers.

Daybreak was approaching and we finally picked up John's date. She looked disheveled as her wrinkled dress and rumpled hairdo was revealed in the early morning light. She sat motionless and speechless in the back seat. Seeing she may need comfort; John hopped over the front seat and gently placed his arms around her. Perhaps there was still romance in the air. But if eyes could kill, John would not have known what hit him. He then jumped back up front and resumed his job as my copilot. We finally dropped her off in front of her house. As my car swiftly took off, her entire neighborhood could hear the chains of my father's old Chevy, rattling and clanging down the street like a disabled Sherman tank.

The epilogue: We were never able to attend the after-dance parties and I was never able to hook up with my cousin. John and I never saw our girlfriends again, my cousin hated me and vowed never to date or get near a PMC cadet again, and finally we were labeled persona non grata at Rosemont College. The weekend was an utter disaster. However, the one bright spot was The Duck. He said he had the best time of his life. He covered all the bases and was prepared. He read Operation Barbarossa and was not going to let cold weather and snow ruin his Junior Ring Dance.

Mike Campbell (as told by Hannah Campbell):
Remembering a special "Punch ... P. J."

Jack and Dora Andreas set Mike and me up on a blind date for September 19, 1970. I'd never been on a blind date, so I had no idea what to expect, but in case this guy was not my type, I went to Gimbel's in 69th Street and bought a very cute Doris Day type blonde wig as a disguise in case he wanted to see me again. When Dora and Jack came to my door, they took one look at me and went "?????" Mike grinned behind them, and I remember thinking he looked like a nice guy.

Off we went to a Phi Epsilon Pi / ZBT Fraternity party with the jukebox in full swing playing Motown tunes, dancing, and the guys gulping beer...until, we girls were served a special punch called "Purple Jesus." My how sweet it tasted over and over again. When the night was over and Mike drove me home, he tried to kiss me and I kissed back and then, he began to run his fingers through my "hair," and I awoke from my stupor and started to hold onto the elastic band attached to the wig. I twirled and twirled trying to remove his hands, almost getting dizzy. Had the wig come off, he would have looked at 37 bobby pins holding onto my normally long dark brown hair. He would be scared to death.

For our next date, I decided I didn't need the wig and when he came to pick me up he asked me, "Hi, I'm Mike...is Hannah home?" I told him I was Hannah and he responded, "No you're not, you're one of her sisters...Hannah is blonde." All that night he kept staring at me as if I were pranking him again. Every time we're asked how we met, I always tell the wig story, and everyone laughs.

William J. Troy:
The Wolfgram Library Inspection

Construction for the new library began our Rook year 1969 and the completed Lieutenant William J. Wolfgram Memorial Library was dedicated November 7, 1970. It is a beautiful triangular shaped building of white brick and concrete with four stories and a penthouse. It just celebrated its fiftieth year of operation. I know, I have the T-shirt!

Lieutenant Wolfgram was a member of the class of 1943 and was killed in Italy serving with the Tenth Mountain Division. It is an imposing structure.

Of course, the building was off limits to students during construction. Bob Leach had an idea to get in and have a sneak preview of the building. He talked me into joining him in an infiltration mission to inspect the new library prior to the book carry and the dedication. We dressed in civilian attire, dress pants, shirt, tie, and sport coat and put on hard hats. I don't know where we got the hard hats, but I still have mine. We had a 50-foot tape measure and a clipboard with paper on it and proceeded to walk into the building. Workmen were still completing the carpeting and some other finish work, and no one took notice of us or asked what we were doing.

We walked through the building, every now and then taking a measurement and writing it down. We went through all four floors. We saw the large stained glass window, "His Master's Voice," the RCA Company's "Nipper" dog staring at a phonograph above the main stairway. I was surprised that no one asked us why we were there. It was a successful infiltration mission!

Mike Campbell (as told by Hannah Campbell):
The Ring Formal Crasher

December 5, 1970: The excitement was palpable as I waited for my date, Mike, to arrive at my home in Overbrook, to escort me to the Ring Formal. Handsome in his Dress Alpha uniform, Mike presented me with a lovely bouquet, and surprisingly, handed my mother a dozen red roses. She was over the moon. As we posed for photos, Mom asked a few times where the Ring Formal was being held to which we responded, "The Marriot on City Line Avenue."

After posing inside the huge painted plywood ring where Mike hung his PMC school ring on a ribbon around my neck, we ducked under the silver sabers arch and strolled to the dance floor for a romantic slow dance. I felt like the cat's meow in my red velvet gown, silver high heels, hair done in French curls, gloves, and pale pink lipstick while my handsome Cadet held me tight. We were surrounded by the other Cadets and their dates, the dance floor moving in rhythm as Colonel Frey watched from the dais. I remember Dora Di, Michael Andreas, and I acting really cute and sweet as we approached Frey's table and plead for our boyfriends to be released from doing tours. No luck.

I heard someone say, "Hey, who's that lady peeking in the door?" Well, it couldn't be anyone I knew, but then Mike yelled, "Hey, Mrs. Dougherty, we're over here!" Oh, dear God, I saw red as she crept across the parquet floor in her ugly brown plaid "car" coat that looked like a horse blanket—only no self-respecting horse would be seen dead in it. Paired with her shabby beige orthopedic shoes, my usually dolled up Mom looked downright dowdy on this particular night in my life.

As Mike met her half-way, she sheepishly and half-heartedly said, "Oh, I'm not dressed, I just couldn't," before he introduced her to our friends, let go of MY hand, and asked her to dance with him. I kept trying to remember the Fifth Commandment: "Thou Shalt Not Kill."

No one else seemed to care about this interloper, but I did and as she often said to me, "You wait till I get home!" In the movie "Stella Dallas", Barbara Stanwyk stands outside the gorgeous home in which her daughter marries, tugging at her teary handkerchief, just wanting to see her daughter happy—only Stella doesn't crash the party in her shabby attire. I'll never forget that night where my mother just wanted to "peek."

Maybe déjà vu'? Family pictures show Mom in her earlier years dolled up in ballgowns, gloves, heels, jewelry, and corsage as she left for dances at the Naval Officers Club with my handsome Dad. Mrs. Betty Dougherty wasn't "peeking"…she'd been the Belle of the Ball long before her daughter.

Hannah Campbell (wife of Mike Campbell):
Artie Hafner

When my then boyfriend Mike Campbell invited me to party at the Phi Epilson House, I met his band brothers in HQ Company and especially the one of a kind, Artie Hafner.

Artie stuttered when he spoke, but on treks to the then old Ponderosa, somehow his gin and tonics loosened his tongue, and his personality came through. Artie was an only child and had gone to military/boarding schools since he was a little guy. His well-heeled parents worked for the PA. Railroad and Owens Corning Companies and were social butterflies…so much so that many times poor Artie's family were his PMC brothers.

Artie visited my parents' home in Overbrook on many occasions, and he particularly hated our dog, "Shamrock." Artie called Shamrock some very #@%^&* terms and we laughed and laughed because we knew Art really didn't hate him. One day I called my mother from my Philly office and Art answered the phone.

"Art, what are you doing there?" I asked. "Well, I was driving by in my car and saw your mother sitting on the outside 2nd floor window, cleaning it so I rang the bell, she came down, and I started helping her."

Art's parents invited a bunch of us to their opulent Berwyn home at noon and we began partying on the back patio, waiting for his parents announced return time of 4:00 p.m. By 7:00, Dora and I removed the one tray of pigs in a blanket from the fridge and baked them…everyone was starving at this point. When the Hafners arrived back at 7:00, Mrs. Hafner asked who had the nerve to cook the pigs in a blanket. Uh, oh. Needless to say, by the time dinner was served, we were all tipsy beyond words and someone drove over a neighbor's mailbox.

When Mike left PMC in his Junior year to enlist in the Army, Artie and Greg Haugens were my faithful friends, taking me to the Pondo, etc. Art and I had one nice dinner and a few gin and tonics and when I went to the ladies room, his mother's Pontiac TransAm had flooded to the seats, thanks to Tinicum Creek. As we scooped out the murky water, he thanked me for paying the check to which I responded I didn't and thought he did. Well, there was no going back that night to pay that $85.00 bill!

Art showed up unexpectedly at my house one night—only I was going on a date with a Navy Cadet named Rocco from Villanova. I asked Rocco if Artie could come along and was met with a long stare…especially after Art got in the front seat and sat on the long stemmed rose Rocco brought for me.

Art welcomed his friends to his house whether his parents were there or not, and I remember many a pool table game. When Mike was stationed at Fort Lewis, Washington, he met up with Artie at a bar and they called me on the payphone. Art had relocated to Washington for Owens Corning and met his bride to be, Carol.

We lost touch after that and I'm so sorry I didn't pursue his whereabouts because by the time I did locate him and we wrote to each other, it was too late. Art had cancer that took his life. But oh the laughter and smiles he left with all his friends, his humility amazed me, his warmth and shenanigans will live on forever.

Greg Haugens:
TKE Sports

My junior year found me as a platoon sergeant in Headquarters Company. If I was a private, I would call myself sort of a jerk in that position! During the first semester, a couple good friends pledged TKE fraternity and did their best to get me to try during second semester. Which I did!! I was totally focused on becoming a brother. As all fraternities at that time did, hazing was the system to root out undeserving pledges. This also included being at fraternity sport events.

I happened to be a starter on the TKE softball team, and a big game against arch-rival Theta Chi was scheduled to be played on a Tuesday afternoon. Preparing for the game, an announcement came over intercom that an Honor Guard was happening at the same time. Being in HQ (the band), I was expected to be at the Honor Guard BUT the softball game was just too important to miss, so I skipped the Honor Guard. The game was fun and more so, we won, thus I was in good mood...until I returned to our Quadrangle where I was met by the Officer of the Day, Sergeant of the Guard, and three POGs, placing me under room arrest. Even had a POG outside my room all night. Wednesday morning at mess, I was instructed to report to Colonel Frey's office asap, which I did once mess was over. Colonel Frey was a bit upset, calling my skipping Honor Guard as AWOL and he was going to get me kicked out of school.

A meeting was set-up with the Dean of Men Thursday morning. I didn't know if I was more afraid of being kicked out of school or having to return home and face my dad. So, I did what I felt was the most logical thing to do. Being under contract and knowing if kicked out I was subject to entering the Army as a private, I started called First Army HQ, even the Pentagon, asking if I was kicked out on Thursday at my meeting could I start basic training somewhere on

Friday. I WASN'T GOING HOME TO FACE MY DAD! Everyone I talked to got a good chuckle, understood, but couldn't do anything for me.

Well, Thursday morning came and I was sitting with the Dean of Men in his office when the phone rang. After the Dean hung up, he said the others required for the meeting on their way up. To my surprise when the door opened the first person to walk in was my dad. Being a Circuit Court Judge in Peoria, Illinois he had to arrange airfare plus getting a replacement for his trial. So, he wasn't too happy. Colonel Frey did his best to dismiss me from school, but my dad convinced the Dean that the crime didn't deserve the death penalty. I got to stay but walked every tour the rest of my junior year (two on Monday-Wednesday-Friday; three on Saturday and Sunday) and senior year and busted down to private.

Maris Eshleman:
Hitchhiking

During the school year 1970-71, PMC adopted an innovative scheduling program. The Fall semester would end in December and the Spring semester began in February. During January, they offered a unique selection of courses that consisted of several hours a day, 3-4 days a week for the four weeks. By having longer classes each day, projects or topics that couldn't normally be handled in the usual shorter class periods of the regular semester were offered.

They called this The January Program. Since it was completely voluntary, the Corps was adjourned and the few of us that took the courses were allowed to live in our own rooms and wear civilian clothes. There was also no meal service available on campus, so we had to forage around to figure out how to get by. Lots of guys got hot plates for their rooms.

I decided to do this because it sounded interesting and an opportunity to pursue learning in a different venue. My best friend in college, Phil DeGroot, also was attending so we spent a great deal of time together.

Since classes were over Thursday noon we had long weekends every week and there were no amenities on campus. As there was no reason to hang around there, we were discussing options. Being poor students, we didn't have cars at the time and little money to travel so we decided to hitchhike.

Phil had met a girl that lived in Wantagh on Long Island, and we thought for our first adventure we would hitchhike there to see her. Her parents agreed to let us stay at their home, so it was perfect. There was also a local club there that was a favorite of Long Island cadets we wanted to visit. We had often done local hitchhiking to other colleges to see girls, so we had some idea of how to do it.

But this was a whole different level of hitchhiking. We decided that we needed to make signs with intermediate waypoints to increase our chances of getting rides. We made up signs and Thursday afternoon walked over to where I-95 ended at the time in Chester and started our journey. It went better than we thought. We quickly got rides at each stop and we made it to Wantagh by about 8pm that evening. All the rides there and back were pleasant and even some single women picked us up for rides.

With one success under our belts, Phil had an uncle and aunt that lived in a suburb of Boston that became our next adventure. We had no trouble getting rides and we were able to quickly move through New York City and up to Boston on I-95. It was the first time either of us had been to Boston. His uncle had an extra car that they let us use so we got to do sightseeing in and around Boston. I remember it being incredibly cold and lots of snow in New England. On the ride back we got picked up by a family in a Volkswagen bus that had no heat. Fortunately, they stopped frequently at rest areas, so we all got into the buildings to warm up. Another fun trip.

For what turned out to be our biggest and last trip, Phil had a girlfriend at Bowling Green State University in Ohio, and he made plans for us to visit her. On Thursday we hitchhiked to his parents' home outside Cleveland where we spent the night and then Friday went on to Bowling Green. Phil was a member of the fraternity Alpha Phi Omega and was able to get bunks for us there and they allowed us to eat with them since they had a fully functioning house. They worked us into the kitchen detail to help out.

On Saturday of that weekend the Fraternity had a "Tea" with a Sorority that happened to be the Sorority of Phil's girlfriend. The Tea was an afternoon mixer with drinks and dancing. I danced with several girls and one in particular that went out with me that night and we double-dated. I saw her several other times after that. Sunday we hit the road and hitchhiked all the way back to Chester. Between Cleveland and Pittsburgh it began snowing. We got a ride just outside Cleveland that took us all the way to Harrisburg through about a foot of snow in the Alleghenies. We got back late after a wonderful weekend.

We didn't come up with anyplace to go for the final weekend and I don't recall what we did. I also don't remember if PMC did a January program the next year. But, in January of 1971, Phil and I mastered the art of hitchhiking around the northeast. We had no trouble getting rides and every ride we got all were great people.

Dave Neimeyer:
The Curse of the X

Many college campuses seem almost to come alive; to be endowed with life and feelings of their own. The Cadets at Pennsylvania Military College soon learned that their campus was possessed of a particularly malevolent personality. Like Egdon Heath in *The Return of the Native*, the campus seemed to sense a person's feeling towards it. Some loved the campus and were content to stay there. They lived lives of total bliss. It was they who would find dollar bills lying by the walkways as they went to class. Their rooms were comfortable and had a pleasant view. They walked in sunshine and warmth the whole day through.

On the other hand, there were those who hated PMC, or "the X" as it was known to Cadets. Cracks in the sidewalk leaped up and tripped them. Mud puddles lay in constant wait for them. The light bulbs in their rooms burned out with amazing frequency. Gloom hung on them, like the dust cloud over Pigpen in "Peanuts" or the dark cloud over the character in "Li'l Abner."

I was one of the lucky ones. The campus and I flourished in mutual understanding. In the midst of my happiness, however, a change was coming. At last, even I was to feel the heavy weight of "the curse of the X."

The sophomore slump was hard upon us, and we were dying for a chance to get away and visit some young, honest to goodness, real live girls. We put our heads together and a plan began to form. I had been writing to some student nurses in Allentown and had the address and phone number of their dorm. Kaj could provide the transportation; he had a car on campus, even if it was only a 1962 Corvair. Kaj and I decided to include Crazy Charlie Kortlang and Wild Man McKelvey, just to round out our number.

It was now 4:45 on a Friday afternoon. By Corps regulations we were supposed to be back in our dorms by midnight. The question arose as to how to find a way to stay out longer. Crazy Charlie had the answer in a moment. It was his roommate's job to turn in the report that night. With a little bit of wheedling, we convinced him to neglect to mark us absent. It was unethical, of course, but very effective, and highly necessary in view of our imperative need for a short vacation.

With that settled, I gave the girls' phone number to Crazy Charlie. A minor hitch developed. The girls were at work, but we were told they'd be off at 9:00. Crazy Charlie left word to tell the girls they might have visitors later in the evening.

We decided to leave campus a little after six. Allentown was a two-hour drive from the X and we didn't want to be late. The journey began well enough. We piled into Kaj's Corvair right on time and pulled out of the parking lot with no trouble at all. We headed north, and ten minutes later were passing through Swarthmore. It was there that we felt the first sting of the curse. A gentle warning, really. The generator light popped on. Car trouble! We pulled over and investigated but could find nothing wrong. The car was apparently in fine condition. Warily we set out again, but soon relaxed as no further trouble occurred.

Suddenly a harsher bolt was sent our way. A moment of confusion at a traffic light and we were off course. Maps were pulled out and examined. We soon worked out a way to get back to our original route with a minimum loss of time. We continued northward.

Now the full curse of the X came down upon us. Our lives would be spared, but our sinful plans must be halted. Thus, it was that as our little group strove onward in innocence, we were suddenly beset. Smoke began coming from the Corvair's motor. Strange engine noises began, and the dashboard warning lights flickered on. We pulled over and jumped from the car, expecting at any moment to be engulfed in flames.

The seconds ticked by and nothing happened. The engine stopped smoking, and signs of an eminent explosion began to fade. We again ventured an examination of the motor. We determined that it could be driven for a short distance, so we started up and headed for a gas station. At the station our worst fears were confirmed. With luck we could make it the fifteen miles back to school. The sixty miles remaining to Allentown were out of the question. With hearts drooping, we realized that our escape had been thwarted. We could do nothing but turn back.

As we drove in gloomy silence, the curse seemed to lift. The engine perked up, and we began to think that perhaps we could make it to Allentown after all. But no, it was not to be. The sinful thoughts had no sooner entered our minds than there was a snap and the generator light popped on once more, to glare at us with fierce malevolence. For the third time we followed the now familiar procedure of pulling off the road for an investigation. As we pulled to the side, the motor stalled, and we drifted slowly into another gas station. Our fan belt had given up the ghost. We could go no further.

The gas station we were at didn't have the size belt we needed, but they told us that another station up the road might. Kaj and McKelvey set out to check, while Crazy Charlie and I sat dejectedly on the hood of our shattered steed. The minutes passed slowly by, like mourners on their way to a funeral. All at once, shouts of joy broke through the gloom. Our companions came running towards us, with McKelvey brandishing a fan belt above his head, whooping like an Indian with a tomahawk.

We quickly set to work installing our new fan belt. After half an hour of pushing, pulling, and prying around with screwdrivers and fingers, we finally managed to get the belt in place. Kaj tentatively turned the ignition key. The engine hummed into life. Everything was working perfectly again. We rushed to the men's room and made ourselves presentable once more, then jumped back into the car and swung northward again. It was now nearing eight o'clock. We would be late. It was decided that Kaj would stop at the next phone booth, and we would call the girls and tell them we were on our way. At this Charlie's face dropped. He stared at us for a minute, then blurted out that he had left their number back at school. We were in a new fix. I had not bothered to memorize the number, and now we had no way of knowing what it was. Since it was an all-girl dorm, the number was unlisted. We couldn't even look it up in the phone book. The curse hadn't been able to stop us, but it was making things difficult.

Another council was held. It was decided that we would modify our course slightly and stop first at my parent's house, which was only a few minutes' drive from the nurse's dorm. We would try calling from there. We hoped to remember the number by then, or maybe we could ask the hospital switchboard operator to put us through without the number. It was worth a try.

It was well after nine when the Corvair pulled into my parents' driveway. We erupted from our seats and shot into the house. I made hasty introductions between family and friends while Crazy Charlie rushed for the phone and attempted to establish a line of communication. We were stalled. We reached the hospital switchboard with a minimum of trouble. Getting switched to the nurse's dorm was another matter. We explained what we wanted. The operator was leery. We told her who we were. She remained leery. We told her how Cadets are fine, upstanding young men, epitomizing all the virtues of American life. She almost hung up. Finally, she agreed to have the girls paged. Within minutes the reply came: they had all left, thinking we weren't coming.

We had sunk back into our chairs, demoralized, our last hope shattered. The curse had won. Our escape was bitter, a meaningless victory. Our only consolation was that the evening wasn't a total loss. Mothers being what they are, we were kept well supplied with cookies, cake, and other goodies throughout our visit. My parents talked and nibbled at the snacks. The four of us ate the snacks and nibbled at the conversation. Both sides were satisfied.

Midnight was swiftly approaching, and the supply of cookies was severely dented when we finally dragged ourselves to the car and began our trek southward back to the X. Our return journey was uneventful.

It was past two as we parked the car and plodded wearily to our rooms. Crazy Charlie's roommate returned our wearied greetings with equally wearied replies, then brightened up long enough to tell us that a surprise "bed check" had been taken, and that we were now assigned several hours of punishment tours for being AWOL.

Ah yes, the curse had truly won after all. It simply does not pay to tangle with forces beyond mortal strength. We had tried and failed, for the curse was stronger. Beware, beware, for mighty is the Curse of the X.

Dave Neimeyer:
Journal Entries: Saturday May 1, 1971 & Sunday May 2, 1971 — PMC Rangers vs Penn State-Ogontz

I am taking the two days as one since I spent the weekend with the Rangers at Indiantown Gap Military Reservation while going against the Penn State and Delaware County (Delco) "Raiders."

We left "The X" by bus about 9:00 and got to the Gap at about 11:30. Weather was comfortable, but not overly warm. We had 35 people, plus Captain Aron and Sergeant Price. Penn State had 20-25 people plus Captain Powell, their advisor.

We set up a base camp, then Berg and Sisco set up a "canned

ambush" for Penn State. When that was over, Verastro and I took our squads out to trigger our "canned ambush". We hit a couple of snipers, then finally found the ambush. Cranston threw a grenade simulator at Penn's M-60 and cut the face of the gunner. Aron then sent Cranston back to be permanent bus guard.

We went back to the base camp, and at 6:00 we went out on recon and LRRP (long range reconnaissance patrol). Berg was a squad recon (by fire), while I split up my squad into two three-man teams: me, Hylan, and Rendeiro as one; Greenhaugh, King, and Sorchik as the other. Plascow stayed at the base camp.

We moved out and bumped into Berg, then moved into an "off limits" area (private property), where we bumped into Greenhaugh. About ¼ mile from there we heard voices and movement, so I left Rendeiro and Hylan under cover and moved in to get a closer recon. I told them where we were on the map, with orders that if they heard a commotion, signifying my capture, they should go to Russ Howald and tell him.

I moved in as close as I could, circling to the far side of their camp. I got within 20 meters and was sure I was seen when three jokers started moving towards me. They stopped, fiddled with something on the ground (a pack, I think), then one guy stood up and combed his hair. When finished, he put the comb back in the pack and moved away. I went back to Rendeiro and Hylan and we went back and talked to Russ. We got held up on the way when we had to wait for other squads that crossed our path. We were right above our base camp when a figure stepped out in front of us.

"Who are you: PMC or Penn State?" he asked.

"Who wants to know?" I replied.

"You're not in much position to argue," he retorted.

"Well, we've got rifles and you don't, so I'd say it's the other way around," was my answer.

"Well, I'm Captain Aron of PMC" he replied. We then talked for a few minutes, then he went clumping off and we moved into the base camp. We went back to our holes in the perimeter and found that Cranston was back. We waited about an hour, till 10:00, then heard mucho firing and cries of "Ogontz in the Cemetery!" (There was a cemetery about ¼ up a hill from the base camp.) A short time later, Sorchik and Greenhaugh came in. King was separated from them. They barely had time to get to their holes when we heard people moving in. It was almost totally dark, so we waited till they were only about ten feet away, then Howald yelled, "Open up!" We did. Cranston, me, Sorchik, Hylan, Redeiro, and Plascow were all bunched together at the apex of their attack, so we fired like crazy. There was a Raider right in front of us, and rifle flashes were all over from behind him. Then one of them hit the trip wire for some grenade simulators we had rigged to trees. Bla-whoom! Most of the flashes stopped. They just barely started up again when two more charges went off. That broke the attack up (as well as some of the Raiders…one kid was knocked off his feet and suffered a broken nose).

We were told the problem was then terminated till the morning. Penn State moved up to the cemetery and met Berg's squad, which was just moving in. "Don't shoot," said the Raiders, "we've got more men than you do."

"Who cares!" Berg yelled and opened up. The Raiders got out of there.

Back at the base camp we were building fires, and that's when the war stories started. Turns out that Greenhaugh & Co. contacted the Raiders in the cemetery right before the attack.

"Who are you?" asked the Raiders.

"We're the National Guard. Who are you?" replied Sorchik.

"We're Ogontz."

King: "Ogontz? What the hell is an Ogontz?"

Ogontz: "Penn State."

King: "Are you camping out, or what?"

Ogontz: "No, we're aggressing against PMC."

King: "Well, Pull My Cxxk!!"

A few minutes more of buddy-buddy talk, then our people moved out. They went about twenty feet, then turned and opened up and yelled "Ogontz in the cemetery!" then beat it for the base camp. King got separated and came in right after the attack was over.

More bullshitting, then we settled down by the fires and went to sleep...all but Kortlang and one or two freshmen. They sleazed over where Ogontz had their cars parked and took berets, patches, and nine of the fifteen artillery simulators we had given Ogontz at the start of the problem. (We later innocently traded six of those for six smoke grenades when Penn said they had run short of artillery. We're too generous.)

The best beret went to Howald...he deserved it.

There was light rain several times during the night and when we were breaking up camp. We moved to the bus, then went to "riot city"—a simulated town to practice house to house fighting. Half the platoon defended against Penn State, then the other half attacked while Penn defended. Sisco, Cranston, and I fortified the top of a stairwell until they busted up, then took off across the roofs of a set of bins. Sorchik hid right above us and blasted after we left. I was last guy out, and got pushed against the wall by a Raider, who yelled "Get out!" and forced me out after the others. We slowly retreated but held half of one building the entire time. Smoke, artillery, and grenade simulators added to the fun. Then we switched. While Penn was holding, the inactive Rangers raided their cars again for more berets. I came back with one grenade simulator, about ten blank rounds, and fifty expended, which I put into split links.

It started to rain just as we left (9:30) but stopped by 10:00. We got back to The X at 11:05 and went to eat as we were. Such fun.

Charlie and I each shot a roll of film with my camera...hope the shots get. Really a great weekend. I had a royal blast. They had four or five people cut by simulators, while the only real injury we had was King, who had his fingers cut when one exploded too close to him.

Really makes up for Penn State sending us a box of kotex when we had to cancel the last meet, after our bus broke down in route to Indiantown Gap.

Journal Entry: Wednesday May 5, 1971

The Animals hit Greenhaugh's room tonig ht. Nothing of Gleeson's was touched, but I hope Greenhaugh likes shaving cream. They applied it liberally to his shoes, uniforms, bed, desk, and even filled a large chocolate rabbit with it. Such fun.

The advisor for Penn State (Major Gallagher) called up Major Beckett today and demanded that we return the berets we took, or he'll call in the C.I.B. (Army's Criminal Investigation Board). Should be fun, cause we ain't giving them back.

Journal Entry: Thursday May 6, 1971

Greenhaugh was slightly annoyed about his room (to say the least). He thinks Kortlang and I did it. Says he's gonna call the cops in and have them fingerprint the place. What a laugh.

Journal Entry: Friday May 7, 1971

Penn State is giving Beckett a lot of grief, so we decided to give most of the berets back. Charlie is taking a hoard over to capture a Penn State Raider to bring to our party and give to Sgt. Howald as a prisoner.

Journal Entry: Saturday May 8, 1971

Well, it rained again this morning, so the practice parade was cancelled. The White Collar turned out to be "Ma" Behney poking his head in and saying, "Keep the room this neat tomorrow when your parents are down."

We weren't sure if the Ranger Party was going to come off, but it did anyway. It stopped raining for it, even if it was overcast. Charlie and his killer squad had no luck getting a "prisoner." They couldn't even find an Ogontz Raider.

Dave Neimeyer:
Spring Days in the Quadrangle

Spring had come to the campus. The weather was warm and filled with sunshine. A light breeze occasionally stirred a few unraked leaves, survivors of the fall and winter of a few months ago. It was, of course, impossible to study. A few diehard academics made a valiant attempt, then they too joined the growing ranks of idlers.

We had indeed been blessed. The three dorms of our complex formed a "U" shape that enclosed a quadrangle fully half the size of a football field. Although a few walkways invaded our refuge, the majority of the area was now sprouting fresh spring grass. The few saplings were also sprouting, providing a contrast of pink and white buds against the green of the grass and the red bricks of the dorms.

The seasonal change had affected the students, too. From the grey, somber creatures that had sloshed through equally grey snow a month or two earlier, the Cadets now blossomed forth too. Standard uniform became cut-off fatigue trousers and T-shirts. Worn out sneakers or bare feet replaced the highly glossed "spit-shines" of normal daily wear. The entire Cadet Corps was swiftly evolving into two types of people: those who joined the relaxed atmosphere outside in the quadrangle, and those who watched from the second or third story windows. No one was slighted. The participants were carried back to an earlier time when love of nature and worship of the new life of spring was an integral part of mankind. They could unwind in the fresh air and forget about calculus, Shakespeare, and the Punic Wars. Those who chose to merely observe could watch as a tapestry of life unfolded before them. The same quadrangle that had previously only reflected the cold, harsh glare of ice and snow was now alive with people.

Frisbees were dredged out from under piles of ice skates and gloves, and soon several of the brightly colored disks were whizzing between expectant pairs of hands, occasionally being diverted from their normal flight patterns to be bounced harmlessly off the stomach or back of an innocent bystander. The usual reaction was for the bystander to make a few interesting comments on the abilities of the current Frisbee tossers, then to pick up the Frisbee and toss it back; the Frisbee game then gained another pair of expectant hands.

Dotted about the area was an occasional sunbather. Throughout the long months of winter's weak sun, they had watched their tans fade slowly away, leaving each as pale and wan as a leprous ghost. These determined souls now set about the task of becoming well-browned before it was time to hit the beaches and pools of summer. The sunbathers were dedicated. They had to be, for theirs was not an easy lot. The door would open, and out would step a young man dressed only in gym shorts, with a blanket over his shoulder. He would look around, blink several times, then slide behind a pair of sunglasses. It was time to select a spot to settle down in.

No homesteader ever faced such a momentous decision. It must be a spot with plenty of sunshine yet shielded from the still cool breezes. Furthermore, it must be a spot unfrequented by the Frisbee tossers and their kind. Sunbathers were frequent targets for the erratically guided flights of Frisbees. It was better to avoid tempting fate and find a nice quiet spot out of the range of fire.

The areas adjacent to the dorms were favored. The walkways had cut off strips of grass seven or eight feet deep and running nearly the entire length of the dorms. Bushes and other shrubbery broke this division into still smaller segments unsuitable for the other quadrangle games, but perfect for those of the unbronzed skin.

With a spot selected, the sunbathers would worm their way through the clusters of people that gathered on the steps of the dorms for the inevitable bull session, and to watch the antics of the others. Sighing happily, the sunbathers then unfolded their blankets and settled down to "soak up some rays." A pastoral Nirvana.

It was about this time that observing became a participant sport. Heads disappeared from third floor windows to return a few minutes later, grinning in expectation. Hands came forth supporting colorful balloons bulging and wobbling from the pressure of the water that filled them. Careful aim was taken, and the hydrous bombs were sent earthward to crash wetly on their human targets below. Soggy sunbathers charged up the stairs, but the culprits usually escaped. Even when the bombers held their positions, more often than not, the doused sunbathers could soon be seen helping direct the fire on his remaining comrades below.

Stickball was another great favorite of the quadrangle games. Thin strips of wood, about three feet long, were brought forth. Someone produced an old tennis ball. The players noisily selected teams, then set to the task of marking off bases. The batter took his position. The pitcher aligned himself several yards away. The outfielders found suitable places and fastened their gaze on the pitcher-batter duel about to take place. The batter's teammates and interested spectators made themselves comfortable along the sidelines, then also settled their gaze on the battle before them.

The pitcher assured himself that the outfielders were in position. The batter tightened his grip on the stick and waited confidently for the first pitch. Both could feel the attention upon them.

The first pitch...a swing...a miss. The catcher throws the ball back to the pitcher. Another pitch...a swing...another miss, but closer. The spectators are forgotten. There is only the ball. The pitcher draws his arm back. He throws. The ball whizzes in. A crack, and it is whizzing back out, to lose momentum rapidly and drop safely several yards from the windows of the opposing dorm. Several outfielders ran towards it. The batter is now the runner. He slaps the light pole that is first base, turns smoothly and glides to the jacket that is second. He starts to run further, then sees that the outfielders have recovered the ball, so he stops and stands firmly on the jacket base. The second batter steps up and the game continues.

Above, the sky is losing its bluish tinge and is streaked with red and gold. Soon twilight begins. Shadows begin to deepen. In the dorms, lights snap on, first one or two, then a few more, then nearly all are lit as the spectators return to their papers and books. Below, the stickball players and Frisbee tossers are decreasing in number. In the deepening twilight the ball is lost several times, then the remaining stickball enthusiasts also surrender to the night and walk away. The sunbathers left long ago and taken with them the groups of bombers who had preyed so unmercifully on them.

The quadrangle lights come on, and in their glow a pair of Frisbee tossers continue their game. Ten minutes pass, then ten more, and the tossers fade into the dorms.

In the lower corner of the quadrangle three people sit on the steps, the remnants of a once mighty bull session. Their conversation becomes slower and more random, eventually dying out altogether as the young men sit and stare thoughtfully into the distance, lost in the deep meditation of the young. In the dorms, the lights are starting to go out once more. The three young men stand and stretch, then go quietly into the dorms.

Another young man, in uniform and carrying a bugle, comes out of a different dorm. He walks to the front center of the quadrangle, then turns to face the silent trees and buildings. He brings the bugle to his lips and wets the mouthpiece, then slowly plays "Taps". As the last mournful notes die off in the darkness, he walks back into his dorm. The remaining lights go off. Night has claimed the quadrangle.

Dave Neimeyer:
The Beauty Contest

Sometime during my Junior year, a local beauty contest asked for Cadet volunteers to serve as escorts for the participants. Visions of gorgeous girls in bikinis oozed through our imaginations, and the contest organizers quickly had enough Cadets to meet their needs. On the night of the competition, about a dozen of us were bussed to the contest venue and paired up with the contestants. Sadly, there was no swimsuit competition.

Of the dozen contestants, one was truly gorgeous, two were above par, and the rest were of average good looks. Our job as escorts was simple. We simply walked with our contestants and escorted them on and off the stage. When the various competitions were done, the young women were arrayed in a wide arc across the stage with their Cadet escorts standing behind them. The host announced the second runner-up. Number 4! I leaned forward and whispered to my contestant (who I mentally had named "the midget gypsy," due to her small stature and swarthy looks). "The second runner up will be number 8," I whispered, indicating the remaining "above par" contestant.

"How do you know?" she whispered back.

"I'm psychic," I replied.

"Who's going to win?" she queried.

"Number 6," I replied, indicating the truly gorgeous contestant.

Sure enough, number 8 was the runner up, and number 6 took the crown. When Number 6 was announced as the winner, the contestant I was escorting turned and gave me a wide-eyed look, somewhere between awe and fear. I remained dead-panned. My psychic skills may have been non-existent, but my ability to recognize good looking young women was top notch.

Dave Neimeyer:
Stage Struck

Also, during my Junior year, a civilian organization used the campus stage to put on a play set in Italy in the 1800s. They requested Cadets to participate as a firing squad for a military execution that was part of the play. When the Cadet firing squad was chosen, I was selected as the leader. We drew M-1 rifles and blank ammunition from the armory and headed over to Alumni Auditorium.

At the appointed time, my four-man firing squad and I marched onto the stage and took our position. I did not know any Italian, and had not been told what to say, so I improvised my commands from the name of one of the upperclassmen: Vito Greco.

"VITO," I commanded. The squad came to attention.

"GRECO." The squad raised their rifles and took aim.

"FUEGO!!" The squad fired. The actor being executed stood shocked for a second or two. I suspect he didn't know that the sound of firing the blanks would be so loud. It reverberated nicely in the closed auditorium. After a short hesitation, he dutifully clutched his chest and dropped behind the parapet wall in front of which he had been standing. (Good way to remove a body from the small stage.) I dutifully marched my firing squad off stage and back to the armory to turn in our weapons. Our brief moment of glory was over.

Dave Neimeyer:
Men of Ice

It was February of my Junior year and things were going badly. For one thing, I had just been "Dear-Johned" by my girlfriend of the moment and I was in a foul mood. The rest of the Corps joined me in my fit of depression when word came that Bob Aldrich, a 1969 PMC graduate, had been killed in a chopper crash in 'Nam. Another 1969 PMC grad, Bob Chinquina, had been killed there a few months earlier, and the effect on the present Cadets was quite sobering. It was decided that the Cadets would hold a special memorial service for Lt. Aldrich. It was to take place on Saturday morning in Alumni Auditorium.

Since Saturday was also the day of the annual Military Ball, this meant that the Cadets would have a hectic time of it. They would attend the service in the morning, then would have to rush like crazy to get ready and pick up their dates for the formal a few hours later. Saturday morning came with three or four inches of snow on the ground and more coming down. At the appointed time, scores of Cadets thrust themselves from their dorms and made their way to Alumni Auditorium. Bundled against the wind, snow, and cold in overcoats, scarves, and other paraphernalia, we must have looked like grey balls of wool against the sugar whiteness of the still falling snow.

By the time the memorial service was over, it was obvious that the Military Ball would have to be cancelled. Long lines formed by all the telephones as the Cadets called to inform their dates of the postponement. We were now faced with the prospect of having to sit in our rooms and stare bleakly out our windows at the unceasing blizzard that enveloped us. Truly a dreary day.

I was perhaps more glum than most. I spent the afternoon working on a reply to the "Dear John" letter. After wasting a considerable amount of paper, I finally decided that she just was not worth the effort. The possibility of resigning from life and becoming a hermit was becoming better looking all the time, when suddenly a snowball smacked into my window. Followed closely by a second, then a third.

I looked out and saw several Cadets standing below me, gesturing for me to come out. I opened the window to talk to them. Wrong move. They greeted my action with movements of their own, and a split second later a hail of snowballs was hurtling towards my window. Some missed. Most did not, including several that shot past me to crash wetly on my bed and the opposite wall.

I bravely stuck my head out the window. "Hey, truce!" I yelled. "Cease fire!"

"Come on out!" one of my attackers yelled back. I needed no second call. I threw on boots and a bulky fatigue jacket, grabbed my hat and gloves, and was halfway down the stairs before the door had finished closing behind me.

I bounded from the dorm and into a scene of icy whiteness. Snow covered everything. I squinted against the glare, then ducked just in time to avoid another snowball. I needn't have bothered. My attackers were on me in seconds, hitting me with several more snowballs, then throwing me down in the snow for good measure. I was hopelessly outnumbered, unable to fight back. Then, as suddenly as they had begun, they stopped their attack to laugh at me as I sprawled helplessly in the snow.

My roommate for the year, Howie Rubinow, stepped forward and stretched out his arm. "Get up, Hobbit. You've just been initiated into our ranks. Welcome to the club."

"Thanks, Howie." I replied, while removing most of the snow from the back of my neck. "Let's find another victim!" cried Bowser Hullitt. "Hoo-ahh, let's go!" someone else agreed, and we were off on our search.

"There's Hasbrouk's window…we'll get him," said Howie, and so Hasbrouk received the same treatment as I had. We repeated the procedure over and over again, and soon a full thirty Cadets were involved in our fun and games.

By this time, the window raids had lost their novelty, so we devised a new pastime: namely, a snowball battle. The war raged furiously. One side would attack, forcing their victims back against the walls to be pelted mercilessly, then the underdogs would rally, and the oppressors would, in turn, be driven back. It was "Cry Havoc!" all the way…no quarter given; no prisoners taken. Total warfare on a blanket of white.

Our spirits rose as the sun sank, yet when its pale face finally faded and gave way to a winter evening, much of our enthusiasm also faded. More and more of our icy horde disappeared into the dorms in search of warmth and dry clothes. Finally, we had dwindled to a mere half dozen or so, and the snowball fight ended for lack of targets.

We stood outside the main doors of Howell Hall and debated our next move. As we mulled over the possibilities, I absent-mindedly began packing snow against the windowpanes on the door. Before long the others joined me, and within minutes we were rolling huge balls of snow to lodge against the doors. We threw ourselves into the new task, and the mound of snow rose, blocking the doors completely.

As we continued to pile snow haphazardly against the door, Skip Chiaventone came from another dorm to watch us. He observed quietly for a moment, then commented. "You're going about it all wrong. Let's give this thing some class."

We stood back and let Skip go to work on the mound of snow. Under his hands, the shapeless heap began to take on a human form. More snow was added here and there, taken off at other places. The minutes ticked by. Finally, Skip stood back to reveal his masterpiece. "There. How's That!" he said proudly. We stared in wonder at his creation. "Holy Cow!" said Howie. "It looks like Colonel Frey."

"Yeah!" agreed Bowser. "Our Commandant in snow. A Snow-Frey!"

"Hey, that's really great, Skip!" I chimed in. "Look at that detail! You've even got buttons on the uniform...and the nametag!"

Skip smiled under the barrage of our compliments. His snow sculpture was an instant success. We continued to admire the figure for several minutes, then I involuntarily shivered. It was well into evening now and the night was cold. I looked over at Howie and saw him drawing his coat tighter.

"I'm cold!" I declared. "Let's go back inside and change into some dry clothes."

"Ok," he replied, and we headed for the dorm. "Feel like going down to the Frat House later on?"

"Sounds good to me," I replied, walking on through the door and into the warmth of the building. "Ya know, Howie," I continued, "for a day that started out so rotten, today didn't turn out half bad after all."

Dave Neimeyer:
Against Whatever Gods May Be...

The door flew open and crashed noisily against the doorstop. My roommate Howie charged into the room, excitedly yelling "Frey's on a rampage again! He's over in Cann Hall now, tearing up the senior's rooms."

I jumped up and flew past Howie into the hall. "Frey's coming!" I shouted down the corridor. Doors flew open everywhere. Various voices called back.

"Frey? Now? Where is he?"

"He's hitting the seniors now!" I cried and dived back into my room. Howie was doing a rush job of making the bed. I grabbed a pile of books and began to shove them back onto their shelves. The smell of pledge and shoe polish began to waft in from the corridor. At the end of the hallway, Joe Spangler was tapping his ring against the fire alarm bell, making a distinctive metallic noise, interspersed with Joe's voice calling "Green alert! Green alert!" through it all, the flurry of activity continued as Cadets furiously attempted to get their rooms into some semblance of order.

"He's coming out of Cann Hall!" yelled Chuck Hasbrouck, whose room faced that dorm. "Oh, Christ, he's coming this way! He's coming in!" Some people took a second look at their rooms, panicked, and fled. Maybe they'd be lucky. Maybe Frey wouldn't have the pass keys with him today. Others realized that the time for flight was past.

Despite a feeling of impending doom, I sat down at my now spotless desk and attempted to look studious.

I heard the door to the stairwell open. Then I heard his heavy tread, and I knew that "The Man" was on our floor. A jingling of keys. He does have the pass keys with him today. Damn! I heard him open the door to the first room. Fred "Pony Soldier" Gerber and Gino lived there.

"Good morning, Sir." Gino's voice. Pony Soldier must have gotten out in time.

"Mr. Ginoski, your hair is totally unacceptable. Get a haircut immediately. Report to my office this afternoon for an inspection."

"Yes, Sir."

The door closed. The next door opened. "Digger" Dell and Shuman the Human. "Mr. Shuman! What are you doing in your rack at this time of day!" He must have caught Norm sleeping. How the heck could Shuman miss our warnings! "My God! Look at this room! Dust! This is a pig sty, Mr. Shuman, a pig sty! Hang your uniform up when you take it off. Don't just throw it over a chair. And those windows!"

The tirade continued. Frey worked Norm Shuman over for a good five minutes, then proceeded checking rooms all the way down the hall. Then our room was next.

The door opened. Frey's massive bulk filled the doorway as I snapped to attention. Behind him I could see Bob Sabochik, the Cadet Adjutant. Bob was carrying a pad of yellow legal paper, and I could see that several pages had already been filled with room discrepancies. Bob was frantically scribbling, trying to keep up with Colonel Frey.

"Well, Mr. Neimeyer, studying I see."

"Yes, Sir."

"How are your grades coming? Having any trouble?"

"No, Sir."

"Good. Don't forget, grades are important. You need them before you can get anything else here."

"Yes, Sir."

The Corps Commandant glanced around the room, then turned back to me. "How long have you worn that shirt?"

"I put it on yesterday morning, Sir." I replied, sweating.

"It looks like you slept in it. Have it ironed. When did you polish those shoes last? And those boots! They've a disgrace, Mr. Neimeyer. Clean them up immediately."

"Yes, Sir."

"You'll be needing a haircut soon, Mr. Neimeyer. I don't want my Cadets looking like a bunch of hippie freaks."

"Yes, Sir," I replied. Should I have said 'No, Sir' I wondered.

"Your room isn't too bad, but those beds could be made better." Frey shifted his weight to his good leg and looked the room over once more, then walked back into the hallway. Sabochik closed my door, still furiously copying down discrepancies. As I heard Frey going into Skip Chiaventone and Bruce Boehm's room next to mine, my thoughts turned to the man who had just left.

Lieutenant Colonel Gerald T. Frey had come to the Corps of Cadets as Assistant Commandant my freshman year. The following year Commandant Ford Fuller left, and Colonel Frey was given the post. Frey was a strict disciplinarian who had lost a leg in Vietnam, and who had long held a complete distaste for hippies, long hairs, and anything that was even faintly unpatriotic. He ruled the Corps with an iron fist, yet under his short command, Cadets had come to be given a greater role in the running of the Corps.

It was at a Corps training session in Alumni Auditorium that Frey best explained his method of handling the Corps. He told us that we would be given the responsibility for planning our own training and maintaining discipline, but that "I will be like Zeus on Mount Olympus, hurling thunderbolts on the scofflaws below."

We promptly dubbed him "Zeus" then went about the job of dodging thunderbolts. We usually didn't succeed. Even if we managed to escape his frequent, unannounced room inspections, there was always the chance he'd be at Mess I or Mess III formation and tear through our ranks there.

The Cadets were unable to fight back. He was too powerful. We chose instead the path of least resistance: we avoided him. We stayed away from his favorite haunts. We learned that the library was a good place to hide during room inspections. We discovered that the upstairs reading lounge of MacMorland Center was great for catching some extra shut-eye during those hours when we were not allowed to be in the rack. By joining extra-curricular activities, it was possible to get out of formations and evade possible confrontations there. We learned a million other tricks, and he'd still find us. Just when we thought we'd escaped him again, Frey would catch up to us somehow. It was utterly impossible to escape the will of Zeus.

Even the elements themselves bent to his will. No one had forgotten our Veteran's Day parade in Media, PA, shortly after Frey's thunderbolt speech. It was a beautiful, sunny day, but just as the Cadets reached the reviewing stand and Colonel Frey, the skies clouded over, and a torrential downpour commenced. In minutes we were soaked completely. With so many wet wool uniforms, we smelled and looked like a troop of drowned sheep. The rain continued until the last elements of the Corps had paraded past the stand, and then gradually tapered off. Five minutes later, the skies were just as sunny as they had been before. Many of the Cadets now spoke in awed whispers. "Frey did it. He really is Zeus."

Frey's rampage of iron rule continued. A few Cadets even took down their dartboards of President Moll and put-up pictures of Frey instead. Crazy Charlie Kortlang made a stencil of a lightning bolt, grabbed a can of silver spray paint, and "redecorated" first floor Cann Hall. No matter what we did, or what happened, Frey reigned supreme, handling all contingencies with ease.

Cadet opinions of Frey varied. All feared him. Many respected him. Others said he was sick and should be put away. "He'll kill the Corps! He's driving people away!" some cried. Others retorted, "He's our only hope. We need someone strong to stand up to the administration!" "He's a fanatic." "He'll save the Corps." "He's crazy." The arguments ran back and forth endlessly. I mulled them over in my head but was unable to decide which was right. Would we ever know the true Frey?

I was drawn from my reverie by the sound of Bruce trying to convince the Colonel that the hamsters he had in his room weren't pets but were part of a biology project. Maybe Bruce would have succeeded if Skip hadn't used some fancy artwork to make their box look like a miniature Nazi SS camp. As it was, Frey wasn't buying the story.

I stood up and stretched. "Oh, what the heck," I thought. "I guess I might as well go get a haircut."

*Artwork by David Neimeyer & the Brigadier Staff

SENIOR (FIRST CLASS) YEAR

Rick Moller:
Halloween 1964

It was Halloween evening of 1964. After Mess 3, the PMC Corps of Cadets commenced its celebration wearing the Uniform of the Day (now evening) of "Dress Whatever." All Line Companies queued up for our traditional out-of-step Halloween Parade on East 14th Street in front of Old Main, to be led by our National Championship Marching Band. This time, however, the Band had one additional marching member. My First-Class Roommate, Harry Carlip (RIP), enlisted his girlfriend to join us in this parade. She was already wearing slacks and Harry and I outfitted her in a Dress Alfa Multi-buttoned Coatee. We had her put her hair up and stuff it inside Harry's PMC Shako.

We got through the parade unscathed and undetected (of course our fellow Bandsmen were abundantly aware of this welcome intruder). However, post-parade we got busted as the three of us literally bumped into The Commandant of Cadets, Major General Biddle. For an older gentleman, his vision was still acute, and he realized one of us was not an ordinary Male Cadet. His mouth was agape with incredulity. We rendered a hand salute and beat a hasty retreat, leaving the General standing there in astonishment. To the best of my knowledge and belief, I believe this was the first time we had a female in our PMC Cadet ranks.

Rick Moller:
Army Logic — The Right Way, The Wrong Way, The Army Way!

Although I was certainly not a scholar (I graduated with a 1.99-out-of-4.00 Cumulative Four-Year Average), I did well in Military Science. In my First-Class year, I was designated a Distinguished Military Student (DMS) and was, hopefully, on my way to becoming a Distinguished Military Graduate (DMG). Following ROTC Summer Camp at Indian Town Gap Military Reservation in Annville, PA, after completion of my Second-Class Year, I received my pre-commissioning physical examination. The eye examination revealed that my vision was 20/500 in each eye.

The ROTC staff then informed me that, while I could be commissioned, I was not physically qualified to serve in a Combat Arms Branch (Infantry, Armor, or Artillery) and must then serve in a Combat Support Branch. I then selected Military Intelligence (MI) Branch as my Army Branch choice. I was disappointed as I had wished to be commissioned as an Infantry Officer. A month or two passed within the academic year and the ROTC Staff called me into their office. They then said I would become a DMG. Great—I would serve as a Regular Army (RA) Officer! Then they said that, because I would be a DMG and then graduate as an RA Officer (not Army Reserve), while on Active Duty, I must first serve a two year Combat Arms Tour before reverting to my MI Primary Branch. So, go figure Army Logic. I picked Infantry (for which the Army said I was not physically qualified) as my two year Combat Arms Branch. I then went to the Infantry Center at Fort Benning for Infantry Officer Basic Training, Airborne School, Ranger School and served my Infantry Tour in the Republic of Korea with the 7th Infantry Division.

David Fiedler:
A Cadet Veteran

In 1964-1965 there was in the Corps of Cadets a senior private who had already served a hitch in the Regular Army. He was a fully qualified paratrooper and had been in the 82nd Airborne Division and in the Strategic Army Corps (STRAC). On his PMC uniform, he always wore his jump wings which impressed the hell out of me. How he ended up at PMC as a cadet I never knew, but always wondered. He had lots of stories about the army and how he and the 82nd Division was prepared to jump into Cuba on very short notice during and after the Cuban missile crisis. This guy knew everything about weapons and tactics you could ever want to know.

The cadet veteran was not shy about telling us what to expect when we went on active duty in the Army and also about how any similarity between PMC and the army was purely coincidental. He continually critiqued both the ROTC and particularly the Commandant's Office. He was particularly averse to two captains in the Commandant's Office who were both PMC graduates. One of those officers had a habit of carrying a "swagger stick" that he found particularly offensive. After weekend training, he didn't hang around with us much because he had a very cute girlfriend and a 1957 Chevrolet convertible. I really envied that. She kept him very busy.

Just before graduation, word got passed around among "the boys" to watch what this guy was going to do at graduation. When the day came it was like all other graduations when I was there. It was held in Memorial Stadium. A platform with a ramp was assembled on the 50-yard line in front of the stadium seating. The graduates were seated in front of the platform between the stadium seats and the platform. When called, the graduates walked up the ramp, their name was announced, and they were handed their diploma by Dr. Moll and the faculty. They were then supposed to march down the ramp and retake their seats in preparation for the tossing of the hats into the air as was the custom!

Our cadet got his diploma and marched down the ramp. As he did, he removed the parchment from its holding tube, unrolled it and just as he came even with me in the audience was heard to say, "Got the damn thing." (or words to that effect). He then continued to march down the aisle past the seats and through the stadium sally port. We were told later by some classmates that were serving as ushers in the stadium that the girlfriend was waiting in the parking lot in the '57 Chevrolet with the engine running and the top down. He got in, she did a wheelie across the parking lot, then did another one under the iron bridge between Old Main and the Chemistry Building. Both were never seen or heard from again.

More than a few eyebrows were raised because of this little show, all the cadets were aware of what had happened, and back in the barracks we had a great laugh. What a guy!!!

Rick Moller:
PMC in Korea

My one and only Infantry Tour (prior to Military Intelligence) was to the Republic of South Korea (ROK) for 14 months spanning 1966 and 1967. I was assigned to the 1st Battalion, 31st Infantry Regiment, 3rd Brigade, 7th Infantry Division (7ID) headquartered at Camp Casey, a US Army Post in Dongducheon, 40 miles north of Seoul, South Korea. At the time, 7ID was designated the Reserve Infantry Division while the 2nd Infantry Division was on-line on the Demilitarized Zone (DMZ).

In 1966, with respect to US Army company grade officers in ROK, most all Infantry captains were either diverted or reassigned to duty stations in the Republic of Vietnam (RVN). When I arrived at the 1st of the 31st, there were three vacant (see prior explanation) rifle company commanding officer billets--Alfa Company, Bravo Company, and Charlie company. Three Butter Bar Military College 2nd Lieutenants (of which I was one) were assigned as Infantry rifle company commanders. I was CO (PMC '65), of Alfa Company, Dick Endicott (RIP—KIA 1968 friendly fire RVN) CO (USMA '65) of Bravo Company, and Chuck Krajniak, CO (The Citadel '65) of Charlie Company.

My first duty as CO was to personally sign for thousands of dollars of equipment—weapons, vehicles, radios, etc. This responsibility was never mentioned in PMC Military Science classes. I asked about responsibility for lost equipment and was told by the 3rd Brigade S-4 that they would garnish my pay until I had worked off the expense. I never forgot that. Fast forward two months when my PMC 2nd Class roommate Max Gayer (RIP) was assigned (similar to my assignment) as an Infantry rifle company CO in the 32nd Infantry Regiment, 7ID at nearby Camp Hovey, ROK. Well, I hooked up with Max shortly after his arrival and we shared some beers and war stories (some of which were true).

Later in the year, the Annual General Inspection (AGI) was about to commence. The AGI was a Bean Counter Drill, and we were expected to have all equipment to be properly accounted for (or paid for by salary garnishment). My First Sergeant and I inventoried all our equipment and we found that I was short a number of bayonets but, as luck would have it, I had a surplus of gas masks. I contacted Max and he was short gas masks but had a surplus of bayonets. We drove our two jeeps for a rendezvous on a back road between Camps Casey and Hovey and made our exchanges. Max and I both passed the AGI with flying colors, and no one was the wiser! Colonel Hyatt would have been proud of us!

David Fiedler:
The Great White Hunter

Upon returning to campus in 1967, I was greeted by two of my classmates that said, "Are you hungry? My mother just gave me a bunch of food that the two of us could never finish, including that Jewish deli stuff that you like. Come on down to our room and help yourself before the rest of the mob gets back and it's gone." When I get to their room, they held open the door and I walked in. I then heard the door slam behind me. As I looked around, I saw that they had covered the desk lamps (that were on) with green cellophane so that the room had a dark greenish glow about it. As my eyes adjusted, all of a sudden I saw two live alligators on the floor of the room. One was over six feet long and the other was more than four feet long. When the six-footer hissed at me and showed me his teeth, I shot up to the top bunk in the room and let out a long stream of choice cadet curses until they opened the door to let me out.

After they had a good laugh and let me out, they explained. One of them had been to Florida where he grew up. In high school he had worked on a gator farm, so he knew how to handle them. As he was driving back he passed a gator farm that had a sign that said, "Going out of business, stock for sale". He stopped and bought the two gators, threw them in the trunk of his car and got them to PMC. After pulling the same stunt they pulled on me a few dozen more times, the question then became, what do we do with them now?

The answer was to hide them in the company rifle rack and keep them as pets, which they did. Unfortunately, gators, even small ones, need water. The answer to that was every night they would stuff up the "gang" shower drain, and fill it to the lip of the shower, thus creating a six-inch-deep pond for the gators to swim in. All cadets were warned not to enter while the gators were in the shower. As the days went on, rumors flew about what was happening (days in various rifle racks, nights in various showers). In order to do this, more and more cadets were dragged into the conspiracy.

There were several gator sightings over a three-week period. The prank was starting to get old, and security was not that good. Those involved, and even the cadet chain of command, pretty well kept mum. Eventually the rumors reached the commandant's staff and LTC Wilson, the Deputy Commandant (who lasted less than a semester but that is another story), was on the hunt for the gators. Several times the gators were moved just ahead of the hunting party's arrival. What brought the whole caper down was one day the boys were a little slow in getting them out of the shower. The shower cleaning crew were of course women from Chester. When one entered the shower to clean it and saw the gators, she freaked and ran from the building.

Outside the building was a construction crew working on something, they armed themselves, and went to look. By that time the gators were gone, and they thought that she was either crazy or drunk. But Colonel Wilson connected all the dots and deduced what was going on. I think it was pretty easy since the shower was full of gator shit. Apparently, the gators liked the Slater food more than the cadets did.

Anyway, one morning Wilson and his henchmen hit all the showers in the "new dorm" complex at around the same time and found the gators. When they did, there wasn't a cadet to be seen in the whole area!! Then animal control came, and the gators were gone.

I well remember that night's mess—III. LTC Wilson got up on the podium and in his deep southern drawl stated, "Well, we finally found the two alligators that 900 cadets didn't know anything about."

The whole thing lasted about three weeks, no cadet ever admitted being part of it, no cadet was ever punished. Wilson was nicknamed the "Great White Hunter" (among other things) and the whole thing blew over. I can name the two cadets that owned the gators if you would like.

A note from another cadet, Richard Borton: "While I would defer on some of the details such as size (four foot and three foot) and their origin, the basics of the story is verifiable. The two cadets lived in what was Spang Hall in the last room streetside and I was through the arch in the first room. Early on in this adventure they kept their mascots in their room. As an add-on to the story, one night Nick Kuzo, who lived in the left on ND5, decided to take a shower in the ND5 (don't know why) in the right-hand shower room. Well, apparently Nick may have had a nip or two earlier that evening and didn't get the message as to the evening quarters of Frick and Frack. They were enjoying the ND5 "swimming pool". Nick got in the shower, not knowing who his swimming buddies were. When he saw them in the shower with him, he let out a howl, ran out of the shower sans uniform or towel, and ran through the reception area of the dorm where a couple of Cadets were entertaining their dates. And such was Cadet life.

David Fiedler:
75mm gun and PMC

In the Fall of 1967, LTC Wilson, the Deputy Commandant, decided that I needed a position of responsibility since I was going to be commissioned in less than a year. I was then appointed, to my amazement, to command the gun crew and what was left of Battery Robinette. Great assignment for a future Signal Officer. Membership had been voluntary, but I was being assigned.

We mostly fired the famous "French 75mm gun" every day at retreat and for football games and parades. Initially we made our own ammunition by taking an old shell casing that had been drilled out to fit a 12-gauge shotgun shell (with the pellets removed) and a small charge of black powder encased in aluminum foil. It made noise but nowhere near what a real 75mm salute round did.

A member of the battery came to me one day and said, "My father works at the Frankfort Armory, and I am sure he can get us real salute rounds if ROTC sends in a requisition." I went to the ROTC supply sergeant, and he gave me the forms. I put my name and phone number down as the POC.

In a few days I got a call from the Frankfort Ordinance office and the guy said he can't fill the order until they inspect the gun. I

Stories and Vignettes from PMC

arranged for him to come over and he showed up with a fluoroscope and a set of gauges and worked on the gun for an hour. He said, "Sound as the day they made it in 1917, how many rounds do you want?" I said 500 and he said okay.

A few days went by and a cargo truck from Frankfort showed up at ROTC supply with crates of ammo. I was there to get it, the supply sergeant was trying to figure out where to put it, and Colonel Fuller the PMS came out to see what was going on. When I told him, he said, "Each of those rounds has three pounds of black powder in it. You cannot store 1500 pounds of that right next to my office! You can have 20 rounds and when you run out, we will reorder." So that was what we did. Colonel Fuller was an artillery officer, and he knew about this stuff. Whenever we reordered, we got it.

The next day was Friday, the beginning of the weekend. We were all excited because now we could make some proper noise. Also, at this time ROTC had just been assigned a new Warrant Officer (WO) that was a helicopter pilot just returned from Vietnam. We didn't know it, but the guy was really shook up and very gun shy. He got the PMC assignment because he was an outpatient from the hospital, I think in Valley Forge. Guess who was assigned as the MOIC the evening of our first big shot.

At mess—III the staff, the drums, and the MOIC took their usual position opposite the Senior Steps. At the proper time, we fired the gun with the three-pound charge. Luckily, prior to firing, I checked the gun for foreign objects which some jokers put in the barrel. It was clear, but I still swiveled the gun a bit toward Old Main because I was afraid of "back blast." Good thing, because when we fired, the plate glass window over the front of MacMorland Center moved but didn't break. After that we swung the gun completely around to get rid of that problem. The power of the blast did wake up a bunch of people.

Meanwhile, over by the staff, the new Warrant Officer leaped into the air at the sound of the shot, then fell on the ground as the staff watched his cap roll into the street. Some thought this was pretty funny and were laughing. The drums then played, and the Corps marched into dinner. One of the staff recovered the WO's cap.

When I got into the mess hall, I got many cheers from those who were impressed by the new sound of the gun. Then the PA system announced, "Cadet Fiedler report to the adjutant." As I walked down the aisle to the front of the mess where the staff was, I got many cheers/comments about how much trouble I was in.

Alfred J. Peck:
What Can Happen on Leave

Call me Ishmael. I sought to open a story with Melville's opening for years. But my remembrance of Pennsylvania Military College (PMC) does not surround whales, or the sea. It surrounds a ubiquitous NCO that was regularly present in the life of cadets at PMC. Like Ishmael, he appeared early in our experience and stood tall at the end.

At PMC you became confronted with a myriad of rules and regulations. No such thing as vacation existed. You traveled on authorized leave. Christmas of my senior year, 1967, I had the opportunity to visit relatives in Ireland. Christmas "leave" from PMC amounted to thirteen days. Back in the day, the airlines suggested a multitude of discount flights. The cheapest flight I could manage required staying at your destination for fifteen days. Do the math, I needed two days added to my leave. What to do?

PMC had the rules of the Regular Army and add to that our cadet rules. I had to request special orders to extend my leave. I filled out the standard forms and submitted them to Master Sergeant Eugene Cloud. I first saw Sgt. Cloud standing off to the side of the auditorium in Old Main during first-year student orientation. He popped in and out of my life for my entire four years. By my senior year, making requests through Sgt. Cloud became common place. The Sgt assured me that the two extra days would not be a problem, so I bought my ticket.

Well, the day approached for my departure, and I had heard nothing about my extension orders. I produced myself at M/Sgt. Cloud's office the day before I planned to depart and inquired what might be happening with my request. He grumbled that the orders had not arrived back yet. On the morning I planned to leave for the airport, the permission had not arrived. I walked to Sgt. Cloud's office and found no one in. Flight paid for, people waiting for me at Shannon Airport. Something had to be done. I designed arrangements with my platoon leader to be put on a special assignment. This allowed my missing roll call, or so I thought. I left for the airport.

As luck would have it, Sgt. Cloud went to Headquarters and pushed the paperwork through. He secured the paperwork and came looking for me that afternoon to give me the good news. Of course, I was no place to be found, including on my special assignment. Cloud was furious. He put me on the report as AWOL. Regulations dictate "Absent Without Leave" starts when you are found missing for twenty-four hours. AWOL does not stop until you set foot back on campus. Regardless of the fact I had thirteen days I could be on leave; it was all AWOL. While all this commotion took place, I am blissfully on my Air Lingus flight to Shannon to meet my relatives.

The time came to leave Ireland. With many goodbyes and an Irish Cable-Knit Sweater snuggly wrapped around me, I left for Shannon Airport. When I arrived at Shannon, I exchanged my Irish pounds for dollars. While in Ireland, the English pound sharply devalued. The Irish pound was based on the English pound. By some quirk of the international currency market, I left Ireland with close to as much money as I arrived. Adding to my airgead (money) were some winnings I had at the poker table in my cousin's kitchen.

As the plane departed Emerald Isle, the captain announced a brewing snowstorm in New York. The captain cautioned we might not land at Kennedy Airport. The possibility gave me pause to worry. Fortunately, we managed to become the last plane to land at Kennedy in the howling snowstorm. My parents picked me up, and we became one of the few cars on the Long Island Expressway during this blizzard. The next day being snowed in, I now had a sixteen-day vacation leave. If you recall, Sgt. Cloud had reported me on AWOL status, to which I remained oblivious. My hope was the snowstorm could be applied as an excuse for the extra day.

The next day I left for school, judging I was in the clear with my extra days. You can imagine my shock when I arrived on campus and promptly ushered into Sgt. Cloud's office. The jig being up, nothing I said impressed the Sgt. For my punishment, he busted me down to senior private and handed me an hour of "tours" every day except Sunday for the rest of the academic year. For the first week of tours, I memorized every crack in the tarmac, marching up and down in front of Old Main for an hour in full dress uniform with my rifle. Tours, according to our manual, helped us remember our transgressions so you would not do it anew. Sgt. Cloud was supremely content with the sanction, but I was not.

One of my classmates, Kenny Wolford's father, was a General in the Air Force and stationed in the Pentagon. Kenny persuaded his father to come to PMC in his uniform for a visit and let the Commandant know he was going to be on campus. By tradition, a visiting General could forgive all non-judicial punishment to the Corps. "Tours" fell into that category. After a week, I was free. The Corps grapevine burned up with Kenny's tactical move. A few days later, after my freedom, walking across campus, I met Sgt. Cloud. I expected a dressing down, but to the contrary, he congratulated Kenny and me for our ingenuity. He said it pays to know a general. But that did not stop him from recommending my MOS be INFANTRY.

Our commissioning ceremony became the next and last time I laid eyes on the good Master Sergeant. He stood at the end of the ramp from the commissioning stage in his green uniform, spit-shined shoes, waiting. As I came to the end of the ramp as a newly minted Second Lieutenant, he gave me a smart salute and put out his left hand. I returned the salute and placed a dollar in the outstretched hand. Another tradition, you pay the NCO that gives you your first salute fulfilled. The Sergeant collected a tidy sum that day.

David Fiedler:
Contraband

Background: In the Fall of 1967, "D" Company had more rooms than cadets to fill them. Because I was a 1st classman, I was asked if I would like to have a private room. I said sure and joked that I was made that offer because none of my classmates wanted to live with me!! Of course, then my room became the gathering place for a group known as "the boys" (sometimes "the lads") who were a collection of malcontents, hound dogs, and general pains in the commandant's rear end. It was great for me because I made up the top bunk perfectly for inspection and slept on the bottom one, so I never had to make my bed. Inspections for senior privates like me consisted of a cadet officer/classmate sticking his head through the door, taking a glance (for formalities sake), and asking "what up all okay with you brother Fiedler."

Background: If you recall, cadet rooms in the new barracks were separated by back-to-back wood partitions that consisted of bookshelves, a cabinet holding a mirror with shelves underneath, and a wall locker for hanging uniforms with shoe rack below. There was also in the corner facing the window above the bookshelves a locker for general use that was almost always not used...in order to get to it you had to stand on your desk. That locker gave access not only to its own space but also to the space between each back-to-back room separator. The separators were joined to each other by screwing them to a wood 2x12 set even to the bottom of the general use locker. So, access to the top locker that no one ever looked in also gave access to a hidden 2x12 shelf the width of the cadet room that was almost impossible to see unless you knew it was there! That space probably should have been covered cutting off access, but I never saw one that was.

Since my room was a popular gathering place and "the boys" (sometimes called the lads) were who we were, the knowledge of this concealed space was a secret I discovered, and we shared. I happened upon it when looking for a place to store a spare army blanket.

The first request I had to hide contraband was for a very small black and white TV set with maybe a 9-inch screen. Since cadets were not allowed to have TV's in their rooms, it went in. A few of us spent many nights watching the late news on it, particularly the news from Vietnam. I can remember a few Saturday nights when I had no date, no money to go to the MAC Theater in Chester, and nothing else to do, so I spent the evening watching a John Wayne movie on that tiny TV and feeling sad for myself. After midnight, two of "the boys" showed up so the evening was not a total loss! We all liked John Wayne. Being an engineering/physics major I did build an antenna that outperformed the "rabbit ears" antenna that came with the set.

The second request for a contraband hideout came from an underclassmen friend who was a bio/chem major and an EMT to hide his medical kit in my overhead because he didn't want it looked at during inspections. This guy was actually building a heart lung machine in the basement of the barracks in his spare time. He had the key to the downstairs somehow. How can you say no to a guy like that, so I just asked what was in the kit that he didn't want seen. His answer was morphine, so it went in and joined a few taped up shoebox sized packages and two 50 cal ammo cans also taped. I never asked what was in them and the guys who asked me never said. We just trusted each other because of who we were. The guy that had the medical kit later became an MD and had a long medical career.

A pretty bizarre request came from a guy I was very close to at that time and still hear from. He was the only cadet I ever brought home to NY to meet my family. Ever since the beginning of the school year, he kept telling me about how when we got out for Christmas he and his high school girlfriend were going to have the greatest Christmas ever! He saw her at Thanksgiving, and they had it all planned out. They lived in the Washington DC area and there were all sorts of events that they both loved going on. His room was festooned with her pictures (not bad looking), he had saved his money, and he was so in love with her that he was gasping for breath. I know he had another hound dog activity also in mind, but we won't go into that.

The minute I got back to the barracks after Christmas, he showed up and before I could even ask how Christmas was, he said with a very pained look on his face, "I need you to hide something for me." I said, "Sure, what is it?" He handed me a white German army snow cape. I said, "There must be a story to tell about why I am hiding this!" He said because it may be evidence in a criminal case. Then I said what would the charge be in this criminal case? His reply was attempted murder. I said her? No, he said, some random guy. Up the snow cape went into my hiding place, but I made him tell me the story. Turns out:

He reunited with the girlfriend in Washington as planned and they went on several daytime dates, but at night, she was sick, too tired, had to babysit for younger siblings etc. After one day date, he brought her home after dark but again she was not feeling well so he could not stick around for the evening. As it turned out, it had been snowing in DC and the plows had left a huge snow pile on the street within sight of the girlfriend's house. Being a well-trained PMC cadet, he began to suspect something so: he returned to the area around 2200 hours, parked his car a few blocks away, wrapped himself in the German army snow cape, and dug himself into the snow pile and waited.

I said you are lucky no one saw you doing what you did, he said empty lots, that's why they piled the snow there. Sure enough after a few hours a car drives up with her in it and some guy driving. In the parked car the cadet could see the traditional after date drop off smooching commence. He became enraged, emerged from his snow hide still wrapped in the snow cape and ran to the car on which he began pounding and throwing around some foul barracks language and somewhat would now be called "terroristic threats."

She began screaming, the guy was too dumb to just lock the doors or drive off, so he got out of the car and the cadet cold-cocked him and left him lying in the snow. While all this was going on, she got out of the car and ran into the house. The lights came on, etc.

Our cadet decided now was the time to go, ran back to his car that was quite a distance away, and took off. Next morning, he asked his parents to take him to the early train back to Chester because he had some work to do in the physics lab. His father said, "No goodbye to the girlfriend?" His answer was, "Said goodbye last night."

Bottom line, my hiding place held cadet contraband, illegal narcotics, and criminal evidence, plus God only knows what was in the sealed packages. Not bad, I guarded it all with my life until graduation when the owners all came to collect their property.

PS—law enforcement never showed up looking for the snow caped crusader. Don't know why. It was probably never reported, his father was an officer serving in the Pentagon so maybe he fixed it, don't know. The pictures disappeared from his room and her name was never mentioned again.

I never thought twice about hiding stuff for "the boys", it was who we were! This was the life we chose!!!

Art Liss:
Letters:

"I remember you one Saturday night when you were CQ on my corridor on the first floor of Terrell Hall and I was a Rook. I noticed your great spit shine earlier and you were working on a pair that night. I was working on mine and couldn't get that Gray look out. When I asked for help, you were flabbergasted that I was in on a Saturday night shining my shoes. You passed on some of your tricks that I used throughout my PMC years period. That was how we met, thank you. Nice memory." *From Byron Daniels a Rook during my Senior year 1966-1967*

"Let's start with one to set the stage. Your single room was about 2/3 down from the street entrance on the quad side. As such, you normally passed my room in the center of the other side of the hall. Whether you knew it or not, you had a reputation of not holding your alcohol; one beer and you were out of it. The main story I remember and have related so many times over the years and around the world as the knight of the Junior Ring Dance my Rook year.

Some of us rooks would volunteer for details on Saturday night so we could miss mess one formation and church. That particular night, we were cleaning up after the formal and found a mouse in the mess hall. Well, we captured it and took it back to the dorm. I don't recall how, but the mouse didn't survive; probably a heart attack from being handled. Now to the crux of the story—we knew this was one of those nights they went drinking but normally come rolling in around midnight or so.

Well, we were ready. I came up with the idea to tie the mouse carcass spread eagle across your doorknob that has the lock in the center. We had lookouts waiting in view of your arrival. We all hid in our rooms with the doors cracked and the hall light out. My memory may have played tricks, but we thought we heard you bouncing off the wall on the way to your room. At the moment you tried to insert your key, we heard the crunch. We couldn't see how you reacted but heard you when you realized what had happened.

A rousing time ensued, and we all eventually hit the racks side note and I don't know if you had something to do with it but when I woke up in the morning, I sensed commotion in my room. Before opening my eyes, I steeled myself for the unknown that was sure to happen. There it was...the mouse hanging from the top rack, a fraction of an inch from my nose.

And, yes, we did realize that you had a hand in keeping Dankowitz under control. You were indeed a stabilizing influence on us for our remaining PMC years and throughout life." Thanks. *From Dave Ling March 10, 2014*

"Thanks for sending me the files on Larry for my review. They are most impressive, and I want to wish you much good luck in having his DFC for valor upgraded to an MOH. In my recollection, we last chatted when you were a Lieutenant, and I was an ROTC cadet at Fort Indiantown Gap between mid-June in late July 1969. My

ROTC company commander was Major Richard Duckloe, Class of 59 perhaps, you met him while you were there. I correctly remembered that you were a Cadet Major and that you were a member of the Second Battalion staff. However, I must confess that I forgot your cadet number and I was only semi sure that you were the Second battalion Executive Officer. I did, however, correctly remember Colonel John Everson's cadet number 142 when I chatted with him and Colonel Steve Reho class of 68 the Cadet Brigade Commander during the 67-68 academic year, at John's office in the "Five Sided Foxhole" in Arlington, Virginia in 1991 during Operation Desert Shield/ Operation Desert Storm. We had fun discussing our individual perspectives of life at PMC back in the mid-1960's.

I often wondered what it happened to Dick Emery, Joe Charles, Brian Labar, Dick Hodges, Larry Martin, and Hayden Wilbur. You may find interest in knowing that my class 1970 had 184 cadets on September 1, 1966—four academic years later, 64 of us were graduated and, of the 64, 40 of us were commissioned Lieutenants in the United States Army. There were fewer than 225 cadets in the Corps after my graduation late in May 1972. You've probably reached your saturation point for PMC therefore I will close. Once again, Art, good luck in having Larry's DFC for Valor upgraded to the MOH. Best, John #51" *From John Blair August 13, 2012*

NOTE: This was about a Demerit SGT Eckard wrote me up for a disturbance after taps in the Quadrangle. Dave had a twin Brother.

"That must have been my evil twin, Cadet Liss…Whoops, I had a real twin there at PMC although he was in your class, not mine…Since I'm older, Brother, and thus more cognitively challenged, I will accept your explanation of the discrepancy in the demerit slip. But, on the other hand, you may recall that I was an officer in Company B in the 1965-1966 year when you were awarded merits by order of our T. O. MSgt Eugene Cloud. Cadet CPT Charlie Eichenberg was our CO. When it came to awarding Merits for "Outstanding appearances and excellent military bearing..." that designation was based on the conflab of the officers of Company B 1965-1966...and I was one of them. I won't say how I voted at the time, suffice if it is to say that based on your outstanding appearances and excellent military bearing, I had the chance to overcome my having given you trivial lousy demerits in the prior year..." *From Dave Eckard August 19, 2017*

"Even though it seemed that Louis Lynn, our Cadre Commander's primary goal was to wipe the smile off my face at all costs, he indeed instilled the Esprit de Corps in me and our F Company Rook class with the values of: "All for one, one for al!" "A unit is only as strong as the weakest link." etc.

I had great respect for CPT Art Liss who lived on our F company Rook Hall and epitomized the grace and gentlemanly aspects of an officer and a gentleman. His calm demeanor many times offset Lynn's sometimes maniacal behavior. I admired our Cadre CPL Al Thigpen who also led with a calm positive attitude. I also admired Everson, Raho, and lastly Bob Grace.

An add on...I remember you and how rational you were compared to Louis Lynn. Louis was brutal the way he dealt with my exuberance. Louis paddled me so hard that I ended up in the infirmary a couple of times. He didn't like it when I would beat him in the hand slap game. I was also too outspoken and reveled in my own enthusiasm. I crossed the line too many times.

I apologize to anyone who has misunderstood my attempts to remember any of the incidents I tried to recall. My time at PMC was intense and somewhat gratifying although incomplete because of my immaturity and the fact that I left without graduating. I spent 3 1/2 years there going full time during the academic school year in the last two summers I was there, trying to raise my grade point average to be eligible to continue as a full-time matriculated student and to continue.

Thanks for accepting me into the ranks of past cadets of PMC. I did not graduate that attended the years of 1966-1969. Left and moved to California." *From a cadet, Jan 20, 2018*

David Fiedler:
"Townies"

I have a classmate (Bill Luckenbill) who at the time we were at PMC was a real animal. He would do hundreds of sit-ups and had rock hard six-pack abs. Also working in the kitchen at PMC during our time was one of Chester High Schools more outstanding graduates, a guy named Claude, who had been some sort of athlete at CHS who also had a six-pack of abs but was not very bright.

If you recall, lunch meal was always served in the chow line off the steam tables and Claude was always there serving when we ate lunch. Bill and I had the same schedule so every day we were in the line together. Every day when Bill and Claude saw each other, a verbal fight would start as to which one of them was the toughest, had the hardest abs, could bend steel in their bare hands, etc. At times they each challenged the other at various feats of daring do like crushing cans and bending or breaking things.

Bill and I both had morning kitchen jobs, so I guess that is how he first met Claude. It probably is also how Bill knew that there were two kinds of knives in the bins on the serving line. One kind was kind of flimsy with a thin shank where the blade joined the handle. The other kind was much more hefty and solid. One day Bill amused us by showing us how he could tense up his abs and break the knife blade at the handle by glancing the blade off his abs like they were a brick or stone. It was a cute trick and he never even cut his shirt or undershirt when he did it.

Sure enough, a few days later we were in the chow line and Bill and Claude start up again with each other. Bill said, "Claude, if you think you are so tough, do this..." He then reached into the knife bin, grabs a flimsy knife, and snaps the blade against his abs and throws the broken parts into the trash can. Bill then reaches into the bin, pulls out another knife, the other strong kind of course, hands it to Claude and said, "There, now let me see you do that!" Claude, being that fine product of CHS then takes the knife and knifes himself in the abs.

Because Claude was in such good shape, the wound was not that deep and the docs at Crozier-Chester Medical Center were able to stitch him up pretty quickly. We did not see much of old Claude for a while after that, but he did heal up. Don't know how he explained the wound to them, but he could have done some serious damage.

About 20 years later, when Bill and I were both in the NJARNG I remember telling that story and asking Bill to repeat the trick with my bayonet, he declined. Just getting too old for that stuff I guess.

David Fiedler:
Shot in the Rear!

As I was returning from a date one Saturday night/Sunday morning about 1AM, I entered what we then called new dorm #4. My room was in the back corner of the building's second floor, overlooking the parking lot behind MacMorland Center. As I got to the hall near my room, I was stopped by two of my classmates who told me to, "Keep silent and don't show any light," then slowly crawl over to the window in the room next to mine, which I did. Two more of my classmates were at the window. They instructed me to look out into the parking lot. When I did I could plainly see a person moving from car to car toward us. Whoever it was fiddled with the car doors and when one opened he dove in and came out with some stuff. Probably loose change or other things of value. The initial plan was for us to go to all the avenues of escape, catch the thief, and deliver a quick beating to him.

One of my classmates then said, "No, wait! I have something better." He left the room and in a few seconds returned with a scoped Model 52 Remington .22 target rifle. I must mention that in 40 years of military service I have NEVER known a better shot than this individual. The cadet with the rifle then proceeded to pile up books on the desk and slowly open the window. The book pile was used as a rifle rest. As the cadet took aim I said, "A .22 long rifle slug can kill you at ranges up to a mile, and I don't want to be an accessory to murder." He said, "Just watch and wait!" We did.

As the thief started on the next car in line, the .22 fired and we could see the target visibily jump and grab his ass. He then took off running. I said, "pretty shot" it was at least 200 feet, not bad for a .22. The gun and the shooter then disappeared. The next day the car owner who was told what happened found a "slim jim" car lock pick inserted between the car window and the door frame, but not a mark on the car.

Later, I looked for a blood trail in the car area but couldn't find one. After this action, the prohibited privately owned firearm was gone from the campus or placed in a better hiding place. Thefts from parked cars on the PMC campus stopped, no one was charged with attempted murder, and someone from Chester had a .22 caliber hole in his behind. A message was sent.

David Fiedler:
PMC Radio Schwenzer/Campus Pirate Radio

From 1964-1968, PMC cadets were not allowed to have television in their rooms. TV could only be viewed officially in the orderly room in the lobby in Howell Hall, even though many had TV's hidden away somewhere in the barracks. Radios in the rooms were permitted as long as the volume was kept at a low level so adjacent rooms would not be disturbed.

Conrad Schwenzer was a cadet in the Corps for over two years. Schwenzer had a reputation for being a bit weird, but harmless. Schwenzer discovered that you could buy what was called a "carrier current radio transmitter" from one of the old radio supply companies that existed before cell phones and the internet. Carrier current systems worked by sending radio signals, not to an antenna for broadcast, but instead into internal electric lines like those in a building. If you had a standard radio receiver connected to the same electric line as the transmitter, you would receive the transmitted signal over any broadcast station you were tuned to. You might have a problem if there was a transformer in the system that would "choke out " the radio signal, but that was rare. Since carrier current radio systems did not broadcast into space via an antenna, they were not regulated by the Federal Communications Commission (FCC) nor did the station need a license or a call sign.

Knowing this, "Radio Schwenzer" was on the air connecting all of the PMC barracks rooms that had radio. Schwenzer's broadcasts were infrequent, but if he was on it was usually around the time the call to quarters sounded.

In the beginning, Conrad was just sending his weird music and a few comments. But as time went on, he changed the format to criticism comments about Dr. Moll, school policy, the Commandant and his staff, the Greater Chester Movement, the cadet chain of command, the need to acquire a nursing school, a law school, and a junior college, and basically came down as anti-school administration on just about everything.

As reports filtered back to the powers that be about Schwenzer's broadcasts, his station and its operator could not be identified for quite a while. Some comments were made by the cadet chain of command about a "pirate radio station" being on campus, but only a few of us engineers/HAM radio operators could figure out where the mystery broadcasts were coming from...and we didn't talk. Eventually, during one Saturday morning inspection, the equipment was spotted and radio Schwenzer was shut down. Conrad Schwenzer did not last until graduation.

David Fiedler:
ROTC ARQ Testing

In early 1968, the Army/ROTC decided that cadets who were about to be commissioned needed to be mentally evaluated, just like any other draftee or enlistee was in order to prove them worthy of a commission. The PMC ROTC detachment was ordered to test all senior cadets using the standard Army Qualification Test (ARQT) known as the ARQ's in early 1968. The ARQ's concentrated on things like word knowledge, simple practical math, general science, numerical operations, and general information on a bunch of other simple topics. The test was given in MacMorland Center with everyone sitting at the 10-man mess tables with no separation and no proctors, just a few of the ROTC NCO's that merely distributed the tests and collected them after an hour.

I am a product of the New York City public school system and believe me when I tell you that my entire 6th grade class could have passed the ARQ's. Imagine our shock about a month later when we were informed that at least two of my classmates (maybe more) had failed the exam, were being counseled, and would probably be dropped from ROTC / Commissioning. It was pretty obvious that those involved did not want to go into the army and were using the failure of the ARQ's as a way out of military service. Remember, this was after the death of several former cadets in Vietnam, including one that had been 1st Captain.

A rumor started that the individuals concerned were told that since they failed the test that they were in ROTC on a probationary basis only. Also, since they were on "probation" that their draft boards would be notified that they should no longer be considered 1D (member of reserve component) but rather 2S (student) and were therefore eligible for military service.

After this "persuasion," we were told that they were allowed to retake the tests and they all passed. The names of those involved were never disclosed and the whole incident was hushed up. I was there, it did happen!!!

David Fiedler:
Branch Selection

The class of 1968 was very close to each other. For the most part we actually liked each other, although every class had at least a few jerks that made them unpopular, so they were mostly ignored. We had very few. Since we were so close, this inevitably led to mass gatherings and some of the best BS sessions I ever had in my life. During my senior year, many of these sessions happened in or near my room, mostly in the hour between call to quarters and taps (9-10PM).

Stories and Vignettes from PMC

Of course, by the Fall of 1967, much of the discussion turned to the War in Vietnam and PMC graduates that were either KIA or WIA. Many of us started having second thoughts about military careers that we had envisioned since boyhood and was the main reason we entered PMC to begin with.

The great military thinkers of the class who rejected the idea of trying to get out of military service, but also did not want to die, analyzed the situation, and came up with this just prior to the ROTC requirement to select three Army branches in order of personal preference. This was done by filling out a form known as your "dream sheet" and the Army, with input from the ROTC/PMS, was supposed to use this to decide which branch you would be commissioned in. Some with strong feelings filled in the blanks with the same branch (ie infantry, infantry, infantry in one case) in order to express extreme desire for a particular branch.

Anyway, the military analysts of the class reasoned that all the infantry was in Vietnam and all the armor was in Germany, SO if you put down armor and got accepted, your chances of going to Vietnam were minimal, going to Europe would be fun, and you would not die unless the Russians decided to invade the west, which was unlikely. Almost everyone that put down armor as their first choice got it and they were very happy.

After graduation they all got their crossed saber brass insignia and went off to Fort Knox to learn about tanks, tank gunnery, and automotive stuff.

A year later, when I was in Vietnam, I heard that many of them were also in the country still wearing their armor brass BUT LEADING INFANTRY PLATOONS!! So much for the military geniuses in the PMC class of 1968.

David Fiedler:
Lock In

In the so-called "New Dorms" (Turrell, Howell, Cann, etc) all of the cadet room doors opened inward. A few of the jokers one day discovered that the doors all had a tiny bit of space between the door and the lip of the door frame that it contacted when the door was closed.

A certain group of cadet jokers (known as "the boys" or sometimes "the lads") discovered that if you jammed an ordinary pencil in the space between the door and its resting place on the lip of the frame, the bolt in the door latch was pushed against the door frame latch receptacle so tightly that it was impossible to turn the doorknob and open the door. If the room was occupied when the pencil was jammed between the doorframe and the door, it effectively imprisoned the occupant or occupants. The jam was so tight and the doorknob so small and hard to grip that not even the strongest of us could turn the doorknob. If more than one cadet was locked in, it was impossible for two people to get a grip on the doorknob and turn it. Pounding on the door frame, if thought of, did not help because it would not release the pencil. In a very few instances, the prisoner was so strong, and his grip was so tight, that the knob finally was forced to turn, freeing the occupants, but this was very rare. In effect, until someone in the hallway pried out the pencil, the door could not be opened from the inside.

Rumor had it that one of "the boys" had gone to a private military high school and he had learned the trick there. In 1966, armed with this knowledge, "the boys" got even with a Senior cadet officer by locking him in his room just before evening formation. He could not turn the doorknob to get out. He just barely made it to formation and dinner by jumping out his window and didn't realize what had happened until he returned and found the pencil in the door jamb. Prior to that, he had thought the door lock had failed.

To my recollection, over my four years at PMC, this trick was repeated at least five times, mostly as a joke and the jokers released the victim themselves after a short time. At least twice however, it was done as an act of revenge for being awarded punishment due to some infraction. In these instances, the prisoner had to be rescued by his classmates or fellow members of the cadet chain of command. I saw one rescue where a cadet officer's saber had to be used to pry the pencil out of the door jam.

Gerald Ferguson:
The Ponderosa Bar

I suppose every class had a favorite watering hole during its 1st class year. For my class, it was the "Ponderosa" located on Chester Pike about one mile from campus. Once or twice a week, especially after ROTC monthly checks arrived, there might be a table occupied by 5-10 cadets in civilian clothes. Pitchers of beer were the usual order frequently augmented with a sandwich. I recall that there was a TV/video player that for a price would play a short tape of a very attractive, semi clad woman dancing to, I believe, a Santana song. After a few pitchers were consumed and usually well before last call, there would be a memorable version of the Alma Mater sung loudly and proudly followed by dismissal, loading up in a car or two, possibly the "Dog Mobile," and hustling back to campus via the incomplete I-95 that ended next to PMC. Unfortunately, the bar closed.

David Edward Ling:
The Chester Ferry Incident

During our First Class (Senior) year, I and an unidentified underclassman were involved in the referenced incident. It involved me, an underclassman (I remember his name, but he will remain unidentified), then1SG Sisto Cicuzza, the Chester Police Department, including the jail staff, and many unsuspecting victims of our "crimes" that night. Before I go on, someone from PMC may observe that I had my '56 Chevy with no reverse; yes, I did, but I must have needed a car as this was one of those times when my car was not up to the task.

I was arrested during my First Class (Senior) year. It began with me taking the underclassman, Cadet X, with me while I drove my Father's VW home and we would return in Cadet X's car as he was from near my home. He drove an MG Midget which will come into play later. We first went by Cadet X's house and he picked up his car then dropped the VW off at my house. At this point, it would bear mentioning that the two of us had been drinking before and throughout the trip. As we left my house in his car, somehow we got the great idea to take some souvenirs along the way.

Here is where Cadet X's car, the MG Midget, comes into play. If you are aware, there isn't much room for cargo. I don't recall how we got so much stuff in the small car, but you will understand just how much stuff I am referring to soon. If an item was too big to fit in the car, we simply broke it into pieces, like the plywood sign at the entrance into the Bridgeport Boat Company (or something like that). After we collected several small things along the way, we approached the Bridgeport-Chester Ferry aka the Chester Ferry and he proceeded to drive onto the Chester Ferry.

At that time, we thought it would be a great coup if we could score a hose from the Chester Ferry. I don't remember who went to get the fire hose, but it was too big for the room left in the little car, so it was settled that we would take the fitting from the front of the fire hose. Little did we know (or care) that the Chester PD was waiting for us on the Chester side. We were near the front of the boat, so we didn't have a chance to escape and evade. As the Chester PD made us unload everything in the little car, the stack at the rear of the vehicle grew and grew, much higher than the car of course. The people waiting to exit the Ferry must have thought the whole situation was funny and, I'm sure, frustrating.

We were transported to the Chester jail and, still pretty drunk, thought it was still hilarious. We were separated in different cells, so I was alone to act out the shenanigans. These included scenes I had seen on TV like running the Styrofoam cup across the bars in which we had coffee (?) served to attract the attention of the Jailer so I could ask what the charges were. When he asked me what I was doing, I told him. He smirked and said he didn't think the Styrofoam cup would attract much attention and that the charges would be read later that night or in the morning.

We also communicated with the other incarcerated folks verbally and when I asked what they were in for (ala Alice's Restaurant), we got the normal drunk and disorderly, etc. until we got to the last guy in the cell next to me and he was obviously hesitant. After some verbal prodding, he said he was run-in for vagrancy, and we booed for that. He then admitted the cops found out he killed a guy in Mississippi; things got really quiet in response. That was the end of that part of our adventure.

As the night was ending, the court bailiff came in and read us the charges—"Larceny and Conspiracy to Sink the Bridgeport-Chester Ferry" and our bail was set at $120 each. Obviously, we didn't have that kind of money so I called my TKE brother whose initials were H.P. which sounded a lot like Harry Papastrat (OK, I said I wouldn't name them but …) and he scraped up the money for me. I don't know how the underclassman got his bail, but suffice it to say, he got his. As I was sobering up, I realized the seriousness of our situation.

Later that morning, we were escorted to the Hearing Room and before we reached it, we were stopped and informed that someone had intervened, and we were being released with no charges as long as we promised we would not get in any more trouble and made restitution to those from who we stole. We also had to pay $13 for room and board. That was a metal cot with no mattress or pillow and a cold cup of something, mostly milk and a small serving of what may have passed for scrambled eggs. Obviously, we agreed.

A side note, I knew that telling my folks would happen shortly as my father always said, "It's better to find out from you." I called home and my Father answered the phone and I proceeded to tell him every detail. When I was finished, he said he would support us anyway he could, but not money. I had to repay my debt myself. I surmise that he already knew of my troubles and it was never spoken about again!

I have since found out that 1SG Cicuzza was the source of the Chester largess, and he pleaded our case. I will be forever in debt to "Pappy". A legend, then-First Sergeant (1SG) Sisto "Pappy" "Buckskin" Cicuzza (RIP) was assigned to Pennsylvania Military College, and I understand he was the highest decorated soldier from the 9th Infantry Division in Vietnam. He was shot several times in the stomach and chased down the Viet Cong and killed him with his bare hands.

1SG Cicuzza got us off since he had friends on the Chester Police Force (the Chief of Detectives) and I was eventually aware of most of his involvement. He got us off with the condition that we returned the stolen material and repair/replace any damaged items. That arrest would have disqualified me from getting a commission and maybe even college graduation.

Years later, when I was preparing for another of my security clearance background checks, I did not enter that arrest as I had not in previous editions. I asked the investigator and he told me to not put it down because it apparently didn't exist. This proved that then1SG Cicuzza did get our records expunged as no arrest had been recorded. Yes, alcohol was involved. Further, he apparently did not report it to the college, the PMS, nor the Cadet chain as I suffered no repercussions during the class year from the incident and even years later. CSM Cicuzza retired from the Army in 1977 and passed away in 1989. The late Command Sergeant Major (CSM) Retired Cicuzza was posthumously admitted to the Ranger Hall of Fame in 2001. If it appears I held "Pappy" in high regard, I still do, as do others.

A closing comment: I have delved deeply into my memory to address this long-ago incident in my life. Not a mean feat for an old guy with dementia and rapidly approaching Alzheimer's.

Gerald Ferguson:
Fran and Nan's

What cadet attending PMC in the 1960's does not have a place in their food memory for Fran and Nan's Steak and Hoagie (not sub) Shop located at the end of 14th Street? For underclassmen who didn't have the option of leaving campus for an evening fast food run, a call to Fran's for a cheesesteak or hoagie was a life saver from a routinely disappointing 3rd mess meal. Typically, a shout would go out in the corridor that an order was going to be called in. Those with cash or guys who could beg a couple of dollars would place their order. About 45 minutes later, the aroma of greasy steaks and hoagie onions would announce that Fran was on the floor and delivering the order. Fran and Nan's is long gone now, replaced by Maggie May's Campus Pub.

John E. N. Blair:
A Masonic Experience at P. M. C.

On 20 August 1969, my 21st birthday anniversary, I signed a Petition to join my father and maternal-grandfather's Masonic Lodge and returned to P. M. C. for my senior-year. However, joining the Masons requires a multi-month approval process, together with several advancement requirements. Consequently, I did not become a Master Mason until the evening of the third Friday in the month of January, 1970 while home for our semester-break.

After returning to P. M. C. shortly thereafter, Professor C. Joseph Chacko, Ph.D., chairman of the Political Science Department of the Liberal Arts Division, asked me if I was a Master Mason and I replied, "Yes, as of last Friday night, I am." Professor Chacko, a non-driver and the Right Worshipful Deputy Grand Master of the Grand Lodge of India, was being honored for his service to Freemasonry in India by the Right Worshipful Grand Master of Masons in Pennsylvania in mid-February, 1970 in Corinthian Lodge No. 2 in Grand Lodge (1 North Broad Street in Philadelphia); therefore, he needed both a ride to Philadelphia and a Master Mason to accompany him.

Although I may have been the only P. M. C. cadet so qualified, I told him that, since I was such a newly 'minted' Master Mason, I might not be able to pass entrance examination; therefore, he told me, "If you cannot pass it, we will return to Chester." In those circumstances, I told him, "Sure!" He received his award, and we had a very nice, highly memorable evening.

Gerald Ferguson:
Graduation-Parting Ways

Senior (1st Class) Year was the most rewarding time for me personally at PMC. With three years of experience to know the "ropes" and having attended six weeks of ROTC Summer Camp at Indian Town Gap, PA (IGMR), I felt fully prepared to fill a leadership role at school. I thoroughly enjoyed those final nine months at PMC. But all good things come to an end and May of 1970 rolled around quickly. I think all my classmates were anxious to graduate and move on, so everyone was happy when they received their diploma and, in most cases, a commission in the Army. For me it didn't take but a few days after that May ceremony to realize that I would not be seeing my classmates again for a long time, maybe never again. Of course, some of us would be together in various military training courses and in a few cases, we crossed paths during our duty assignments, but I found that parting ways with my PMC brothers was a sad but inevitable conclusion to my PMC years.

After graduation, most 1970 grads filled service commitments resulting in guys settling all over the U.S., from New Jersey to Alaska. It made alumni gatherings difficult. When coupled with the converting of Pennsylvania Military College to Widener University and the disbanding of the Corps, PMC alumni functions tend to be poorly attended. A shame.

Bob Kukich:
A PMC Education

Recent events have caused me to reflect upon the education we received at PMC. I believe the education and experiences we enjoyed at

PMC were meant not for a career but for a lifetime. Jack Gale (1970) shared, "The education and experiences we enjoyed at PMC could never be replicated at a civilian college—it would be like comparing apples to oranges."

Bill Feyk (1970) wrote, "Our Education was of two types: 1) Academics which gave us the means to secure a career and 2) Military Discipline which taught us about standards, self-discipline, withstanding pressure, and leadership. This second aspect served me better than the first, not only in my military career, but in the civilian world as well."

From our first days as Rooks to graduation, the standards that were set for us, the self-discipline required of us, the leadership skills taught to us, the positions of increasing responsibility and authority offered to us, these developed within us the traits that would last a lifetime.

In those first days as a rook, our class was pushed as a group into an Old Main assembly room for a class on cadet rules and regulations. And on the wall in that room was a quote which read: "When wealth is lost, nothing is lost; when health is lost, something is lost; when character is lost, all is lost." Years later, I would read similar words which I believe were taught to us, experienced by us and instilled in us as PMC cadets:

Watch your thoughts, for they become words.
Watch your words, for they become actions.
Watch your actions, for they become habits.
Watch your habits because they become character.
Watch your character, for it becomes your destiny.

Prior to PMC, most of us had little experience or exposure to a disciplined lifestyle. Few of us had been required to demonstrate much in the way of respect for authority, self-discipline, responsibility, or working as members of a team. Little did we know that by adhering to our cadet rules and regulations, we would come to understand and embrace these traits, the conditions under which we were expected to demonstrate them, the standards required, and the self-discipline required to live them on a daily basis—even when no one was looking.

When we were awarded "Old Man" status, the upperclassmen congratulated us and welcomed us as members of the Corps of Cadets, an organization in which we discovered a new sense of pride, both collectively and individually. We also discovered that with our recognition as PMC cadets, we had become members of a band of brothers, all who together had successfully experienced a year of change, a year of growth, and a year of maturity unlike any other previously.

The years that followed at PMC were years of further growth. We were afforded opportunities to lead and hone our leadership skills commensurate with our ability and demonstrated performance. As upperclassmen we became not only cadet leaders, but more importantly mentors. And during those years, the traits of self-discipline, responsibility, leadership, and mentorship became engrained in us to the extent that they would become traits for a lifetime, not just for a career.

Gerald Ferguson:
And then You Were in Charge

One of the objectives of a military school education is to train its graduates to be leaders, whether that is in the military or civilian world or both. Over the course of four years at PMC, there were many opportunities to build leadership skills. It didn't require that you "have rank" although being a corporal, sergeant, or officer made leadership a formal part of your everyday activities.

As a Rook or 4th Classman, those men who wore the gold braid on their service caps and had all those chevrons on their sleeves were admired and in many cases feared. Those guys knew the ropes, they had confidence in their abilities, and an ease interacting with classmates. Their orders were obeyed without pause.

Jump ahead three years and now myself and my classmates are the guys in charge. We interpret the policy and enforce the rules. Of course, most of us had completed the ROTC summer camp assignment at Indian Town Gap and were loaded with military knowledge and confidence. But as I drove to the College on that first day of the Rook orientation, it was sobering to realize as a company commander, I was responsible for the 40 or so cadets in my unit. I was confident that I was ready, but apprehensive as to what the school year would hold.

Over the course of the next nine months, the 1st Classmen fine-tuned their leadership skills. Yes, we "practiced" on the cadets under our command, but our actions were usually well intentioned and correct. By the time graduation and commissioning rolled around in May, we were confident that we could hold-my-own against anything the Army or life could toss our way.

Gerald Ferguson:
Branch Assignments

Early in our senior year, those cadets who signed contracts to go into the Army were given the opportunity to select the branch of the Army they would like to serve in—a wish list. This required that the senior cadet complete the six-week ROTC summer camp at Indiantown Gap Military Reservation, have a satisfactory GPA, and was generally seen as having respectable military performance during the first three years at PMC.

The selection process stipulated that each prospective 2nd Lieutenant (regular Army or reserve) identify his three preferred branches. One option had to be a combat branch (infantry, artillery, armor), one a combat support branch (MPs, signal, etc.) and one a support branch (finance, AG, etc.). Several weeks later, we would find out what was assigned. In my case, I selected MPs as my first choice, artillery, and a support branch I don't recall.

In 1969-1970, the Vietnam War was still going full tilt and the demand for combat branch officers was high. Therefore, it wasn't a surprise that I was "awarded" an assignment in Field Artillery. I assumed that as a Distinguished Military Graduate I would receive my first choice, but the Army in its infinite wisdom didn't agree. I suspect anyone who requested a combat branch received their choice.

It was a PMC tradition that 1st Class Cadets with branch assignments would wear the emblem of that branch on their cadet uniform collar. The Field Artillery crossed cannons promptly appeared on my uniform. I was proud to be in the Army Field Artillery for the four years following graduation.

William J. Troy:
Education Really did Happen!

We should not forget that in addition to our military experience, we were in college. As students, we had many college majors and studied under different members of the faculty. It is appropriate that we highlight some of the most memorable professors we learned from over our four years.

As I remember, all of the entering Cadet Rooks had Military History. The class was first up in the morning and held in the Alumni Auditorium. It was team taught by Major Carl R. Morin, Jr. and Dr. Benjamin Franklin Cooling III. Major Morin was a soldier's soldier! He was born at Ft Eustis, Florida and graduated from Melbourne High School, Florida, and The US Military Academy. Major Morin received his master's in history from the University of Florida and was assigned as an Assistant Professor of Military Science in 1967. He was impressive! He was an artilleryman and had served in Vietnam. After our Rook year, Major Morin was reassigned and returned to Vietnam in 1970. Dr. Cooling was also impressive! He was born in Washington, DC. He was an ROTC cadet in Coolidge High School in DC and in Rutgers University where he earned his bachelor's degree in history. He was a member of the Scarlet Rifles Drill Team at Rutgers. His Master's and Doctorate degrees are from the University of Pennsylvania. Professor Cooling was commissioned and served in the Army Reserve from 1957 through 1963.

The fact that they both were thorough, informative, and even interesting history educators was lost on me and I struggled to pass, although I had enjoyed history and especially military history since elementary school. It wasn't their fault. I made it through the class and especially remember them because they were impressive men and excellent examples for us to emulate. Major Morin had an outstanding career, retiring as a Brigadier General in 1990. He had a successful civilian career after retirement until his death on May 24, 2010. He is buried at West Point. Professor Cooling went on to teach at the National Defense University and the Naval War College. He has written numerous books. I have read three of them, Forts Henry and Donelson—the key to the Confederate heartland, Symbol, sword, and shield: defending Washington during the Civil War and, Jubal Early's Raid on Washington!

I failed Algebra I the first semester of my Freshman year. Math was never my strong point, and it didn't help that I initially had a professor whose accent I could not fathom. Then I found Professor Mary Wolfe! To this day I refer to her as the "savior of the flunky!" I went from failure to a B grade for both Algebra I and II. She made math simple for me. I owe her a lot, possibly even graduation.

Dr. John A. Jenkins in History was a classic. He always wore a Greek Fisherman's hat and usually had his overcoat thrown over his shoulders rather than having his arms through the sleeves. I was always impressed by how he entered the classroom, took off his overcoat, opened his briefcase, and removed a manila folder, placing it on the desk. He then took out his pocket watch, opened it, and placed it on the desk. He proceeded to lecture while walking around the desk, never looking at either his notes or the students. To ask a question, you just had to speak up. He finished his lecture, picked up his notes and put them into the briefcase, put on his coat and hat, closed his pocket watch, and returned it to his pocket and beat the students out the door when the bell rang! It was masterful! He was very interesting, and I learned a lot about American History from him.

Dr. Carlos Allen was another History Professor. He taught early American history and often brought in music from the Colonial era. He would swing his arms as if he were conducting the music. He made that history interesting.

Dr. Hope Goodale was my Spanish instructor. She was tough and had us read Don Quixote by Miguel Cervantes in Spanish. I survived but just barely. She spoke Spanish with a Castilian accent. I had trouble with her accent! My high school Spanish teacher was Cuban.

Joe Lowe taught English. Professor Melvin R. Lowe was great. I don't know why he was known as Joe Lowe. He was well liked and the 1970 Sabre and Scroll was dedicated to him. The dedication states, "An excellent instructor, An involved faculty member, And a friend if you so desire." He had taught in Saigon, so he was almost a Vietnam Veteran. He made college English enjoyable.

I was a liberal arts major, so I took Earth and Space Science—sometimes called science for dummies. I think Professor Richard Boekenkamp taught it, but I'm not sure. I passed and that was good enough. Professor Boekenkamp was the faculty advisor for Lambda Chi Alpha fraternity. I pledged and am a member. Professor Boekenkamp was a very nice man and a friend of the Cadet Corps.

Professor Bill Zahka, with a thick Boston accent, taught Economics. He was fun in class and made economics easy to understand.

Eugene Cloud was the Director of the MacMorland Center. Our Dining Facility, the Bookstore, and importantly, our mailboxes were in the Center. It was the Student Center, so we students often ran into Mr. Cloud. Master Sergeant Cloud was formidable was my first impression. He appeared stern and harsh, but I soon found out that he was friendly and helpful. He was a friend to Cadets and civilian students alike.

My major was Political Science with concentration in American Government. Dr. John Hopkirk was the Chair of the Department. He was very knowledgeable and informative. I learned a lot about Constitutional Law from him.

Dr. Joseph Chacko taught International Law. He had the greatest attitude and demeanor, a true gentleman. I answered one test question and his comment in the blue book was, "very interesting, though it did not answer the question!" He gave me half of the points for the question.

Dr. Martin Goldstein was an interesting professor. He argued against support for Israel in a class debate. His argument developed the reasons for supporting Israel, especially that it is a democracy amongst monarchies, and that it was in a strategic location in the Middle East. I found that technique interesting and used it when I taught Political Science courses for Southern New Hampshire University. He has written a number of books. I have read, *America's Foreign Policy: Drift or Decision.*

William Madison Rolofson taught a few of the political science courses I had. He was interesting and his classes were informative and enjoyable.

These are some of the faculty members who made impressions on me and added to my knowledge. I found that my college education was sound and on par with other college graduates. I went on to earn a Master of Public Administration from Golden Gate University and a Master of Science in International Relations from Troy University (I couldn't resist). I taught Political Science Courses for the University of Maryland Overseas Division when assigned in Italy and for Southern New Hampshire University Online. My Critical Thinking skill and ability to express my thoughts clearly and logically are grounded in what I learned at Pennsylvania Military College. They helped me succeed in my twenty-eight-year career in the Army and Army Reserve and my thirty-two year career in management for Northrop Grumman Corporation.

James H. VanSciver:
Girls

Not surprisingly, the major issue permeating through the minds of most members of the Class of 1972 (perhaps all classes) through their four years at Pennsylvania Military College was girls. Here were hundreds of testosterone-fueled young men restricted to a campus on which, during their freshman year, there were approximately a dozen members of the opposite sex open for competition. This could have easily erupted into some unfortunate situations if not for the clear-headed and strong-willed leadership inculcating a strong set of values on these late teenagers.

True, some of the classmates had girlfriends. But, for most, cleverness, persistence, and a good sense of humor were in high demand if one was to ensnare a date for a Saturday evening party. The college must have realized this, as strange social events called "mixers" were organized on a monthly basis. One must wonder what was going through the minds of the ladies as they boarded buses from neighboring places of higher learning and headed to the middle of Chester for an evening of polite and cordial courtship. Had they any idea what awaited them?

These opportunities greatly expanded the odds for the poor fellas seeking some female companionship and it was apparent shortly after the arrival of the busses and before the music began careening off the walls of MacMoreland Center that ambitions gave way to actions.

Did girls really prefer the swank look of Dress Charlie or were they mesmerized by all the shiny brass buttons on the formal regalia? Surely the hat and brightly polished shoes would be a hit!

The problem next became what to do with a female once you got one. There was little time until she had to return to her transportation and a trip back to her campus. Get her number? Give her your number? Make plans for a future rendezvous and find a way to make it work? There wasn't time to sneak her into one's dorm. That was risky business with a hefty penalty if caught and there were plenty of voyeurs ready to laugh as you were discovered.

A romantic stroll down the street to Fran and Ann's for a cheesesteak was all some fellas could put together. Nothing like the taste of cheddar cheese on the lips of a loved one. And there was always the presence of alcohol, that damning fluid that loosens one's values and opens the door to acts of malfeasance the like surely to embarrass one's parents.

Options improved as 1968 became 1969 and so on. As the civilian population at the college grew, so too, did the numbers of the opposite sex. Girls even had their own dorm! This presented those so willing with new opportunities for promoting oneself and gaining entry to the most important building on campus. Yes, the doors were locked but crafty individuals used their ingenuity to work around that illusionary obstacle. If you wanted a relationship, you had to work hard to get it.

There was another challenge. As the civilization population grew, so did the quantity of males on campus. The race was on!

Fortunately, many classmates met their mates during activities off campus or after graduation. Amazingly, many are still married to the ladies they met during college or shortly thereafter! Incredible!

William Troy:
Commandant and Military Science Departments

I had little interaction with the officers and sergeants of both the Commandant's office and the Military Science Department in my Rook year. Most of my direction came from the Cadet Cadre of Echo Company, the best company to which I was assigned. All of the Rook Cadets had World Military History taught by Major Carl Morin, but the Professor of Military Science, Colonel Ford Fuller, the Assistant Professors of Military Science, LTC Grayson Yetter, Captains Thomas Jones and Clarence Bell were figures I saw and maybe learned from in Military Science class. SFC Ragland was the ROTC Staff NCO and I probably saw him when we were issued supplies and weapons. First Sergeant Sisto M. Cicuzza was the most memorable of the group. He was a cigar chewing Non-Commissioned Officer of the old school. He was quick witted and full of comments. He did set an example. When we had rifle qualification at Ft Dix, NJ (I think) he was in charge of the Pits. We had to raise and lower the targets and mark hits. Although protected by a steep bank, it was like being under fire. 1SG Cicuzza would walk back and forth along the pit smoking his cigar and yelling at us to hurry up. He was very close to the area off limits, and I swear a few rounds hit the ground near him or just over his head on the other side of the pit. On Memorial Day, I was detailed to help take down the Garrison Flag. The flag is huge! As we were pulling it down, I asked 1SG Cicuzza, "Where did this flag come from?" His immediate answer was, "Top of the pole!" I learned never to ask questions like that again!

The Commandant of Cadets was Colonel Edward Cleary. The Assistant Commandant was Colonel Charles O'Hara. The Adjutant was Captain Charles Alter and Captain George Lynch was the Operations Officer. 1LT Gerald McAteer was the Counselor. I saw them during inspections and parades and during training, but really had no interaction with them. The purpose of the Military School is to train future officers, so almost all of our direction came from the Cadet Corporals, Sergeants, and Officers. The Brigade Commander and Staff ran everything.

In my sophomore year 1970, the Commandant and Professor of Military Science were one-in-the-same, Colonel Ford P. Fuller. It seemed much bigger. Now Major Lynch was essentially the Assistant Commandant. Captains Reasor, Pollak, and Arthur were on the staff. There was a slew of Non-Commissioned Officers. First Sergeant (1SG) Cicuzza was still there in Operations (S-3). Master Sergeant (MSG) Behney was the Adjutant. 1SG Hite was the S-4 (Supply), Staff Sergeant Poff (SSG) was the Supply Sergeant. Staff Sergeant. SSG Koense was the S-2 (Intelligence). 1SG Goodermuth was a Senior Instructor. Sergeant Major (SGM) Bugdon and Specialist 5th

Class (SP-5) Hindert were also assigned. I'm not sure if Sgt Bugdon was a Sergeant Major. I don't remember him at all.

The most memorable member of the Military Staff this year to me was Sergeant First Class (SFC) "Hurricane" Louis Price. He had been wounded in Vietnam near his hip and he carried the crushed bullet taken out of his leg in his wallet. He had a thick Southern accent and was really the epitome of what a Platoon Sergeant should be, although I didn't recognize that then. Once on active duty, I realized the example SFC Price set for we Cadets.

Lieutenant Colonel (LTC) Gerald T. Frey joined us that year as an Assistant Professor of Military Science. He will be more memorable next year and my senior year. He was an interesting instructor. I enjoyed his classes. He had been wounded in Vietnam and had lost his left leg from the knee down.

I find it a little more difficult to put together the Commandant and Military Staff for 1971. The Yearbook is devoid of information! I do know we had Colonel Ralph "Slow Ralph" Smith as the Professor of Military Science. Colonel Smith was called Slow Ralph because of how slowly he spoke. He had a deep Southern accent. I think LTC Frey took over as the Commandant. Major Lynch was still in the Commandants office. SSG Koense was still there. I'm pretty sure SFC Price was there. I'm not sure if Major Ronald Beckett and Captain Aaron joined us that year in the Military Science Department. Cpt. Aaron was an Armor Officer. I remember a story about Colonel Smith and Cpt. Aaron taking some of the Seniors to Liberty Park for horse racing. Cpt. Aaron thought he knew all about handicapping horses because he had been to the Kentucky Derby! Col. Smith bet on horses because of their color or tail or mane. Cpt. Aaron bet by handicapping. Col. Smith always won! Again, most of the direction for the Corps came through the Cadet command structure.

My senior year, 1972, I had more dealings with the Military Staff and Commandant. I was a Cadet Captain commanding C Company. Lieutenant Colonel Alden W. Jahnke, Class of 1951, became the Professor of Military Science. Affectionately known as, "Big Al" because of his size was an impressive soldier. He was an Engineer and a combat veteran. LTC Frey was the Commandant. Sadly, this was to be the last year of the Cadet Corps and the two of them had to manage that transition. Thankfully, Widener University embraced the Reserve Officers Training Corps (ROTC) and is the Headquarters for the Dauntless Battalion, a name harkening back to the days of the Cadet Corps. The Dauntless Battalion is a march written by John Phillip Sousa in 1922 dedicated to the Corps of Cadets and Staff of Pennsylvania Military College.

Major Ron Beckett was an Infantry officer who had served a couple of tours in Vietnam. He had commanded a company that deployed in helicopters before the Air Cavalry influx. He had been a District Advisor also and had many interesting stories and perspectives on the war in Vietnam. When we were choosing our military schools and duty assignments, he advised me to select training like the Motor Officer's Course rather than Airborne and Ranger School. My Basic Branch was Transportation Corps. I did. I kind of regretted that choice then, but in the long run my career as a logistician was benefitted more by the Motor Officers Course. I commanded a Medium Truck Company on active duty.

Captain Aaron had graduating seniors over to his house one evening for dinner. He had a dog and we started to give the dog beer surreptitiously. The dog eventually staggered around and collapsed, fell asleep, and started snoring. We all got a good laugh over that. LTC Frey was disliked by many of the Cadets, and it didn't help that the Corps was ending. In the winter we had a large snowball fight, and someone sculpted a life size "Snow Frey" complete with a wooden leg! That should be the subject of a different story from another Cadet.

I will state that the Corps, inclusive of the Military Science and Commandant Staff, prepared me well to be an officer in the US Army. I did not report to active duty until September 1972. I was sent directly to my duty station at Fort Hood, Texas. Usually, an officer first reports to a training center for an Officer Basic Course. I knew how to be an Officer. I was scheduled to go to Officer Basic in November 1972. In the meantime, I became a Platoon Leader, 3rd Platoon, B Company, 66th Armor, 2nd Armored Division. As a Regular Army Officer I was detailed to Armor Branch for one year before going to my Basic Branch of Transportation. My Pennsylvania Military College training put me in good stead to lead my Platoon through Field Training and Tank Gunnery before I went off to Armor Officer Basic at Fort Knox, Kentucky.

At no time did I feel inferior to any other officer, whether they had graduated from the Military Academy, a Military College, or ROTC. PMC prepared me well!

Gary Sisco:
Significance

Let me ask you, what did you experience in your time at Pennsylvania Military College that you regard as a lifelong takeaway, as something of importance, as a compass for your actions? When Bill Speer first asked me to write up a short piece on the experience of attending PMC, I thought that it would be fairly simple. As I started to think about those four years that I had spent many years ago, I came to realize that there is no simple, homogeneous answer. Being a member of the Corps of Cadets was both a communal and an individualistic experience, but it is often through the communal that strength and endurance grows in the individual.

Perhaps I should consider the very fact that I managed to graduate with a college degree as my most significant achievement of attending PMC. I was no scholar then and I am no scholar now. I do have some regrets concerning my scholastic efforts, but I really cannot complain too much. No, the activity that I worked the hardest for, the thing that pulled and pushed and drove me was the PMC Ranger Platoon. I decided early in my Rook year that I wanted to see if I could earn that round pin R that I saw a limited number of upperclassmen wearing on their shirts. I knew that I was going into the Army. I knew that our country was at war at that time, and I knew that there was a good possibility that I would be responsible for the lives of others. I wanted to prepare myself the best that I could for that task. The Ranger Platoon was not open to Rooks. I would have to wait until my 2nd year to try to join.

When I returned to school in the Fall of 1969, I was a private in Bravo Company. Tom Regeness was the Ranger Platoon leader and the previous year he had been a cadre Sergeant in my Rook Company. A number of fellow classmates from my Rook company also elected to try out for the Ranger Platoon. Each day, Monday through Thursday, Bill Troy, Pat Verrastro, Ed Reed, Xavier Wauters and myself, along with about twenty other 2nd year cadets would assemble for training. There were also about fifteen 3rd year cadets who had earned their positions as PMC Rangers the prior year. Regeness had broken us up into three/four squads. I remember Russ Howald, Bruce Hotter, and Kevin McHale, all 3rd year men being squad leaders. Bill Troy and I were placed in McHale's squad.

We did a lot of running, a lot of PT, and we worked on learning small unit tactics. We learned the importance of having a solid mission statement, of articulating the action plan to all members of the group, and of having an after-action critique to examine strengths and weaknesses to better perform in the future. There was a period when our runs were getting a little long. Thirteen miles doing the airborne shuffle in combat boots was about the longest run that I remember. When we ran, we sang cadence. Looking back on it, some of what we sang would probably not be considered politically correct today.

We learned to rappel and practiced that skill off small cliffs, school buildings and, not exactly legally, off of a train trestle down by Swarthmore. We learned to use ropes to cross creeks and/or just forded them. We learned how to set and deploy ambushes, to conduct recon patrols, and utilize fire and movement. I learned the value of teamwork and the enhanced strength of an organized and inspired group. I learned about friendship and about leadership. I learned about endurance and about the importance of perseverance. It was a year in which I learned many things that I like to think have served me well in the various roles I have since found myself in. It was in the Spring of 1970 that the candidates for the PMC Ranger Platoon stood at attention on the parade field and received our small round pin with an R. We were now PMC Rangers and to me that was significant.

In my 3rd year at PMC, I returned to the Ranger Platoon as a squad leader, but that is another story with another cast of characters for another time.

Gary Sisco

Disclaimer: If anyone reading the above article feels that I have strayed from the facts, forgotten to mention significant individuals, or have left out pertinent information, I ask you to please remember one thing—I'm old, leave me alone!

William J. Troy:
The Kidnapping of Phil Lewis

When we first arrived at Pennsylvania Military College there were Blue Laws on the books in Pennsylvania. Bars had to be, if I remember correctly, two miles from campus. That changed and the Blue Laws were lifted, again if I remember correctly, our junior year 1971. By our senior year, there was a beer hall on campus in the basement of Howell Hall called the Ratskeller. There was a good bar off campus at 1601 Providence Avenue about a block away from the Wolfgram Library. Many an evening the gravitational pull of Walios would suck in students who otherwise would have gone to the library.

Phil Lewis was not one of those who was sucked into Walios. Phil was an exemplary cadet, outstanding military bearing, and strong academic prowess. On top of all that, he was and still is a nice guy. He went on to Medical School at Johns Hopkins University and became a doctor. He had no time for the frivolity of a diversion to Walios. He went to the Wolfgram Library almost every night to study.

One evening a number of us less studious cadets in civilian clothes were on our way to Walios—it had great meat pies, not to mention beer! Chuck Ketchel, Bob Sabochik, Bob Frutchey, and I saw Phil walking to the library carrying a number of books. We decided collectively to grab Phil by the arms and take him to Walios with us. We hurried up alongside Phil and grabbed him and hauled him to Walios. We had our beers and meat pies, and he drank water, but he sat there and enjoyed our company and us his. We did let him escape and finish his evening at the library after an hour or so. It was his first experience in Walios, and I believe his last. He could now leave college having had a well-rounded social experience.

Stories and Vignettes from PMC

James H. VanSciver:
Contradictions and Confrontations

For those of us in the Class of 1972 attending Pennsylvania Military College, there was one situation that stretched the limitations of the Corps to the fullest. That was pledging and being accepted into a fraternity, particularly the most rambunctious and perhaps notorious on campus, Tau Kappa Epsilon.

The dichotomy of philosophies could not have been more profound. From the military perspective, life was about obeying rules, order, and self-discipline. The behavior of the TKE fraters demonstrated anything but. The rule of the day was self-indulgence, playing outside the rules, and not even the smallest hint of discipline.

TKE cadets were constantly being pulled by the edicts of the Corps and the enlightenment of the fraternity. From formations to weekend parties; from late nights at the house to early morning reveille; from sharply pressed uniforms to worn out civies, it appeared that every choice was a contradiction or a confrontation. It took equal parts courage, ingenuity, and evaluation to maintain the balance of a highly regarded cadet and a fun-loving frater.

We were able to pull this off largely because of our intense loyalty to the Corps and our unyielding dedication to TKE. While it would be difficult to sort those commitments into a hierarchy, we were sufficiently alert to understand when pushing the bounds of one to satisfy the requirements of the other would compromise our standing in both.

While some might have remembered this as an extremely stressful period in our lives, we celebrate the challenges and fondly reminisce of the regular push and pull of this dynamic at each homecoming. True, some of the antics of the fraternity life resulted in our spending more than a little time on the blacktop behind MacMoreland Center with a rifle on our shoulder and an excessive indulgence at the expense of the fraternity would result in unfavorable ramifications at the TKE house.

More than a few of these instances involved two triggers, girls and booze. For girls, it was always how to get them, what to do with them once you got them, and how to cover up anything that your parents might not be proud of learning that you did. It is well known that alcohol has a way of compromising one's values and injecting too much of it into the two-legged cocktail that is your person results in behavior that afterwards is always deemed regrettable. Further, mixing girls and alcohol will always bring out the worst in you, but the absolute best stories for the week following, even if they may have to be enhanced by a small dose of hyperbole.

Some fifty years later, it is with fondness and regret that these memories pass through our minds. Fondness because of the joy we had in creating and recalling them and regret at the realization that those opportunities are presently beyond our grasp.

Bob Schneider:
Jim Vandever's Promotion to Platoon Leader

Everyone remembers Jimmy—I believe he set the record for walking the most tours. (Jimmy played on the PMC football team offensive line with Joe Fields (NY Jets All-Pro) and Billy "White Shoes" Johnson (College Football Hall of Fame and Houston Oilers Pro. My wife had a crush on him.)

Jimmy and I were battery commanders in the 42nd Artillery Group in Giessen Germany (1975—1978) and over beers one night at the officer's club (he, of course, was always a hit at the O Club) we were laughing about our days at PMC. I asked him if he knew the story of how he had been promoted to freshmen company platoon leader. He said no. (We, of course, had to discuss old crazy peg legged Lt Col Frey—I think the man lost more than his leg in Vietnam.)

Lt Col Frey was having a Corps officer staff meeting in his office and one of the subjects was the need for a new platoon leader in the freshman company. Jimmy was a 3-year private and wasn't one of Frye's favorite cadets. Lt Col Frey got a few recommendations and when he got to me I immediately recommended Jimmy for the position. If Lt Col Frye had had two legs, he probably would have jumped across the table and choked me. He said in his unique way of expressing himself in the English language what he thought of my recommendation. After some further discussion, he finally relented and gave Jimmy the job and the stripes. I remember to this day what he said, "I'll give that #@$&* the job, but if he screws up, I'm taking his stripes and yours."

Jimmy did a great job, and he was also a superb battery commander in Germany. He is missed (Jimmy not Lt Col Frey) Note: We all knew Frey was out of touch with reality—I think he came to PMC because he thought he could mold us into a real fighting machine—I think we just let him be him so we could enjoy the humor and the crazy memories 50 years later.

Do you remember—one of our classmates invented a way to lock our room doors using a bent coat hanger. My wife (girlfriend then) was staying on campus over a holiday my senior year for Jack Andreas' wedding and I used that invention so that Frey couldn't get into my room when we were there. It really worked because he came to the door, tried his key, and commenced to say every curse word available out of frustration.

James H. VanSciver:
The Evolution of the Alumni Experience

Few experiences in life have a definitive and known ending. We may count the days until a job interview, review the calendar in preparation for our upcoming nuptials, or keep track of the time until our vacations begin. But, for the most part, our lives simply evolve around routine and circumstance. Not so for the four years of undergraduate study that were our Class of 1972's time at Pennsylvania Military College.

We knew the day, date, year, and place of graduation the moment we entered the school but, for most of us, that information was lost in a whirlwind of activities, classes, extra-curricular programs, military training, and the like. At once, it seemed like an eternity and an ephemerality. In the end, some classmates found themselves shocked by how little time they had left to qualify to walk across the stage, to submit that final paper, or to complete that last project. Others had been checking off milestones for months, the extant academic requirements, the ultimate formation, which concluding class, the decisive exam, the last practice, and the career ending game.

Then came that final act in the Class of 1972's four years. With jubilation and ceremony, each member participated in the closing undertaking of his career at Pennsylvania Military College and was catapulted into the world as an educated individual.

What followed was an interesting evolutionary development that may be described in terms of generalities but not absolutes, the alumni experience. While not all classmates participated in exactly the same way, the cohort that has come to be known as the Class of 1972 did exhibit some familiar and predicable behaviors.

The initial phase was very similar for most classmates. They returned to celebrate homecoming for about five years, brought their wives, and participated in the university sponsored and developed programming, broom drills, meetings, tailgating, football games, visitations to the PMC Museum, browsing through the bookstore, walking the campus to inspect new construction, and so forth.

Again, in a general sense, the next phase saw most wives no longer participating and leaving their husbands to sporadically attend the homecoming activities, renew friendships, and begin to formulate smaller groups identified by academic focus, fraternity allegiance, sports team, or some combination thereof. Participation in university sponsored activity gave way to group formulated programming which may best be described as a collection of rooms at a designated hotel with an adjoining room in which a collection of a dozen or more alumni spent the time not involved in selected activities engaged in consuming food and drink and reflecting on their college-day activities. During this time, the football hits became more ferocious, the stories of activities with members of the opposite sex peppered with hyperbole, and the classes that were conquered more taxing. Small wonder why nearly all wives are tired of this blabber. But these activities served to strengthen the bonds between participating classmates with more communication taking place during the rest of the year becoming more frequent.

The following phase is an adaptation of the middle one. Classmates had mourned and celebrated the passing of classmates through the years, and, during this period, which is becoming more common. Another feature that takes place at this juncture is a function that time has on the brain. Classmates actually remember experiences that really never took place! Through debate and conversation, they have the ability to create an entirely different occurrence than that which took place from 1968 through 1972.

Finally, the 50th reunion took place, and a committee of classmates formulated a robust and stimulating itinerary designed to provide comfort and support for the members of the Class of 1972 and their wives. Celebration, fellowship, and remembrance were the themes of the weekend as the alumni gathered to honor their time at Pennsylvania Military College and the relationships they had established, nurtured, and sustained.

William Troy:
100th Night

One event that Seniors looked forward to was 100th Night! This signified that only 100 days remained until graduation! On February 9, 1972, we seniors moved out to celebrate! Gary Sisco had a car and four of us decided to join him on a trip to the new Ponderosa Bar in Essington if I remember correctly. Bob Frutchey, Angel Monk Rivera, Tony Tamburello, and I accompanied Gary to the Pondo! We celebrated wholeheartedly.

Returning to campus on the early morning of Friday, 10 February 1972, our celebration came to an abrupt halt. We came off I-95 a little too fast and failed to make the turn on Chestnut Street. The car slid sideways on to the southern side of the overpass. Gary and Bob were hurt badly and were taken to Crozer-Chester Medical Center and put in intensive care. Monk, Tony, and I ended up in the Campus infirmary. We were released Saturday. Bob and Gary recovered and returned to campus after a stay in the hospital. We were very lucky!

Bob Schneider:
Reporting for Active Duty B

God Bless president Nixon (I didn't like him but) and in no way am I forgetting the immense sacrifices of several PMC graduates or all the other vets who served in Vietnam. On the day of commissioning, I was signing my paperwork to finalize my orders for reporting for active duty. I had originally asked for an October report date but during the signing I asked the Sgt Major if I could change my reporting date. Carol and I were getting married in October. He said yes after I explained the reason. He suggested January 1973—I said that sounded great. Remember Nixon signed the peace accord in November 1972. So instead of heading to Nam with the October Field Artillery basic course graduates and being a FO in the jungle, I ended up in Fort Dix pushing the first troops in the NEW all-volunteer Army. I honestly believe it was a God thing.

James H. VanSciver:
Leadership and Personality

Nearly three-quarters of a century in the making, I am what I am at this moment as a result of all of the experiences I have collected. A huge foundation for that took place over fifty years ago at Pennsylvania Military College. As my career has constantly flowed between the impact of leadership and personality, it was interesting to look back at some of the influences I received as a student in the Class of 1972 at Pennsylvania Military College. Only, this time, I'm going to look outside the realm of the military experience.

Through watching, reading, listening, and experiencing, I've learned a lot about leadership through the years. It is important; it can be lonely; it can be exhausting, and it can be fun and helpful. There is positional leadership and there is personal leadership. Those who have both are inclined to be the most successful. Leadership must be situational, with those who are most effective being capable of determining their followers' readiness level in the context of a given situation, being able to consider a vast array of leadership behaviors, and adroit at implementing the one deemed most appropriate.

From where, outside the marching, formations, and inspections, did this inspiration come for me? Extricating some exactness from the vast array of happenings over a four-year tenure was not an easy task, but the following five individuals, in no particular order, surfaced from my memory.

George Hansell was a busy man. He was the athletic director of the college, with schedules, games, fundraising, and all of the other responsibilities that go with that position pulling at his every resource. He was also the one to whom I reported for my work-study experience. Always charming and never rushed, he taught me that I was not the interruption of his work; I was the purpose of it. That lesson I carried with me through my entire career.

Few people probably ever noticed him, but I did. Smoker was omnipresent at football games and sometimes at practice. Always adorned in a coat and tie with a half smoked, half chewed cigar protruding from his mouth, he just stood there and watched. A fixture cemented in my memory, I think about devotion and commitment when his image comes to mind. Also, if you ever did talk with him, which I did, you found a mountain of information about Pennsylvania Military College football for the past decades.

Art was an African-American custodian that I seemed to encounter several times every day. Whether I walked to or from classes, going to a lunchtime meal at MacMoreland Center, or finding my way to another activity on campus, he always seemed to be there. Each time I happily yelled at him, "Yo Art!" His rejoinder was always the same, "Won't be long now." His likeable disposition and engaging smile taught me how to treat people in every encounter I had.

Eugene Sparrow was my sociology professor. Presenting as Morgan Freeman in the movie *Stand by Me*, he was direct when necessary, accommodating when appropriate, and always caring. Using the book, *Talley's Corner*, he led us through deep and rich conversations about society, culture, and life. He was a master of both substance and style, a message I will never forget.

Situations can develop quickly in a football game. Talented coaches have the ability to slow the game down in order to dictate their vision and priorities in given conditions. This was the forte of head football coach Bill Manlove. From him, I learned to never let a situation become more important than it deserved to be, that keeping emotion at arm's length even during the most heated moments, is a cornerstone to success, and to always treat people as if they were family. What a role model for life!

A pitcher experiencing some challenges on the mound expects a visit from his coach to be a friendly and helpful encounter. Not so with head baseball coach Harry Miller. He used a fiery and direct approach during such encounters which motivated his pitching staff to do anything and everything to avoid having them. Harry never told us he cared about us; but he showed us. I've often, in schooling teachers and graduate students, said, "If the local police came into your school and arrested you for caring, could they get enough evidence to get a conviction?" That was Harry's impact on me. Not only was he an astute baseball tactician, but he was also a players' coach. I won't ever forget him.

I believe, from time to time, it is right to reflect on those who were most impactful on our lives and why they were so. These five individuals, from the civilian side of my Pennsylvania Military College years, have left an indelible impression on me and how I view the world. My deepest thanks and appreciation go to each of them, as they probably didn't even know they were touching me.

Bob Schneider:
Mari Gras and Racism (March 1972)

As band members, we had all heard about the PMC band playing in the Rex Parade in 1968 at Mardi Gras in New Orleans. We contacted Mardi Gras and got an invite and the PMC financing for our return trip. We would be the lead band in the Rex parade. We were all really excited and the trip by bus was very arduous (the roads through the south were not the roads we enjoy today). We stayed on a small Navy ship in the harbor and of course had some adventures in the city before and after the parade.

I had been raised in a small farming community in New Jersey. This was during the time where racial issues, like antiwar issues, were appearing everywhere, BUT my hometown hadn't really taken heed to the issues. New Orleans and the parade director opened my eyes to these issues very quickly. When we got to New Orleans, I had to go to a meeting at a lawyer's office to discuss the logistics of the parade. I remember the room vividly and as the meeting came to an end, he asked us how many members were in our group (there was a formal dinner dance in a downtown location that evening), how many "black" members we had, and then distributed tickets to the parade ball for that evening (minus a ticket for our "black member"). I was shocked—I had never experienced such deep prejudice before. I immediately handed back the tickets and informed him that we would not be attending—"If all members couldn't attend, then none of us would attend." I've been proud of that stance for 50 years. That little incident taught me a lot and made me very aware of the issues America has faced over the years.

William Troy:
Field Training

I was sitting on the edge of my foxhole looking out over a snow-covered S72 field and woods in beautiful Indiantown Gap Military Reservation (IGMR) eating my delicious C-Ration meal of Beans W/ Meat Balls in Tomato Sauce B-2 Unit cold, thinking to myself, "Gee I love this stuff!" We were on a Field Training Exercise. We weren't allowed to light fires to cook our delicious C-Rations because it might alert the enemy to our location. C-Rations were great! You got a meal, crackers, a dessert, chewing gum, matches, cigarettes. Everything you needed in life. I didn't smoke, so the cigarettes were a great trading item. I could trade them for another dessert or sometimes another meal. But this isn't about C-Rations. This is about the field training we received as Cadets.

The biggest field training I remember as a Rook was rifle qualification, I think it was on Fort Dix, New Jersey. We spent a lot of time on the rifle range qualifying with our M-1 rifles. The hardest part was working in the pits. In the pits there were two of us who were responsible for pulling down the target and marking hits and patching the holes then lifting the target back up for the next round of shooting. We were constantly pushed to speed up. It was hard work. Cleaning our weapons was the next hardest thing. We had to pass a Cadre inspection, then another inspection by the Army Supply Sergeant or one of the other NCO's.

We learned about tactics in our Military Science Classes taught by Captains from the ROTC Staff. We practiced tactics led by our Cadet leaders. Corporals and Sergeants led their Fire Teams and Squads respectively and Lieutenants led their Platoons, Captains their Companies. We usually started at the Fire Team level. Because we all were to become leaders, all of us were given opportunities to lead at each level. As Rooks though, we were usually being led.

I remember practicing squad tactical formations in Washington Park off Melrose. There were some woods, and we were able to practice movements through the woods. This was rudimentary training, repetitious to learn how a squad was organized and led, the basics. It was after our Rook year that we did more.

I joined the Ranger Platoon. We had additional physical training and tactical training. We rappelled in many different places, even within the campus. Hanna Hall is where the Rooks lived, and I was on the third floor looking out over I-95 and the Delaware river. On that side of Hanna Hall the drop is four levels to the parking lot. One day Rangers led by Sergeant Tom Regeness and Sergeant Dan Murphy commandeered Rook Bill Speer's room for rappelling.

The desks were moved away from the windows and the ropes tied off to the posts of the bunk beds. They began to rappel. That is where I first rappelled! Another time we went over to Kirkbride Hall. It has a large pillar structure over the entrance. It is three stories and we gained access through a window and rappelled out over the entrance. I don't think we got in trouble for those incidents. Later Bill Speer's room was used a few times!

Another location that we travelled to rappel was a train trestle in Swarthmore (I think). We would climb up the legs of the trestle to reach the top. The drop was probably 70-100 feet. It was an active track and often we would be on a rope when a train crossed. One could feel the vibrations on the rope. There was another cliff, and I don't remember where it was that we went to once. While arriving we witnessed a man on rappel push off from the cliff face and have his line severe about ten feet down. He fell about 50-60 feet and landed in some trees, breaking branches, then landing on brush instead of the rocks at the bottom. He survived. Paramedics arrived and he was carried off. The trees broke his fall enough and kept him from the rocks. He was using hemp line instead of nylon and his line was frayed in a few places below where it severed. We practiced safety first and never had any accidents. When I attended ROTC Summer Camp, the rappelling tower was not an issue for me nor was the slide for life, thanks to the Ranger training!

The Ranger Platoon travelled by bus to Fort Pickett, Virginia for a Ranger competition. Major Morin accompanied us. We conducted patrolling, ambushes, land navigation, perimeter defense, and assaulting positions. I remember we navigated in darkness through a dense forest with many thorn bushes and silently approached our objective. It was a bivouac site of another unit. We could see a number of men sitting around a fire. Our two squads maneuvered into attack positions and on a signal began firing our M-16's and M-60's, charging out of the forest yelling at the top of our lungs. My most vivid memory was that of Boris Matisziw firing the M-60 machinegun from his hip, bandoliers of M-60 rounds crossing his chest as he charged towards the fire and the collection of enemies. Needless to say, our assault was successful. I know Major Morin enjoyed it. He was very complimentary.

I returned to Fort Pickett much later as a Major in a Reserve Support Command Headquarters for a couple of Command Post Exercises. I always remembered our Ranger assault on those occasions, but I could never locate the site of our attack. It was a great experience.

What I learned about tactics and field training as a cadet and as a Ranger in the Cadet Corps served me well in the Army. The lessons taught by upper class leaders like Tom Regeness, Dan Murphy, Russ Howald, Kevin McHale, Rich Mulhern, and others stayed with me and helped me lead the Platoons, Company, and Battalion I commanded as well as when I taught the Transportation Officer Basic Course.

William Speer:
Snow Frey

My senior year, we had something called the January Program, basically an independent study month. I'm not sure who came up with the idea, but I liked it. I was working on my project in my room when I heard LTC Frey come storming into the hallway demanding to see the highest-ranking cadet officer on campus (which very well could have been me at that moment). I turned off my lights, locked the door (only Rooks had to keep the key in their door) and just sat there until he left. The story has been told elsewhere here but he was looking for cadets to tear down the "Snow Frey" with entrenching tools. He found some Rooks and someone to supervise. The rest is history.

Paul S. Lewis:
Firing Squad at the Opera

A visiting theater group came to PMC in my senior year to perform the opera Tosca. A dramatic scene involved a firing squad executing the hero. The group arranged with PMC to provide several cadets with rifles to perform the deed. My role as the Duty Officer that day was just to ensure that the rifles made it back into the arms room without incident. In exchange for this duty, I got to watch the production from the wings of the theater in Alumni Auditorium.

The firing squad was made up of a 2nd Classman leader and two or three 3rd Classmen equipped with M-14 rifles and blank rounds. Their Class A uniforms were slightly modified to look more Napoleonic. The script called for the squad leader (David Neimeyer, I recall) to give the commands to the riflemen to fire one volley, being careful not to aim directly at the actor so he wouldn't be hit by the hot gases emitted by the blank rounds. The only problem with this script—nobody anticipated how loud the blanks would sound inside the theater! The firing squad performed flawlessly, but the shots were so loud that people in the audience jumped, put their hands to their ears to stop the ringing, and complained to their seatmates, not that they could hear anything for a few moments.

If the group were to do a second show, I bet they would make one change: one rifle fired outside the building at an open door would have been sufficient. But this was a one-time production. The theater group folded their tent and left town. The rifles were safely returned to the arms room; my duty was completed.

Maris Eshleman:
NOLA (New Orleans, Louisiana)

One of the best memories from PMC was our band trip to New Orleans to lead the Mardi Gras Rex Parade in February of 1972. It was our senior year, but I believe for all of us in the band it was the highlight of our time at PMC.

I began playing trombone very early in school. I don't remember what year it was but throughout elementary, middle, and high school I played in bands and orchestras with some success. So, when I got accepted at PMC it was only natural that I would apply for a band scholarship.

At PMC, the Band was a separate and distinct organization within the Corps of Cadets. We were Headquarters Company. We had our own barracks; we lived together and spent a lot of time together. We came back early and began practicing before the Corps returned from summer break because we usually had a full schedule of activities in the Fall.

Besides the football games, we did parades. Lots of parades. We did parades for the football games, community parades, military parades and often performed for the Corps going to mess. When I went home for Thanksgiving break my first year, I remember on Thanksgiving morning my father calling me to get up and watch the parades. I just rolled over in bed and said I've been in enough parades. I don't need to watch any.

During our four years in the band, we had heard about the PMC Band performing in Mardi Gras some years before and there was always the rumor that we were going again. But we never did, even though we were invited.

Then sometime during the Fall of 1971, it was announced that we would be going to Mardi Gras. Everyone was stoked. Then we got the news that we would have a Greyhound bus take us down and back. At that point we were just really happy to be going. In a later conversation that I had with Clarence Moll, the President of PMC Colleges, he told me that Fitz Dixon, the Chairman of the Board, had donated the money for the bus. He also told me that Dixon had offered to charter a plane to fly us down, but Moll persuaded him not to so that it wouldn't reduce the money he was otherwise giving to the College. They agreed we could go by bus. Through the Military Department it was arranged that we could stay on a Naval Amphibious Assault Ship at the New Orleans Naval Base, but for meals we were basically on our own although I do believe we got breakfast on the ship.

We left PMC early on the Sunday morning before Mardi Gras under cold gray skies and traveled all night and arrived at New Orleans Monday morning after the all-night ride, stopping in the big cities along the way. We stopped in Richmond, Raleigh, Atlanta, Montgomery, and then on into New Orleans. For most of us, it was our first exposure to inner city bus stops and the activity that went on around them.

I don't remember the exact itinerary, but I know we had some free time when we all visited the Quarter, we returned for a rehearsal, and then went back down to the Quarter. When we got to the ship, we were given a security briefing about NOLA. In fact, when we arrived, another band was leaving because several of their students had been assaulted and robbed. Crime in NOLA has always been an issue.

New Orleans in 1972 was all it was purported to be. We visited all the high points, there were women on the balconies soliciting for entertainment, clubs, strip-bars, female impersonator bars, and all sorts of entertainment was everywhere. For guys that had been in a military college for a while, it was a very target rich environment of opportunities. One junior member of the Band had met someone and arranged for a later rendezvous. Several of us went with him to see this female Goddess. She arrived at the corner, and they walked off. A cop on the corner was laughing and just made a comment that he thinks he has a girl. About a block down the street, they stopped by a female impersonator club, and 'she' told him that's where 'she' works. He caught up to us quickly.

The next morning we were bussed to the point of beginning for the parade. I don't recall exactly but it was somewhere down in the Garden District. During Mardi Gras in NOLA there are lots of parades, but the Rex Parade is the longest and goes until midnight and features the King of Mardi Gras. We were very pleased and excited to be leading the parade.

The parade stepped off pretty much on time, but we had frequent stops. The parade route was lined with throngs of partiers celebrating Mardi Gras and each time we stopped, people from the crowd would penetrate our ranks offering us beer or wine to drink. Most of us refused, being disciplined and all.

The parade wound around the City for about five miles and the bus picked us up and took us back to the ship where we quickly got out of our uniforms and headed back to the annual pre-Lenten celebration. Truly, a lifetime event. We partied way into the night and made our way back to the Ship. The bus left early the next morning to take us back to the real world.

We left warm and fun New Orleans and returned back to cold Chester and back to school. For two days though, that seemed like weeks, we experienced the thrill of a lifetime. I've been to NOLA many times since over the decades and it is nothing like it was then. I'm glad we got to see it before it really grew up.

John Semertzides (published in The Brigadier, March 1970):
Rangers at Camp Pickett

On the morning of 7 March, the Ranger Platoon went on a field exercise at Camp Pickett, Virginia. The Rangers were to have been trained in various combat practices by members of the Special Forces. Lt. Regeness was the platoon leader, Sgt Howald served as XO and squad leader, and Sgts Hotter and McHale were squad leaders.

The platoon left by bus at 0800 hours Friday and arrived at Camp Pickett at 1330 hours. Trucks sent by the Special Forces picked up the Rangers and took them into the training area. The Rangers completed setting up the base camp and security by 1600 hours. Recon patrols were sent out to establish their exact location and the location of an ammunition cache. The Rangers' mission was to help the S.F. demolitions men blow up a wooden truss bridge, the Sweeney Road Bridge, by 0500 hours Sunday.

Some S.F. jumped in to help the Rangers and set up their base camp next to the Rangers. The Rangers found that they were only a few hundred meters from their objective. The Rangers set up an O.P.

overlooking the bridge, then pulled out to a safer location. The new base camp was completed at approximately 1200 hours Saturday. The S.F. then gave the Rangers classes on ambushes, patrolling, demolitions, and personal hygiene.

At 1500 hours, the aggressors attacked the Ranger base camp, and made a sizeable penetration. However, it was only a small force and after a brief battle, the aggressors were driven out. Two of the aggressors were captured and quickly released. It was then decided to find a safer base camp and the group quickly moved out to occupy a new area. After security had been set up in the new camp, plans were laid to attack and destroy the Sweeney Road Bridge. The attack on the Sweeney Bridge was supposed to be synchronized with a larger attack made by other schools on the Kennedy Bridge.

The plan called for McHale, Mulhern, Gross, Tinklepaugh, and others to charge across the Sweeney Bridge. Simultaneously, the main body of Rangers would attack across the highway in support of the first attack. The S.F. demolitions men would then move in and set the charges. The Rangers would then retreat by sections and the bridge would be blown.

However, the Kennedy Bridge was attacked an hour early and the aggressor guards at the Sweeney Bridge were withdrawn to meet this attack. Consequently, the Rangers were able to blow the Sweeney Bridge without opposition. The attack on the Kennedy Bridge was repelled. After withdrawing to their base camp, PMC's victorious Rangers hiked to the highway, were trucked to their point of departure, and boarded their bus for P.M.C.

James H. VanSciver:
Where is He Now?

He was as ubiquitous as leaves blowing in late fall. He was everywhere and nowhere...like an apparition. He would jump out from behind a hedge, run at you from an alley, or be riding on the rear bumper of a slow-moving car making its way through the campus. In a heartbeat, he was gone. You never knew when he would again appear.

He was "The Kid" from the 1990 Warren Beatty movie *Dick Tracy*. Annoying and persistent, he was always warming up to you. He was the epitome of the "Chester Urchin." For some reason, he had a propensity for football players and TKEs. Many were one in the same. We only were aware of his first name, Jimmy. He was seven or eight, maybe nine years old. Where he lived was another unknown. And, why his parents allowed him to roam the campus at all hours of the day befuddled all of us. It seemed like going to school was not an item high on his agenda.

His was a one-word vocabulary and he screamed it constantly. "Snack!" was his calling card. We were not sure if someone somewhere offered him a tidbit of a cracker or a half of a sandwich but, whenever he saw you, the same word came pouring from his mouth. Unfortunately, in the beginning, without knowing it, we reinforced this dependency on us as we saw him kind of as a poor Oliver Twist and felt sorry for him. With this he advantaged himself.

He was so omnipresent that we came up with a new name for him, Jimmy Snacker. When we saw him coming, we began yelling, "Snacks!" Upon reflection, it is difficult to understand how college-engaged teenagers would behave in such a way, but such were the times. So routine were his appearances that he became sort of a mascot for a group of us. It was difficult to not feel something for him with his dirty clothes and constant outstretched hand.

It has now been over fifty years since the word, "Snack" echoed in my brain. Jimmy is now in his late fifties or, if we misjudged his age, his early sixties. I wonder what he's doing. I have this image of him driving a Lance truck and stocking shelves in grocery stores or filling vending machines in mom-and-pop shops. I wonder if he announces his arrival by yelling, "Snacks!"

Maris Eshleman:
Concerts

During our time at PMC, concerts and major entertainment was coordinated by a student group called the Social Activities Committee, composed of civilian students from Penn Morton and Cadets. The group was provided an annual budget by PMC Colleges for entertainment and they selected the groups to perform and coordinated the activities. Usually concerts. MSG (Ret) Mr. Eugene Cloud who was the Director of the MacMorland Student Center was our adviser and had legal authority for the college to enter into contracts for the entertainment. I was on the Committee for three years.

At the beginning of each school year, we were given a list of entertainers that were in our price range. PMC at that time was not a large college, so our budget was limited, thus the groups we could afford was limited. The available groups were usually well-known but not the big names of the day. After reviewing the list, we would select a list of acts that we wanted to book for which dates and Mr. Cloud would contact our booking agency and try to arrange them. Most of the time they were available because they weren't the groups in high demand. We worked through the well-known William Morris agency for talent booking and since most of the concert attendees were students, we raised very little revenue from these concerts, despite publicity.

When the date came for the event, we would arrange accommodations for them and often they required food and drinks in their dressing room. We would enclose an area from public access as many times in addition to eating and drinking they would do drugs before performing and we kept everyone out of the area. At the appropriate time, we would usher them on and off the stage. We often heard comments from the entertainers that wouldn't be repeated. For example, in spring of 1971, Billy Preston refused to go back on to play any encore numbers because he didn't feel the audience "appreciated" him.

My senior year at PMC I was the Chairman of the Social Affairs Committee. Our first performance was scheduled for homecoming weekend in October. We had scheduled a joint concert with John Denver and Mary Travers.

John Denver was a well-known folk-rock singer in the 1960's and 70's who was known from several groups he performed with and many songs he had written and other artists had performed. A song he wrote and made popular was "Country Roads" and a song he wrote that was made popular by his co-star's group was "Leaving on a Jet Plane." Mary Travers was the Mary of the famous folk-rock trio, Peter, Paul & Mary who broke up in 1971 and each went on to individual careers, although they weren't extensive. The two performers were each successful on their own and when they came up as a possible concert, the Committee very quickly jumped on the chance.

This concert was scheduled for the newly opened Bernard Lee Schwartz Field House. It was the first concert to be held in the Field House and there were many concerns about damage to the newly installed super material on the floor, particularly from cigarette burns since smoking was allowed in school buildings. We tried to have a no smoking or drinks policy for the concert, but it was difficult to enforce it in the dark among the crowd sitting on the floor.

The concert was scheduled for Saturday night during Homecoming Weekend. Of course there was a football game and my obligation to the Corps and the Cadet Band had me in the stadium until after the game. Midway through the game, one of our students from the Committee came to me and said that Mary Travers manager had arrived and was complaining about many of the characteristics of the Field House. I pointed him to our agency contact, who resolved her issues as far as I knew.

After the game, my girlfriend and I had dinner and then went to the Field House, arriving about 6:30. When we got there, Mary Travers had already arrived and was rehearsing. I went to her dressing room, met her, and chatted with her and her manager who were both now happy with the venue and would be ready to perform at 8 pm.

When I walked out into the Field House, I asked about John Denver who had not yet arrived. In the late 1960's and early 1970's, it was common for performers not to show or arrive very late for concerts. So when John Denver wasn't there, I began to get concerned.

I found his manager and asked about John not being there yet and he smiled and said, "Don't worry. He'll be here." I asked him about every 15 minutes after that about John coming and each time got the same casual response.

About 7:45, I again approached his manager, then I noticed this guy walking in the door with a buckskin jacket, leather cowboy hat, carrying a guitar case who walked up to me and said, "Hi, I'm John Denver. Can you please show me to my dressing room?"

I experienced a mix of relief that he showed up, awe in meeting this great musical talent, and overwhelming admiration for the modesty of this star. As we walked to his dressing room, he asked if I could bring a few people back to him in about five minutes to get some local color, which I did.

John went on first, pretty much at 8:00 pm. He was so comfortable with himself that he simply took off his coat, got out his guitar, and was ready to play. A totally different type of entertainer than we had ever had before. In about an hour, Mary Travers came out and they performed several songs together and then Mary Travers did her solo performance. I thought it was a great concert. Probably one of the best I've ever seen.

After the concert, we had a press conference with several local media reps with the two of them. It's not hard for me to convey after all these years the stark contrast between the two performers. Mary Travers was the epitome of a Hollywood professional with flamboyant expressions, opulent demeanor, monopoly of conversation, and insincerity.

John Denver, on the other hand, was genuine, modest, down-to-earth, and very soft-spoken. When I talked to him when he first arrived and after the concert, he just seemed like a really nice guy that you could sit down and talk to over a beer. The personas he portrayed in his movies and television shows is exactly who he was. I was very sad when he died in a plane crash. The world lost a great person. He loved to just play his guitar and sing and make people happy.

James H. VanSciver:
That Little Blue Booklet

It's a fact of life that students attend institutions of higher learning to get an education which will catapult them into a successful career. That means they will enroll in classes each semester they are on campus. Each class has a professor; each class has a syllabus; each class has a curriculum; each class has a specified day and time to meet; each class has a designated meeting place; and each class has an exam.

For the members of the Class of 1972 attending Pennsylvania Military College, those exams were administered in the Armory, with desks in columns and rows. Cadets were assigned days and times to appear at the end of each semester in accordance with the particular classes in which they were enrolled. Once seated, directions and assessments were distributed, and a small blue booklet was slapped down in front of them. This booklet was to be used to capture everything and anything related to the class assessment that the cadet could recall.

It's doubtful that today's students, with their need for therapy dogs, safe spaces, and protection from acts of microaggression, could have survived the stress involved with this situation. That dreaded little blue booklet would have ended it for them right there.

Cadets were resourceful in preparing for these examinations. Some had formed study groups, some offered prayers to the divinity of their choice, while others pulled all-nighters, cram sessions with a few friends (and sometimes alcohol) which left them sleepless and ill-prepared to deal with the rigor of what awaited them. It is important to point out that this strategy is in direct conflict with College Board recommended protocols for preparing for the SAT exams. Still others used a novel and nearly forgotten approach...they actually attended class every day. Nonetheless, they all marched into the Armory each semester and took pen to paper inside the covers of that little blue booklet.

It was critical in one's freshman year. The weight of the exam was a major factor, overshadowing all other grades for each class. Beginning your college experience with a subpar grade point average meant an uphill battle for the remaining three years. On the other hand, a handsome GPA in your first year lifted a tremendous academic burden from one's shoulders.

One other factor played an important role in this process, the Honor Code. As it was revealed to all new cadets very early in their orientation, one had to ward off any challenges to veracity as they could lead to expulsion from school. Next came the kicker. One could also be expunged for knowing and not reporting some act of malfeasance on the part of a classmate. Hearing this shook the spines of everyone who let the words flow to their spirit.

So, there they sat, some clueless as to how to answer the questions, some with somewhat of an idea of how to formulate an answer, and others ready to ask for a second booklet in order to complete the writing of their deep and rich responses. Amazingly, most survived and are proud to now be counted among the Class of 1972 alumni of Pennsylvania Military College.

James H. VanSciver:
The Legacy of the Class of 1972 and Pennsylvania Military College

Entering the ranks of the Corps of Pennsylvania Military College in late August of 1968, it is doubtful that any of us would have known what was to take place a mere four years later. Consumed with the challenges of surviving the Rook experience, establishing a credible grade-point-average, and joining one or more additional programs, our lives and thoughts were more focused on the present than the future.

But the seeds of change had been sown. Public resentment to the war in Vietnam had evolved into an anti-military mood in the country. Protests were more evident, speeches were made, and interest in joining the armed forces began to wane. During the tenure of the Class of 1972, the government established a unique lottery and draft for each state and, as U.S. troops began leaving Vietnam, active commissions were becoming more difficult to secure.

At home, surrounding Old Main, unforeseen developments were also taking shape, developments that would have a profound impact on the future of Pennsylvania Military College. As interest in the military continued to decline, so did enrollment in Pennsylvania Military College. The college had already morphed into a dual experience, one for the soldierly and one for civilians, Penn Morton College. In fact, the institution was now called PMC Colleges with students from both groups participating in classes, sports teams, and other campus programs. An established female population was also growing on campus. The school's mascot changed from the Cadets to the Pioneers.

As part of the plan to maintain operations, members of the school's board and administrative team sought donors who would be able to provide resources to keep the Chester, Pennsylvania institution active. One such donor was the Widener family. Contributing a substantial amount of funding resulted in the school renaming itself Widener. The new brand's mascot would be the Pride.

It is often said that commencement means that out of an end becomes a new beginning. However, with the spring graduation of the Pennsylvania Military College came the end of a lengthy tradition from which thousands of alumni have distinguished themselves and made tremendous sacrifices for their country. The most notable remnant of the military's existence on campus is now the Pennsylvania Military College Museum, to which alumni make a pilgrimage each year during Homecoming.

What happens next will depend on the interest, energy, perseverance, and creativity of the alumni. There is a legacy committee that has been formed and there is elevated interest on the part of several members of the Class of 1972 to, not just have the legacy of Pennsylvania Military College survive, but to have that heritage thrive.

David Neimeyer:
Slipping and Sliding on Route 202

Things were looking up. It was the winter of 1972-1973. I was a senior and had a car on campus. It was Saturday morning and the bulk of the weekend lay ahead. The weather report was a bit iffy, with some wintry weather ahead of us. A few flakes dropped like paratroopers from the overcast sky, but other than that, everything was fine.

Bernie Yanos walked into my room. "Hey Hobbit, I need a favor. Can you drive a bunch of us up to my parent's house?" Bernie lived in Pottsville, about an hour or so north of the college.

"Sure," I replied. "Sounds good to me."

"Great! Let me round up some of the other guys and we'll be set to go."

About twenty minutes later Bernie, John Studinarz, Eric Sorchik, and I climbed into my car and headed out of the parking lot. The snow was falling pretty solidly by now. But hey, this was Pennsylvania. Snow was nothing new.

We wound along local roads, and eventually made the turn onto Route 202, which would head us north towards Pottsville. The snow had slowed down a bit, but there was a bit of sleet mixed in with it now. Traffic was light. Everyone was proceeding cautiously. Actually, the cautious and prudent drivers had all stayed home. We continued on.

About twenty minutes later things seemed to be looking up as the snow continued to slacken. However, the roads were slick from the earlier precipitation, and temperatures remained low. Up ahead, the traffic came to a halt. I slowly put on the brakes.

"Whoa! Hobbit!!!" Bernie gripped the arm rest as the car fishtailed on the icy road. In the back seat, Eric and John braced themselves. I regained control and crept to a stop. "Don't worry," I assured them. "It was just a little slippery there." The cars ahead started moving. I slowly pushed down on the gas. The wheels spun futilely, then begrudgingly gained traction and the car eased ahead.

The process repeated itself several times over the next few minutes. We'd slowly slide to a halt as traffic backed up. I became adept at avoiding the fishtailing, but kept my speed low, and avoided sudden braking. Tap...tap...tappppp on the brakes; let the car creep to a stop. It became harder and harder to get the car moving after each stop. Traction was degrading rapidly. We weren't quite halfway to Bernie's parents' place.

Our conversation slowly died out as we each concentrated on the weather and the road. Finally, I broke the silence. "Hey guys, it's getting pretty bad out here. We better head on back to school." The others begrudgingly agreed.

We turned around and headed back to school. Finally, after one stop, the car simply would not get any traction. The wheels spun ineffectively on the icy road. "Wait a minute," said John. "I'll give you a push." He and Eric jumped out and moved to the rear of the car. I slowly gave the car gas, and we started to creep forward. I stopped and waited till my buddies were back in the car, then gave the car gas. The wheels spun ineffectively. No traction. Apparently, any time we stopped; we'd never get moving again.

John, Eric, and Bernie jumped out again. After a moment of pushing, the car got traction and began moving. This time I kept the car creeping along. Bernie ran alongside, then jumped in the front seat. John and Eric did the same in the back. With all aboard, I picked up to traffic speed. We repeated this tactic several times as we slowly drove along. Occasionally, we'd even help out other drivers. I'd slow to a crawl, the guys would jump out and push another motorist with spinning wheels, then would jog back to our car and jump back in. Amazingly, no one fell beneath the wheels, or was run over by another motorist.

Finally, the college parking lot loomed before us. We slid through the entrance, and gingerly pulled into a parking space. It had started snowing again.

"Man, I'm glad that's over," said Eric

"Me too," I agreed. "That was getting a bit hairy."

"Hey!" shouted John. "Snowball battle! Let's go get into it!"

"Yeah," we shouted in unison, grabbing handfuls of snow from the surrounding cars. Well-armed, we headed off to the fray. One adventure ended, but others lay ahead.

David Neimeyer:
Quotes to Remember

"To whom it may concern: I wish you good luck throughout your years at Pennsylvania Military College. These will be years of trials, and there will be many pressures placed upon you. Above all else, maintain your personal dignity and honor. They are irreplaceable. Have no fear; meet events squarely. Remember the Golden Rule and practice it often. Otherwise you will be a hollow man with nothing more than a stained record. You will make mistakes but learn from them by not repeating them. Face your shortcomings and strive to correct them. May God bless and keep you safely."—*Found inside a locker door, Room 210 Turrell Hall*

Oh, for the days when Cadets were Cadets and President Moll was afraid to come out of Old Main during Mess III formation.—*Bill Znidarsic*

"Almost" only counts in horseshoes and hand grenades.—*PMC Proverb*

Win some, lose a lot.—*James McKelvey*

A girl is but a girl, but a frog is a friend for life.—James McKelvey

You can pick your nose, and you can pick your friends, but you can't pick your friend's nose.—*William Znidarsic*

Remember: only forest fires can prevent bears.—*Ernie Frazo*

People forget that to be a good stud, you have your failures, too. For every girl I get, I have fifty failures; like at a dance: some guys quit after one try. I don't quit until the dance is over and then, if I see something good in the parking lot...—*Joe Bartholomew*

You don't have to practice being miserable.—Steve Simon, on Army summer camp

You can peacefully co-exist with a lion in a cage as long as the lion is not hungry. As soon as the lion gets hungry, you've got a problem—unless you're a bigger lion.—*Lt Col. Gerald T. Frey*

It is my contention that the world is not going to end in nuclear war, or conflagration, but will grind to a halt, choked to death by hair.—*Lt Col. Gerald T. Frey*

The only way to learn about sex in New England is to move out of there.—*Howard Rubinow*

For full indeed is Earth of woes; and full of seas; and in the day as well as night diseases unbidden haunt mankind, silently bearing ills to men...so utterly impossible is it to escape the will of Zeus.—*Hessiod*

Ed Albertson:
PMC Remembered

So, many stories come to mind, and as my memory focuses, one that is etched in my mind for all time is this, from when I was the one and only Rook Bugler for my entire Rook year (1969-1970), right up through the graduation of that year's seniors, despite being recognized on Mother's Day.

On Hundredth Night, 1970, I was returning to Hotel Turrell

from having played my rendition of Taps on the porch of Old Main, I entered the Quadrangle sidewalk leading to Howell Hall and suddenly, through one of the windows of a corner room of what I recall was Cann Hall, an entire student desk emerged, having been thrown with full force through the window of the room of a normally quiet, reserved, Senior Company Commander. Stunned and immobilized by that feat, I stood there to witness in succession, a student chair, a PMC lamp, and a flurry of uniforms follow the desk onto the Quad, each toss being separated by merely a few seconds. Drawn to this spectacle, Cadet cheers erupted from the dorms and a few members of the Guard detail entered the Quad, only to quickly return to the safety of Howell Hall. Caught in the Quad alone, I hid behind a tree and continued to watch as more room items appeared through the broken window, accompanied by an unearthly howling from within the room.

Within several minutes of the beginning of all this, four (yes FOUR) Chester Police cars pulled up along the street in front of the Quad and Old Main. As law enforcement assessed the magnitude of what was going on, they gingerly approached the room to find a single, Senior Cadet Company Commander who had "snapped out" and was finally beginning to wind down his energy level. From my vantage point, it appeared the officers took him into custody and spirited him away from the PMC Quad and a serene silence settled over the entire area. At the following day's Mess Three, a much anticipated SPO was announced for said Senior Company Commander and that was the end of the issue. The window was repaired and left resumed at "the X."

Stories and Vignettes from PMC

PMC Cadet with Widener Lion
© Newman 2020

ODDS & ENDS

John W. Stealey:
Basketball and Sports

Since I had not done well with the ladies, I decided to try out for basketball at PMC. I made the team as a good number eight or nine player. I was not great, but very enthusiastic. So, whenever the other team had an exceptional shooter, I was sent out to get my five fouls and piss him off so bad that he was angry and not making many good shots. It was the same job I was good at in high school basketball. I played four years of first team, Lacrosse Crease Defense at the Air Force Academy with the same skills! I was ready to hit the enemy with a big stick and run right over them. Worked way better in Lacrosse than basketball!

James H. VanSciver:
Riding and Reigning

As one who had a job exercising a neighbor's horses when I was a teenager, you can imagine how excited I was when I found out that Pennsylvania Military College had a mounted troop. Crazy as it seems, with the classes, the military requirements, sports teams, school newspaper, and fraternity life, I somehow found the time to squeeze in some time for the ponies. This was not an easy task as the stables were located in the mountains between Chester and West Chester and the troop, under the command of Frank Giorno, rotated responsibilities for caring for the steeds.

For those not close to an experience of this kind, the responsibility faction, about 80 percent, greatly outweighs the satisfaction faction, about 20 percent, unless you are one whose entire fabric of life revolves around these animals. One horse is like having five dogs. Horses must be fed and watered each day and groomed constantly. They need exercise and there is the matter of having to muck out the stalls on a regular basis. True, the babes dig the colorful uniforms and the confidence one commands when astride the saddle of one of these creatures is fantastic, but one must enjoy it while he can.

Under the tutelage of our commander, our acumen with respect to our chores was stimulated to a very high level. We were paired with one horse and expected to develop a relationship with that animal. Mine was a large white four-legged with one blue eye and one grey eye. We did bond and I spent a good bit of time stroking him and talking to him. Perhaps, using that kind of strategy would have been helpful in saving my first marriage. The rotation system worked like clockwork; our horses were provided the necessary attention; and we were able to participate in several community events.

I had known, and not completely forgotten, that horse behavior is not always predictable. Confronted with some unexpected auditory or visual stimulation can turn a horse into a raging bull in a very short period of time. Once, when quietly and deftly walking in a main street parade, the sound of a 21-gun salute so startled our steeds, that we may have looked like Custer's unit at the Little Big Horn for a few minutes until we got them under control.

I remember it perfectly. It was the worst snowstorm to hit the area in years. We received a telephone call that our horses had escaped their pen and were wandering around the mountains. Off we went, into the fray. And spent the next number of hours rounding them up. We couldn't get mad at them. They were just doing what they do. It was a very cold night.

Before college, I had never had the opportunity to load a horse into a trailer. Once, after a parade, I found it impossible to get my ride into his trailer. Coaxing, a carrot held just out of his reach, and a stern pat on the backside were all unsuccessful. So was grabbing the reins and attempting to tug him in. Officer Giorno happened by and exclaimed to my surprise, "Horses won't venture into the darkness. Turn the trailer so the sunlight shines in and you'll be fine." Brilliant! As has often been said, sunshine is the best cleanser for the truth. It also is helpful in getting your horse into a trailer.

I've long turned in my golden gloves, put away my riding boots, stored my hat, and outgrown my uniform, but I will never forget those days of riding and reigning, all as a result of Pennsylvania Military College.

STORIES AND VIGNETTES FROM PMC

David Fiedler:
Service Cap with Visor

An integral part of the U S Army officer's uniform for decades was the service cap with visor. It was worn with class A uniform (greens) and class B uniform (tropical tans and short sleeve shirt etc.). At PMC these uniforms and this cap were worn most of the time by both the Commandant's Staff and the ROTC staff for most activities since their duties were mostly administrative or teaching. The army green uniform was also the uniform worn by cadets on commissioning day in May, which also ended the academic year.

The cap was made by a company called Bancroft and officers' caps were covered in what was called "fur felt". It was kind of similar to today's microfiber in texture.

When entering places like the faculty dining room, classrooms etc. it was common for officers upon entrance to leave their caps on the hat rack/coat rack provided outside the facility. At least two officers I knew also left their "swagger sticks" with their hats and coats.

In those days, company grade Bancroft hats went for about $15.00. This wasn't cheap. Company grade officers' caps had a plain black visor. Majors and higher ranks had visors with gold embossments (nicknamed scrambled eggs). These were not of interest to about to be commissioned cadets.

Company grade caps, however, were another story. If you were going to be commissioned you needed one. This made it "open season" on company grade service caps. Caps disappeared on a regular basis from coat racks, open closets, and even unguarded offices. Interestingly though, caps were never stolen from officers in the ROTC detachment, only from junior officers on the Commandant's Staff, many of whom were not well respected. I can attest to six or seven cadets who were commissioned wearing stolen service caps. Great way to start a military career.

If you were going to ask, NO I was not one of them. I bought my own cap. One day in 1965, however, while pretty much alone in MacMorland Center I came across General Biddle's cap and swagger stick on a coat rack outside the faculty dining room. I was fully alone and could have easily concealed and walked off with both. I looked at them for a long time and a little voice in my head said, "You haven't got the balls!" and I let them be!!! Pretty smart of me in hindsight, I would have been risking everything for a joke.

Gerald Ferguson:
PMC Baseball

I loved to play all the major sports, but baseball was the sport I loved the most. I certainly didn't attend PMC expressly to play baseball, but I knew the school fielded a team in a small college conference so when spring rolled around and I saw a notice about trying out for the freshman team, I was excited. Not that many guys turned out for the freshman team, so no cuts were necessary. As practices progressed, no schedule was forthcoming—very odd. We soon found out that someone in the Athletic Dept. had failed to schedule any games for the freshman team and it was too late to develop a schedule. We continued to practice every day and on occasion would scrimmage the varsity.

I played on the varsity team for the next three years. We had a reasonably good team with a winning record each year, as I recall. I was selected as a co-captain my senior year.

A couple facts about the baseball program that would seem odd to today's Widener players:
- On game days, cadets could obtain permission to "sleep-

in." This allowed me to sleep through morning formation. A slip of paper from the athletic dept was attached to the door as evidence.
- No overnight trips. The longest away game was probably Washington College in Chestertown, MD.
- On away games, we would get a meal allowance of $5.00 in cash as I recall. The bus would stop at a roadside diner for an evening meal.
- There was no baseball field on campus. Practices and home games were played at the Sun Oil recreation complex located around three miles from campus. Coach Harry Miller would drive those without transportation.

Dan Gascoyne:
Pershing Rifles — The Sash

This story takes place during my sophomore year, Sep '66 — May '67.

We were finishing up the competitive season at the Boston Bean Pot Invitational Drill Meet, sponsored by Northeastern University and Boston University, always a huge and tough meet. It had been a very successful year, winning all of the meets in which we had participated.

On the seven-hour bus trip from Chester to Boston, Bill Luthke managed to lose his per diem meal money quickly, playing acey-ducey. This completed the cycle of Bill losing his meal money, always promptly, on every trip his senior year!

Our toughest competition was Seton Hall University and Brooklyn Polytechnic University, both outfits must have practiced as much as we did and took pride in their drilling, both basic standard and trick drill.

We were preparing for our trick show and getting into our standard Delta Blouse and White Trousers (girls wear pants) with sash uniform. Pledges were running around, securing rifles, and helping guys get dressed. It was important to have your sash pinned to your trouser leg so that it wouldn't fly around during quick step—Leroy Eaton '69, (RIP) was pledging and ran over to me and said, "Gas, I'll pin your sash." I'm sure I said, "thanks."

We went onto the drill floor, did our opening thing where we close up and quick step then halt, and Jim Riser pops out to sign in and request to take the drill floor. We would be in a position of looking down with our rifles on the floor and held with both hands, the butt between our feet. I saw my sash wrapped around the stacking swivel and the bayonet stud. I was hidden from the judges, so I tried to unravel the mess, but it only got worse! I tried pulling and ripping it, but no luck. Jim Riser gets back into the formation, hits his rifle butt on the floor and off we go—up to right shoulder arms and go 10 steps and go into "winds." I couldn't get my rifle up to right shoulder arms so I held it as high as I could and got through that move. The next move was a lot of steps and separation, and we ended up doing the four-count manual individually, wide open, and I was done! I went down to a position of attention, kept counting, and got back into the formation at trail arms.

When we went to the machine gun line, I was next to the last man, Sario Caradonna. I extended but ended up a quarter step back so Sario, on my left, and either Chuck Cantley or Ron Spuhler, one of which was on my right, could see when to make their moves. It went well and through the rest of the show, I carried that M-1 at trail arms.

Now Jim Riser has requested to leave the drill floor and we're heading out. We get to the finish area, stop, go to port arms, and march off at regular cadence to our forming area. Leroy is frantic! I was frantic! He thought his screw up would get him blackballed, I thought his screw up would cost us the meet!

In the end, we got second in Trick, won overwhelmingly in Basic Standard, and won the Overall Trophy, which, I may add, we won the next two years and retired the Boston Bean Pot Trophy during my senior year with three wins in a row!

Leroy didn't get blackballed and became a brother, but I never let him forget the pin job! We had lots of laughs about it over the years!!

Bill Luthke went on to a career playing cards in Vegas!

James H. VanSciver:
Precise, Exact, and Confident

Word had it, when I was wandering around the Pennsylvania Military Campus from 1968 through 1972, that those interested in trying out for the Pershing Rifles Company had to have a certain weight and height. That wouldn't surprise me since it would contribute to the exactness of the outfit in still another way.

Everything about the 15th Regimental Headquarters, Q-15, and Company Q-5 was the same, from the way they dressed to the way they performed. The members epitomized the thinking that a military unit had to think and act as one. It showed and it worked.

Securing more than fifty trophies including seven national championships is "proof of the pudding" that these guys knew what they were doing. They completed in basic drill, quick drill, and advanced drill competitions. Watching them was a sight to behold.

Their uniforms were indicative of their exactness, down to the creases in their shirts, the glimmer of the bills of their hats, the polish on their shoes, the shine of their brass, and the perfection of their gig lines. Hell, even their sashes swung in unison during drill competitions!

It was their performance that brought fans to their feet. Every pivot, each step, every arch of the ankle, each stiff leg, every rifle routine, and each salute had the crispness and precision of a very well-oiled machine.

How'd they get like that?

Like with all successful organizations, it begins with a vision and uncompromising leadership. All members were passionate about and loyal to the code that justified their existence. They ate it; they slept it; and they worked at it. For them, perfection wasn't a place; it was a direction. Like highly successful football coaches who meticulously study game film after each contest, I'm sure the members of this group reviewed and reviewed video of their performances to reveal nuances not recognizable to the ordinary onlooker.

Practices had to be brutal and unrelenting. However, knowing that an individual's performance cast an aura over the entire group was motivation enough to keep them all going.

Often did I think about what was going on in the minds of these young artistes. How did they find the impetus to continue, day after day, month after month, and year after year? What elixir had stimulated their confidence to know exactly what move was next in each routine, how to execute it, and do so in the most convincing manner? With these matters my mind grappled each time I enjoyed a performance of Company Q-5.

But they are gone now.

The anticipation of the crowd as they march onto the field, the flamboyant jerks and about faces as they perform their drill are fading into memory. That's both special and tragic since the hold Company Q-5 has on our recollection is firm and justified; yet it is only that...a memory.

We will not see their likeness in action again.

Dan Gascoyne:
Pershing Rifles — Change in Drill Commands

We were flown by PA National Guard in a C-130 to Wright Patterson Air Base to attend the U of Dayton Meet. We stayed in the BOQ of the air base and after dinner at the Officers Club, had our pre-meet meeting.

Jim Riser and Jim Concher attended the meeting for the participants and reported that, unbeknownst to anyone, we, and only we, had received the incorrect basic standard drill commands for tomorrow.

This meant that we had practiced the wrong sequence of commands all of the prior week. During our meeting, the thought of leaving came up, which put Jim Riser in a frenzy—he gave a speech to us all about what it meant being in Company Q-5 and we weren't quitters, and if it takes all night, we'll learn the new routine! Sure enough, there we were, at midnight, cutting into precious beer drinking time, practicing basic standard in the hallways.

The next day, we took the floor and, don't you know, kicked ass with 1st place in Basic, 1st place in Trick, and had five guys in the top 10 in individual drill. That trophy was a Springfield Rifle with bayonet, mounted on a beautiful stand. We ended up winning that one three years in a row and during our senior year, retired that trophy also!

Clyde Tinklepaugh:
Life on the Third Corridor

Hotel Turrell, third corridor, was shared by part of Alpha and Charlie Companies. Alpha company cadre were Rich Urban and Fred Troutman, Charlie company, Bill Bennis. There were also a couple of senior cadets living on the floor, Dennis Dixon and Steve Vassak. Vassak was the studious type, constantly studying, even when sitting on the toilet and never really bothered the Rooks. One never knew what to expect during a step out party, bracing, green chair to name a couple. Things got really interesting when Dixon and Troutman came back from a night of serious drinking. Phone cords got pulled out of the phones and it was common for Dixon to pitch a fire extinguisher down the corridor, water spraying everywhere.

One of the first military training exercises that we took part in was a forced march through Washington and Chester parks, up and down hills, through the mud and water. All Rooks were to attend except those on EMD. An exercise such as that builds comradery in more ways than one. All of Charlie participated except three, Two EMD, the other just weaseled out. After the conclusion of the march, everyone returned to the corridor to scrape mud from your boots and body and get a shower. As we were all getting cleaned up, the one weasel showed up, smirk on his face, which didn't last long. Out came a PMC red blanket and proper punishment was handed out. I believe he left at the end of the semester.

Another Rook stepped out of line, the name and reason I cannot remember. He was rewarded with the fish. Unfortunately, it affected the entire corridor. A large room was divided into two cadet rooms by a wooden portion that that was part bookshelf, wall locker and a cabinet for toiletries underwear, socks, and folded shirts. To get back at the person who did not toe the line, a cadet marched into Chester and purchased a whole fish. He pried a piece of the bookshelf off and dropped the fish into the cavity. Very few knew of the existence of the fish until after a few days when it started to stink. PMC maintenance had to remove part of the shelf to get the fish out, which by now was covered in maggots. Unfortunately, the stench hung around for several days.

Another individual was not toeing the line, for what reason I cannot recall. Someone decided to defecate in his shoe. The affected individual cleaned up the mess just in time for Mess 1 formation. There was a company inspection of the rooks each morning. The inspecting officer said, "Mister, your nails look like shit" if he only knew what had transpired previously.

For Homecoming 1967, all organizations made floats. Charlie decided to make a huge coffin. The first challenge was where to obtain material. Several rooks obtained a car and headed off campus to a building site for a midnight requisition of 2 x 4s. Once returning to campus, the material needed to be out of sight in case the police showed up. Bill Bennis had a single room which had an access panel to the ceiling. All material was placed up there out of sight. A few days later, construction started. The completed floats were paraded through the city of Chester and upon return placed in the quadrangle. Charlie carried this huge coffin which must have weighed several hundred pounds. The reward was worth the risk, we won first prize!

Homecoming 1968. There was a tank sitting in front of the Hyatt Armory at the corner of 14th Street and Melrose Avenue. A group of seniors, led by Leroy Eaton, decided it needed a new coat of paint, pink in color. The next morning, several rooks either volunteered or were "volunteered" to repaint the tank green. I have a photograph of the volunteers, Mike Jessick, Richard Deadorff, and myself. There was at least one more, the person taking the picture and there might have been others, but I just can't recall. The tank was eventually moved to a less conspicuous spot, between the end of Howell Hall and MacMorland Center. The tank lives on at the Pennsylvania Military Museum in Boalsburg, PA.

In 1968 the Vietnam war was raging, and many antiwar protests were taking place throughout the country. Someone got word of a

Peace protest that was going to be held in Philadelphia. Under the leadership of Lou Ogus, we took a trip to the "zoo." Someone procured a PMC maintenance truck, which had no seats, no lights, and no windows. So off we go to the "zoo," standing in the back of the truck. We eventually got to center city Philadelphia to the location of the protest, disembarked from the truck, and dispersed into the crowd. Needless to say, we stuck out like a sore thumb as we were all in dress Echo with white shirts. The only Cadet that I can remember was Dennis Yurcisin. As I recall, nothing happened. We loaded back into the truck and returned to PMC.

Sophomore Year

My room was in Cann Hall, 3rd floor, at the end of the building facing Howell Hall. A perfect location for launching water balloons, not to LTC Frey's liking. Other members of Charlie Company lived in Cann as well, two that were roommates, Homer McGee and Kevin Fay. Kevin had a pet monkey that would occasionally get loose and run up and down the corridor.

Junior year

My residence for this year was in Dorm 5 which had three doors, one on each end of the corridor and the third near the center of the building which faced the quadrangle. The door on the end of the corridor allowed passage from Dorm 5 into Dorm 4 through a short passageway. Boris Matisziw had the end room which was strategically placed to allow for females to sneak in. Boris and I brought in two girls, we no sooner got them into the room when Gerry Ferguson knocked on the door, we were caught red handed. No formal punishment was meted out, only a company article 15.

I joined the Ranger Platoon in my Junior year. One of the exercises that took place was at Camp Pickett, Virginia with part of the US Army's 6th or could have been the 10th Special Forces group acting as the aggressor force. Boris Matisziw and I were assigned to the M-60 machine gun. Other than the machine gun, the only equipment we had were canteens, ponchos, and field jackets. Needless to say, the weather turned cold, so cold that the water in the canteens froze. One poncho was used for shelter, the other as a ground cloth. Shared body heat was used to keep somewhat warm as we awaited the attack that never came.

Part of our Junior class training was a bus trip, first to the Engineering School at Fort Belvoir, Virginia and then to Aberdeen Proving Grounds in Maryland. At Fort Belvoir, we had the opportunity to see Bailey Bridges being constructed. After mess three, all were invited to the O club for much drinking at no cost to the individual. Breakfast the next morning was typical army food with scrambled eggs being the mainstay. After the barracks got squared away, we loaded the buses and were off to Aberdeen. Entering the gate, Hunley leaned out the window and promptly emptied his stomach of scrambled eggs!

Atlantic City 1969

Most fraternities obtained a room in one of the hotels to serve as a party room. The alcohol flowed freely. I believe a civilian student or maybe a local civilian had a few words for Mulhern, a fight ensued, with Mulhern getting the better of the action, knocked the guy out, threw him into the elevator, and pressed the down button. I can only image what was the reaction of anyone in the lobby who witnessed a knocked out, bloodied individual laying in the back of the elevator.

Dan Gascoyne:
Pershing Rifles Ears

On the trip to Dayton during my Junior year, Sep '67—May '68, we were again flying from Willow Grove in a C-130, piloted by PANG pilots. In the plane we sat on the sides against the walls of the plane.

Over the middle of PA and until we landed, we flew through a snowstorm. It was unbelievable, the plane was all over the sky—we'd be swinging to the left then swinging to the right, dropping down and getting bounced up—all over the place.

Rick Beals was pledging at the time and on the trip. Unfortunately, he was the only guy on board who couldn't get his ears to pop, and he was really struggling. He looked like his head would blow off! Everyone was giving him advice—swallow, hold your nose and blow out, whatever they could think of to help him. He was in a lot of pain and there was little we could do for him. Eventually we got low enough when landing that he got his ears straight—I don't remember anyone getting sick to their stomach, probably a result of Rick's malady that kept our mind off of throwing up!

Vito Greco:
Stage Struck

Also during my Junior year, a civilian organization used the campus stage to put on a play set in Italy in the 1800s. They requested Cadets to participate as a firing squad for a military execution that was part of the play. When the Cadet firing squad was chosen, I was selected as the leader. We drew M-1 rifles and blank ammunition from the armory and headed over to Alumni Auditorium.

At the appointed time, my four-man firing squad and I marched onto the stage and took our position. I did not know any Italian, and had not been told what to say, so I improvised my commands from the name of one of the upperclassmen: Vito Greco.

"VITO" I commanded. The squad came to attention.

"GRECO." The squad raised their rifles and took aim.

"FUEGO!!" The squad fired.

The actor being executed stood shocked for a second or two. I suspect he didn't know that the sound of firing the blanks would be so loud. It did reverberate nicely in the closed auditorium. After a short hesitation, he dutifully clutched his chest and dropped behind the parapet wall in front of which he had been standing. (Good way to remove a body from the small stage.) I dutifully marched my firing squad off stage and back to the armory to turn in our weapons. Our brief moment of glory was over.

Bob Kukich:
Golf as a PMC Cadet

In my sophomore year, I competed for a spot on the school's golf team. Although I had captained my high school golf team, I was skeptical of making the PMC team, thinking that college level golf was for PGA tour wannabees. Boy, did I have a lot to learn—Welcome to Division III golf.

Division III golf at PMC provided few perks—no free golf balls, no team shirts, no team bus, no practice facilities. But it provided advantages to me as a cadet: I could skip Mess III formations—"Hey,

I have to practice some time"; I could eat and enjoy meals at the athletic table—"Hey, I am a member of the golf team"; I could wear civilian clothes on campus—"Hey, I'm on my way to the course"; and I could enjoy a beer or two at some nice golf courses—"Hey, we need to celebrate wins"; etc.—Welcome to Division III golf.

As a team, we were pretty good, with a record of 9-2, the best in school history. I won't mention names, but our Captain was not only a talented golfer, but he was also the school's starting quarterback and starting basketball point guard. Our number two and three players received some athletic scholarship money to play golf. The remaining golfers, like me, were "walk-ons," happy to be playing golf—Welcome to Division III golf.

One of the more memorable events happened competing against Towson University. Traveling three hours, in two cars, our coach could only keep his eyes on the players in his car. While hitting putts on the practice green prior to the match, I noticed our three best players giggling and having more fun than usual—then it dawned on me, they had been in the car without the coach, and they were stoned—Welcome to Division III golf.

Playing golf well is difficult, playing stoned even more so. Still giggling, our Captain took the tee to play his match against their best player. As we all eagerly looked on, he hit the ball about 300 yards down the middle of the fairway, whew! He went on to easily win his match as did most of us, giving us a win for the day—Welcome to Division III golf.

Alan Hilkene:
Pershing Rifles

PMC joined Pershing Rifles in late 1953 or early 1954. Memory slowing down at 90 here!! Anyway, we had formed a drill team earlier under the guidance of Bert Mazzio who had been a member of a drill team at the Nuremburg trials after WWII. We flourished under Bert's experience and did exhibitions at football halftimes, parades, ceremony firing squads (no ammo), and escorts of honor for visiting brass!! PMC is listed on Pershing Rifles roster as the 5th Regiment, 2nd Battalion.

Our part in the early 50's was to establish a capable drill team by learning the ropes needed to excel. As the 50's continued, our stake in Pershing Rifles became more and more established as a prime factor in this field. Before the 60's arrived, PMC was winning tournaments with increasing skill and soon became the number one in the competitions. Am I correct that there were consecutive titles for a long spell and the class of the crowd!! Makes it worth the exercise with the Garand rifle when one can toss the sucker like a play toy!!

And to show how it stuck for me, I remember the serial # on mine!! It was 3332171. And in our performing PR team in 1954, Bob Pierpont and Barry NcDermott and several lieutenants and sergeants.

And a monster HURRAH!! to all the Pershing Rifle teams that brought honor and prestige to college and themselves for performance skills!!

Tally HO Lads!!

Bob Kukich:
Track Competition

In the spring of the 1966-1967 school year, the PMC Track Coach, Harry Durney, conducted a track meet between the PMC Track Team and the college as a whole. I am unsure why, but I suppose his intent was to find and recruit hidden talent among the student body.

Students came out from the dorms and competed against members of the track team in almost every event, but one event caught my eye—the high jump. As the bar was raised higher and higher, the PMC track team member made quick work of his competition, finally eliminating all comers before the bar reached six feet.

As Harry Durney was about to proclaim him the winner, one tall, lean cadet dressed in sweatpants came forward to state, "I have not yet competed. Would you please move the bar to six feet two inches?" Without removing his sweatpants and with no warmup, Senior Cadet Private Bob McMinn of HQ Company cleared the bar to the astonishment of Coach Durney and all observers. When Coach Durney discovered that McMinn was a senior, he asked Bob, "Where in the hell have you been for four years?" McMinn calmly stated, "Sir, I am in the band and an Electrical Engineer student. I simply don't have time for track."

Frederick H. Beals:
A PR Drill Meet

I pledged Company Q-5 in my sophomore year, having been afraid I'd be cut my Rook year. Several of my classmates pledged as Rooks. I remember fellow Foxtrot classmate Gordon King, along with Jack Gale, Ron Hoehn, John Greene, Jim Howard, Peter "the Machine" Leonard, and the late Freddie Walker all got in that first year. Oddly, the only name that comes to mind of us Sophomore pledges who made it was the late Col Alvarez, and me. Of course, there's a good chance I don't remember. What was it like? I guess we all have our takeaways, but here's what I recall.

We're going to a Drill Meet! That's what I remember; the excitement of it all. We're boarding an Air National Guard prop transport with some seats in the back and here we are leaving school, out in the world, and flying to Dayton or Cincinnati, or someplace I've never been. It was my first time traveling by plane. To me, the fun of getting away for the weekend was seeing what other teams were like, but mostly enjoying the attention of representing PMC, enjoying sometimes momentarily indulging in the fantasy that we're going out to "kick some butts" and party out of our minds. All this was pretty darned cool to this somewhat hesitant, soon-to-be 20-year-old raised in a family that reflected my father's upper middle class roots and standards.

My first drill meet as a brother was held in downtown Philly, the same place we won when I was pledging the previous year. At that meet, which we probably won, Rick Carmen warned me against the danger of staring at my reflection in the glass perimeter that shielded fans from the Philadelphia Flyer hockey pucks, and yes, Rick, the following year when I was on the floor, I stared, looking for my reflected image and was late on the machine gun line. Some guys never learn!

But Philly seemed too familiar, and only a train ride or car ride away to get much excited about. Flying to Cincinnati, or even bussing through the state roads of Pennsylvania and up to Buffalo, NY was different. It was special. It was Q-5, Pershing Rifles National Champions coming into your town to party and win. Just us, baby!

Most of those trips took several hours, and while I stood 5'9/12", 125 pounds with barely a size 29 waist, my appetite had always been like hungry piranhas. I'd stare at a roadside dinner like in those old black and white Westerns with the vultures circling ever lower, desperate for food– and yet I don't remember eating any dinner, lunch, or breakfast at a meet ever, except once after a meet, when I sat near Paul Lenhart at breakfast as a pledge.

For some reason, like how imposing and stern he could look at you. Well, that was my suspicion that at any moment he was either contemplating behind his no nonsense stare whether he was going to rearrange my face or whether to smoke a cigarette. I had no clue! Anyway, that dissipated over breakfast that morning when he explained to all listeners the benefits of steak and eggs for breakfast. Did he also chug down a beer? Naturally, I copied him. I began to see Paul Lenhart as an OK guy.

Regardless of the city, our first night's hotel experience followed a predictable pattern: the team would scatter into two or three smaller groups. It was cards and beer, but I suspect a couple of the older guys found transportation into town for bigger things. Pledges had to spit shine shoes before being allowed to party, and they'd drift in to join the brothers as best they could. Once there, they were pretty much treated as equals, with a few exceptions.

Besides shining shoes, making a successful beer run was an important and honorable part of any road trip and presented new opportunities for additional bonding, or temporary relegation to merely pledge status. Voicing to get Budweiser's' received near unanimous grunts of approval, with peripheral opinions meekly expressing support for Michelob. Pledges would be handed a few bucks, maybe the keys to the rental car, and disappear under strict orders.

Even if they returned quite promptly and bore a bounty of multiple six packs, they could be greeted with sneers and insults if they demonstrated their utter incompetence by purchasing the likes of Genesee Cream Ale or Utica Club: twin sisters from a waste stream outside the local laundry mat. I swear that I could taste soap suds during each guzzle.

Card playing, the other indispensable activity was a given. In one city, I remember we stayed in an aging hotel. The beer run itself had generally been agreed on as successful, having scored Pabst Blue Ribbon instead of Bud. The Brothers slouched around the worn furniture, both excited and relaxed at finally wearing civilian clothes and focused on the coffee table that no doubt bore witness to many parsimonious guests. For it was here the Brothers were hard at playing Hearts, or Crazy Eights (I forgot). Regardless of its name, it was THE game of choice, with the Queen of Spades being the one card you could drop in front of the player to your right in unbridled triumph? Or maybe you were supposed to keep it? Or both? Either way, I can tell you that doing so was always followed by an eruption of testosterone-driven jeers of approval, screams of revenge, or vile but good-natured cursing for one's bad or good fortune, depending on the circumstance. Being college upperclassmen, the game was given a brutal, succinct name.

Away from the card game, the room itself held no interest, with its dimly lit chandelier over the coffee table, its wide, frosted glass bowl diffusing the tattered yellow light adding to the surreal feeling of not being where we should. That is, until all attention turned to the new-found activity of tossing one's empty beer cans up into the voluminous chandelier bowl, in undeniable proof of one's daredevil and hand-eye coordination. Great stuff! I imagined Knicks announcer Marv Albert repeating renditions of his famous "Swish" and "two Points" at every successful toss, while suspecting we'd all end up in trouble.

The fun came to the logical but unfortunate end as the swollen bowl began swaying noticeably after each beer can found its target. Then suddenly our eyes locked in unison at the groaning chandelier to watch physics in an instant: the ceiling chain seemed to stretch just so, and then crash! The beer-bloated thing just fell to the floor with a thud. In stunned surprise were heard shouts of, "Oh no", and "We're screwed," but mostly of beer lubricated howls of laughter.

Hey, we're Q-5, we party drill and we win! Anyway, that was partially just a façade we sometimes liked to play on peoples' admiration to create an image portraying a certain aura of "outrageous/cool." I went to my room and fell asleep.

Mornings on meet day were understandably quiet and measured. I always stayed in bed, proving I understood the infantry's creed never to ignore good rack time! A few guys diligently woke up early and went to the arena to compete in the individual drill competition. This started before the team competitions began, and attendance wasn't bad, just on the light side. What do you expect for starting at 8:00 am? The competing drillers typically consisted of 100-200 hopefuls, volunteering from the 12-15 schools, their shoes spit shined (or spray shined), collars buttoned on their ROTC issued uniforms, and ready to compete for their team.

Facing the one or more lines of drillers, the military officer in charge, I suppose he would be the Drill Instructor, would give commands such as; "Left Face" "Right Shoulder Arms", or "Present Arms" etc. and continue until one or more would commit a mistake. A kind of "Simon Sezz" while lugging a 9.5 pound weapon while standing at attention. They might have faced left, instead of right, or obeyed an impossible command such as going to Inspection Arms from Present Arms, and they would be forced to drop out.

The remaining competitors would consolidate the ranks before the commands would start again: "Port Arms" "Right shoulder Arms." "Inspection Arms" was the fastest way of removing people and the real "go to" favorite of impatient DI's because no one, certainly not I, enjoyed jamming their left thumb against a bolt to open the chamber, only to later stick their right thumb on a spring-loaded plate so it would snap shut with unforgiving force. Please don't crush my thumb! A few would have always had trouble with that one and were duly eliminated.

At one meet, I actually got dressed in time to watch individuals competition wind down. I saw the Drill Instructor finish up with his whittled down group of only four or five remaining drillers, bark out, the old "Port Arms" "Inspection Arms" there goes the thumb again, before completing the nasty trilogy with "Port....Arms", allowing trace amounts of smirk to come from his voice. After the expected mix of "clicks" and foreboding silence from pulled and unpulled triggers, he approached each of the remaining drillers respectfully, but in a military fashion. After a short pause, I suspect he thought, "I wonder what I'll find here," then slowly released their triggers one by one. Of course, there shouldn't have been any sound. But sounds he would hear, and yes, boys, Life in the Big City, etc., and dismissed they were.

A few commands later it was all over, with Jim Howard, fellow class of 70, Rook MDC, who once startled me with a "Vive la Q-5" in the lobby of the Danbury, CT Hilton in 1983, awarded First Place Individual Drill Competition. Pretty awesome of Jim, but no surprise because he was serious at what he did and good at it.

As a respectful footnote, and with no disrespect to Jim, I think some of us wondered how James Hogg, who was a year older, had the bearing, the appearance, and the mechanics of what lots of us thought were the near poster image of a Pershing Rifle drill competitor, fell to 3rd place. We occasionally referred to him as "Hoagie" but with respect because we did respect him.

If the Individual Drill Competitions were early and focused, the mid morning's start of the Basic Standard Drill competition had a louder buzz, with several schools showing a mix of what we thought was a false bravado, coupled with their visible nervousness from looking over their shoulder at us, we assumed.

We, of course, would get dressed in our Alphas, cool tunic or whatever it is called with brass buttons, block collar revealing traces of white, white trouser, brass belt buckle affixing a wide white belt and tar bucket. We wore (?) the red sash and pinned it above the knee. Unlike the other teams, we also wore white cotton gloves which made it tricky to maneuver our gas operated, clip-fed, semi-automatic shoulder weapons on the drill floor without so much as a slip.

Quick Aside: I believe that's what happened two years earlier at the bi-annual Nationals. Roy Eaton, class of '69 and later author of "Soldier Boy" (I'm there in a group picture!), had his sash get tangled in the rifle sling and he had to "carry arms" his rifle for much of the show, his M1 hanging along his right leg from his shoe top to above his hips, supported by only three overly stressed fingers and a thumb.

Back in the locker room, one of our little mantras was the "shock value" of our appearance in dress Alpha. We'd tell each other not to leave the dressing room early; let 'em see us march on the floor. Shock Value!

Basic Standard Competition was performed using government issued M-1 rifles. Company Q-5 brothers used the same M-1's issued as to every PMC cadet as Rooks; rifles that all of us marched with in the Pulaski Day Parade as freshmen, fired at Fort Dix during rifle instruction, and for us, at Q-5 practice Monday—Thursday through most of the school year. In today's environment it seems unimaginable that our rifles were actually kept in the locked Pershing Rifles team room, along with a TV a ratty worn sofa, bunches of trophies that tradition expected seniors to pilfer, and the ever-present water bugs.

Maybe because all PMC cadets have practiced the Army manual's Basic Standard rifle moves, we may have questioned why we had to practice the manual ourselves. This practice had stopped the previous year or two because, well, we cadets did plenty of Basic Standard. However, a very good Seton Hall unit had actually beaten us in Basic Standard a year earlier, and the senior Brothers agreed we better polish up our skills. The story later was told that we lost at Nationals over a disputed score because of the liberties the Hall took with interpreting what the manual specified—basically by substituting their Trick moves and substituting selective standards of the pre-WW II Army manual. Basic standard marching and moves are to be at 120 beats per minute and not vary: they should have been heavily penalized for all the non-compliant moves but won instead.

A Drill Meet's Basic Standard routine consisted of a set of marching and rifle commands that was distributed to all teams in advance. So, we practiced the Basic Standard routine and became very competent. Heck, even the sound of our hands grabbing the rifle stock would generate a crisp, solid, reassuring sound as if a single hand was at work. Serious! On the other hand, at one Meet we were actually penalized because we happened to execute "Sling Arms '(??) so uniformly that some judges thought we had choreographed it, instead of recognizing we were just good at it.

So, we'd finally get to the staging area ready to execute Basic Standard requirements, do our thing, and because no one was quite as good, we won. Frankly, we felt happier getting off the drill floor and relaxing than in having been just better than the other teams, which we really were.

Back in the dressing room, as we got dressed for our TRICK show, the atmosphere among the brothers became more focused. It wasn't from so much worry about doing what you were supposed to do, as wanting to concentrate on doing everything really well. It wasn't nervousness about the outcome, it was the concerns of each person to stay alert and execute. We wore dress Charlie, our blue-grey tunics with white duck trousers, white cover over our Officers Caps. We covered our rifle slings in white adhesive tape, turning them a uniformly crisp white.

Once dressed, tension would build up to another level. I fretted that my shoes might come untied, that my zipper might open, and my tunic bunched up behind my shoulders. Most of all, it was reminding myself to keep the count! .... after Flame Out, then do 16 steps to begin Open Winds, etc. I would hit the Men's Room every few minutes. I wanted no distractions. I was confident but fidgeting.

These drill meets were well organized. Every team was given a time to arrive, get access to which dressing room, where to wait, the minimum and maximum durations of each show. Judges were positioned on the floor looking for small errors, fingers that were spread apart, open mouths, momentary false moves. After each team completed its routine, it would leave through the staging area, often a hallway opening on to the drill area and leave the proximity. Once a team had left, the next team would assemble, then step into the drill floor for the signal to begin their program.

Every team, including Company Q-5 would march into this area at Port Arms, although this was not part of the scoring. At one Meet, I think it was Nationals, where we spotted an intimidating looking (to other teams, no doubt) DI approaching us at the staging area and asked us questions, such as what class you were in (we were told to say "Senior") or "what is your 3rd General Order". That question was slightly worrisome as we never bothered with that stuff and the Army had just consolidated from 10 General Orders to 3. Anyway, we knew how to respond, and the DI left the staging area.

With their start time several moments away, teams would stand at rigid Parade Rest, each member not daring to so much as turn their heads. I could just imagine sweat running down their backs. Young enthusiasm! We, on the other hand, would go from Parade Rest, to Rest. Heck, we'd scratch, adjust our caps fidget; kind of like San Francisco Giants Jesus Alou, seemly paying no mind to any pressure while giving ourselves those last minute reminders to keep the count, keep our mouths closed, and our fingers together. On lookers must have wondered if we even cared about this being a drill meet.

Then we'd hear the command to go to attention and we'd Dress

Left. In Trick, it was Dress Left, and all marching commands started with your left foot. We'd dress the ranks. "Ready Front" and "About Face" were commanded. Now facing the arena, a timer would sound and we'd take the floor.

"Right Shoulder Arms" was the initial, drawn out command as we'd tease the crowd using a ¾ speed Basic Standard cadence. "Right Shoulder…Arms" was commanded aloud, followed by similarly voiced commands of "Forward…March," at our cloyingly slow pace. A few yards in, we heard "Company, Halt." "Order Arms" done the Army way, again executing the Basic Standard move slowly, making sure to slap our rifle stocks and this time slamming to the ground to the surprise of most and a prelude to the show that followed.

Immediately we'd begin our Trick Show by closing our ranks to the left, pivoting left as we extended our rifle barrel forward and again slamming them down every time we stopped or turned. I remember hearing those sounds starting with the last action of "Order Arms."

It was…Slam, Slam, Slam, Bam, thank you, Ma'am and we were off! I had never really experienced the instant electricity that lit us up when I heard the rebel yell as we began our 220 beats per minute Quick Steps bringing our rifles to an upright version of Right Shoulder Arms in four steps, our right arms bent 0 degrees to hold rifle butt against our upper chest, our left fist closed and half turned forward, knuckles aimed at the direction of march. The left arm itself was straight and moved in short unison back and forth like so many machines. By comparison, the Army Basic Standard specified 144 beats a minute.

Our routine was a "silent drill" meaning no spoken commands, at least, not so anyone could hear them. Every move was based on how many steps you did before starting move "X," and how many the row behind you would do before going into "Y".

By contrast, nearly every other team tried to copy the Army's Old Guard drill routine of rifle twirling and marching to the beat of Basic Standard and spoken commands, sometimes slowing it down to exaggerate certain moves. Most of them featured a separate commander marching alongside the company carrying a sword (go figure!), barking out commands, and climaxing with his strut between opposing lines of spinning and tossed rifles that threatened flowing blood. These routines were performed in several variations of costumes, from quasi-WWII MP outfits to dressy fatigues with ascots showcasing their open collar shirts. Some had white rope under their shoulder patches, some wore long shiny boots. Most, if not all, drilled with non-operating replicas of the WW I Springfield rifles with or without gleaming bayonets. Springfields were beautifully balanced props, light weight and with their loosened hardware tried to imitate the sounds real weapons made when handled with force and precision.

In Silent Commands routines, movements were based on the number of steps you Quick Stepped to begin a move, such as "The Winds" and once completed, how many to the next. Actually, our show was not totally silent; but the audience and scorers couldn't hear our Silent Commands, however our XO, Danny Gascoyne, would whisper them anyway. I don't know if that had always been the practice or not, but in my first drill I lost the count, taking in the moment, if you will. I had often considered the panic I feared I would experience if something like this happened, a lone team member marching randomly by himself, leaving the rest of the company crisply executing a move. We would have lost, finishing low in the standings, I would be totally ashamed and embarrassed, and I might have been kicked off the Trick company. Maybe that's why Gasc always whispered the count or maybe all XOs did it. In any case, Thank You Danny Gascoyne, because when I blurted out, (but quietly! "I'm lost,"

Gasc instantly stated the move we were going into and counted off the numbers. It went like this:

(Me) "I'm lost."

(Gascoyne)…"Confusion" 12 13, 14,15 and by step 16 we executed "Confusion" without the least being confused and there was no damage. Thanks, Gasc!

Yes, It was crucial that everyone keep the count. The individual routines themselves, were so often practiced and their rhythms so natural, there was no way to forget them. Today, 54 years later, I recall Flame Out, Open Winds, Confusion, Q5 Rear March, Marching Marine, Machine Gun Line, Q5 Rear March, (did it have a name?), Squads and Files, Screwed UP Rear March, Black Out, the ACS (after Rudy ACS, its creator, class of 65?)

At the end of our show, roughly 15 minutes, we'd march off the floor, always hearing the thrilled appreciation of fans, opponents, and parents. It was all a great rush and super exciting. The routine's last silent command being given, the company came to a Quick –Step halt, followed by our three moves to order arms and the last rifle butt would slam and we'd walk off back to the staging area and then instantly unwind: Hats off, tunic unzipped, hey, mission accomplished, and we were spent! At the same time, we were temporarily juiced from the high of doing well and electricity and sounds generated from the crowd.

Depending how many teams would perform after us, we had time to carouse through the arena, walk through the stands scanning for interested girls, and enjoy a few moments attention from those we hoped were impressed onlookers. Then it was back to the dressing room and talk about going out later. What a life!

As a pledge attending my first show, The Boston Beanpot, which we won three consecutive years and were later dropped from future invitations, was where I met my first "Love." Her name was Courtney or Corkie, something or other, who drilled (or parading) for the Pershing Rifles Female Cadet sorority club at one of the Boston area ROTC schools. She was classically stunning, I was stunned head over heels, and she returned my feelings, and we held each other and kissed like newcomers all through the party her club was hosting. It was heart-sick puppy love at its newest and most memorable. Hey Corkie, it would be crazy cool if you read this! But the next morning we would fly back to school.

The Trip Home. These weren't memorable. Yes, we were happy to win. In retrospect, I generously compared ourselves to the basketball players at UCLA's NCAA Champs under John Wooden, who also were the annual dominators in what they did. Our flights home didn't include Brothers jumping up and down reliving our victory. It was more like feeling vindicated, because we had arrived fully prepared, relaxed, and were good! So we felt we were the best team and should win, which we certainly did. But with our road trip over, the fun concluded, it was back to PMC and going to class.

What was it like to be in Company Q-5? At first, not as cool as expected. All of us began as pledges, whether we were Rooks, Sophomores, or Juniors trying to get in. We practiced away from the Brothers, and those first two weeks of Pledge practice were the most discouraging as our DI, Chuck Cantwell (for my pledge class), had to instruct about 100 or so of us, mostly brand new PMC Rooks in Basic Standard and learning how to Quick-Step. Those first two weeks quickly thinned the ranks as we realized we were such a rag-tag group. But the rest of us, maybe excepting one or two, stayed with it throughout winter and all were rewarded by joining the company on their trips to actual Drill Meets.

Were we all buddies? I certainly wasn't. I didn't click with most of the brothers, but it was natural that we got on best with the others in our pledge class, especially if we were in the same academic class. I liked Jack Gale, a fellow sophomore who was already a Brother, but I hung out more with the late Colonel Alvarez, a fellow sophomore in my pledge class. But just as with any team, when drill season started, and the Brothers were together, we stood together. Not many of us get the thrill of winning an organization's 350 or so members schools' bi-annual national tournament of champions. Winning is sweetest when the work is demanding. enough to justify feeling unbeatable, especially when you personally contribute to supporting a twenty-year tradition of being "the team".

To this cadet, being on the drill floor as a member of Company Q-5 was just awesome.

Alan Hilkene:
Odds & Ends

All of us currently upright and taking nourishment have memories galore of our exposure at PMC! Almost every one of them was favorable and legal, though on some occasions they were less so. One from that category was cheating on pay phone calls when fares were five or ten cents. It consisted of holding a penny in the coin slot and spinning it forcibly with a pencil to mimic a nickel dropping and energizing the call function. Sure, it took many spins to perform but usually not a long time involved. A sign of success was the hoard of pennies in the coin box and the dorm allocation by room to make up the missing funds! Earning some spending money also involved being a waiter for Slater Services, the meal provider in the basement of Old Main. I remember it was quite a modest provider of spending money.

Also did some typing of professor's study plans and notifications of expected bedroom projects of study subjects and any questions raised by the project. Also paid modestly, but little went far in those days. Once we reached our junior year, the ROTC provided a monthly stipend that went pretty far in keeping us in smokes and eats. My roommate Andy was a gem of a cadet in so many ways. He convinced Coach Ludwig (football) that we could take game film at home games from the dome of Old Main with him doing the filming. I was his donkey for on the job needs of film, umbrella, or whatever was needed. Also ate at the team meal table, so that worked out well! Andy also did ALL the cartoons and yearbook scenes tailored for everyone and also made some special sketches for occasions that cropped up. A very versatile and talented "roomie"!! One other touch of class was marching to church on Sunday mornings and having our soul massaged for improvement and adjustment!

Let's summarize the truly outstanding benefits of PMC for all of us. First, the duty of the military system is to develop character with ability. Now all of us learned that big time. In addition, all of us learned that combat and weapons are only necessary when smart minds don't pay attention to world events and changes. Plus, all of us have developed friendships, in our case in the 1954 class, which have matured and strengthened for some seven decades now, with more to come. Many of us have made our 50th, 55th, 60th, and 65th reunions. There is a compound of PMCers in the Ft. Myers area that attempts to have a monthly lunch together and once had a cruise to the Caribbean from Tampa. Whatever the future holds for us, nothing can remove PMC and its values from everyone. Thank you everyone for being the best and most faithful reflection of life and friendship possible. Yes, we truly love each other, our families, and the experience of comradeship with the guidance of PMC!

Dan Gascoyne:
A Habit of Winning

In an eight-year span beginning in 1955, Q-5 competed in more than twenty-three major tournaments and was awarded some forty-eight trophies, including the title National Champions. In 1969, Company Q-15 won the Pershing Rifles trophy for the seventh time. The trophy was then retired to PMC's trophy case. (From Google).

The National Championship Drill Meet was held every two years. Between 1955 and 1969, 14 years, Nationals was held seven times, and as stated above, we won all seven and retired the National Champion Trophy. Gannon University hosted the 1969 event in Erie, PA. All the major players were in attendance, Seton Hall University, Brooklyn Poly Tech, Fordham University, Clemson University, as well as several regulars that could win on any day. Approximately 40 teams competed at Nationals.

It was no secret that we had won Nationals consistently. In the 1968-1969 drilling season, PMC had won every meet we attended—and had a remarkable record in that we retired the trophies of the St Peters (NJ) Invitational Meet, University of Dayton Invitational Meet, and the Boston Bean Pot Invitational Meet, as we won those meets for three successive years. We had also won the University of Illinois meet at their Champaign-Urbana campus and the 15th Regimental Meet in Philadelphia.

At the end of the Nationals meet, all the teams parade onto the drill floor for the announcement of the results. We were pretty nervous as there was quite a history to uphold. We came in first in Basic Standard Drill and second in Trick Drill and first Overall!

What a thrill, what a year, what a three-year stint for the six of us who pledged and were accepted our freshman year and the four other seniors who had pledged during their sophomore year. What a thrill for all the underclassmen who also drilled and had more to look forward to!

Pershing Rifles is a brotherhood, just like a fraternity, and created a bond between all the brothers. The bond strengthened at PMC because of our commitment to practice hard and often and maintain the high standards.

John Czekner, Bill Feyk, Terry Fadem, Stu Perlmutter:
Being a PMC Bugler

When Theodore Hyatt founded the Delaware Military Academy in 1858, Richard Triggs was on that first faculty as Professor of vocal and instrumental music. Hyatt's belief in the necessity of music on campus began with cadets playing fifes, drums, and bugles. Historically, fifes and drums were used to provide music for the military as well as being an integral part of the unit structure. These instruments were used to regulate the daily activities of the Cadet Corps, signaling when the Cadets would rise in the morning, when to eat, when to assemble, and when to go to bed.

In 1864, the legendary John Robson Sweeny, who had been a Union Army Bandmaster, came to the school and reorganized the fife drum and bugle squad. Throughout the latter part of the 19th century and into the 20th century, the school boasted a drum and bugle corps. By 1875, the bugle began to replace the fife in the U.S. Army. Historically, a bugle was used in the Cavalry to relay instructions from officers to solders during battle. PMC with its equestrian history certainly took advantage of this musical instrument.

In 1920, the famed bandmaster John Phillip Sousa, along with future President of the United States Warren Harding, were both awarded honorary doctorates from the school. Subsequently, in 1922 Sousa wrote a march dedicated to Colonel Hyatt, faculty, and the cadets of Pennsylvania Military College. The march was called "The Dauntless Battalion." Perhaps Sousa was inspired by our drum and bugle corps which would have likely performed at the degree ceremony.

In 1935, under the direction of Professor John Norris, Class of 1884, the PMC Marching Band was formed. Virtually from the beginning of Pennsylvania Military College, buglers were needed to alert the Cadet Corps to attend daily events by playing musical tunes. Each particular bugle call was used for a specific purpose. A PMC bugler was needed to sound the call indicating when to wake up (reveille) in the morning to when to go to bed (taps) in the evening. Numerous other bugle calls were necessary as well.

The incoming freshmen trumpet players would be assigned the task of performing bugle calls during their first year at school. Our bugle calls were played on trumpets which have valves that are used to play music with multiple notes. Having no valves, bugles are capable of producing only four notes for military "calls". Trumpets are able to produce many notes which include those used in the bugle calls. These "buglers" were part of Headquarters Company (also known as the band) which was composed solely of musicians.

As incoming Rooks in our freshman year beginning on September 6, 1966, the trumpet players who were in Headquarters Company were the buglers for the Corps of Cadets. For that future Class of 1970, the buglers were John Czekner, Bill Feyk, Stu Perlmutter, and the late Terry Fadem. Every morning at 6:30 AM, one of those buglers would go into the basement of Dorm #4 accompanied by the Sergeant of the Guard. In the R.O.T.C. area near the Commandants office was an amplifier. A switch would then be turned on and the bugler would play Reveille into the attached microphone. The tune then would be played over the loudspeaker system throughout the dormitories to "wake up" the cadets.

The next bugle call would occur ten minutes before the Mess I (breakfast) formation at 6:50 AM, as the Corps gathered around the flagpole on the macadam horseshoe in front of Old Main. The bugler would walk up the steps onto the porch facing the flagpole and play "First Call" followed at 7:00 AM by "To The Colors" as the flag was being raised.

The next bugle call happened when the Corps gathered on the horseshoe for Mess III (dinner) formation. The bugler again positioned himself on the porch of Old Main and played "First Call" at 5:50 PM. At this end of the day formation, the Cadets are put at a Parade Rest formation and "Retreat" is sounded. Then the Cadets are brought to attention with the command "Present Arms" followed by the final rendition of "To The Colors" as the flag is lowered at 6PM.

In the evening at 10:15 PM, another call was played. The bugler stood on the "senior steps" and while facing Howell Hall, Turrell Hall, and Cann Hall would play "Tattoo," a rather long bugle call. The last call of the day was "Taps" played at 10:45 PM, with the bugler again positioned facing the dormitories.

There were quite a few ceremonial occasions off campus throughout the year that required a PMC Bugler to play bugle calls. The buglers playing their trumpets were part of the band which performed in concerts as well as marching on our own parade field for ceremonial events. The band during our time at PMC traveled to major cities representing the school. We marched in the New York Saint Patrick's Day Parade, the Cherry Blossom Festival in Washington D.C., as well as the annual Pulaski Day parade in downtown Chester.

One significant performance occurred during our years at PMC when we as band members led the Mardi Gras Parade in New Orleans, Louisiana. As a northern band, we only played one song numerous times continuously throughout the parade. It was a tune called "Dix-ie!" Events were held with PMC Buglers playing at the Liberty Bell and the Union League in Philadelphia. During our years at school, an honor guard and bugler attended the funerals for the local PMC alumni who were killed in Vietnam. A PMC bugler played "Taps" at those funerals. The commanding officer of the Honor Guard then would give the grieving widow the flag that had been draped over the coffin saying, "From A Grateful Nation."

As buglers, we paid daily tribute to the American Flag and through our performances played an important part of the cadet corps' daily life on campus. While the solitary bugler was rarely seen, his musical voice, floating through the air, was heard by all who were cadets at Pennsylvania Military College.

Being a PMC Bugler was an honor that we cherish to this day.

Abraham J. Gale:
Pershing Rifles Q-5/Q15

Pennsylvania Military College's Company Q-5/Q15 compiled an unmatched competition record of (consecutive) National Drill Championships between 1957 and 1972. To put this into some perspective, imagine the same football team winning the Super Bowl every year, year after year after year for nearly 15 years.

Drill Competitions consisted of Trick Drill and Basic Standard Drill. Trick drill required a minimum time (usually around 15 minutes on the drill floor) in at least a 16 man formation (sometimes 24) while the Basic Standard portion required a set series of commands to be performed by a platoon and judged against each team where points were deducted by D. I's for each series of commands the team followed from a starting total.

TRICK DRILL: There are many stories about pledging, competition, practice, etc. regarding the Brotherhood of Q-5/Q15 (Some of which can actually be repeated). To demonstrate how remarkable the precision was in Trick Drill, for example, consider this one example: The entire Trick Drill performance was done to the "quick step" cadence; roughly four steps per second where each row in the Unit was separated by about 2.5 feet. Then picture this: the late Rudy Acs 1966 dreamed up what became known as "The Acs" which was performed about halfway through the trick drill sequence. "The Acs" consisted of splitting the Brothers into two groups where each group passed within each other in formation no more than two feet apart two consecutive times on a diagonal at four steps per second, without commands (no oral commands were ever given after the unit was called to attention to start the performance).

The margin of error given the speed, cadence, and the "Acs" formation to avoid a collision between cadets carrying a 9.5 lb. M-1 was approximately one half second. If you were off by more than that, a collision happened. Usually, one collision in practice with an M-1 rifle and another Brother at speed cured any timing errors in the future. Of all the things we did in a silent Trick Drill performance, "The Acs" required the most immaculate timing and precision in my opinion. To my recollection, no collision ever occurred in competition over my four years at PMC.

BASIC STANDARD DRILL: The Corps was less familiar with this since it was performed at Drill Competition to a set of commands that were established by the Pershing Rifle host command of the competition. The Basic Standard Drill performance differed from competition to competition. I'll relate what we did at The Boston Beanpot Competition in 1968-1969 for example. This competition drew competitors from all over. It was traditionally one of the largest field of competitors in the country, drawing teams from all over.

The 1968-1969 team that year was led by Jim Hogg '69, the First Captain of the Corps. Each team started with 300 points. The DI's deducted points for each maneuver / command required during the entire Basic Standard Drill sequences governed by FM 22.5. Q-5/Q15 scored 1,492 points out of 1500 points after five Marine DI's scored the team's roughly 15 minutes on the drill floor. We retired the Beanpot rifle trophy for three wins in a row that year while the nearest competitor in second place was about 20 points behind us. The remaining teams were even farther behind. On the flight back to PMC, we joked that we didn't know where the deductions came from! The Basic Standard Team always personified perfection.

Helpful to appreciate that by the time a brother graduated from PMC, he had probably spent more than 1,000 hours in practice or competition and knew that no one else could compare with the results that this dedication to perfection produced.

There are so many stories to recall and relate about Q-5/Q15. These are just two.

Mark Billen:
The PMC Mounted Troop

The PMC Mounted Troop was founded by a group of dedicated cadets who wanted to bring the tradition of the horse cavalry back to PMC after an absence of almost 26 years. In the Fall of 1967, several cadets began borrowing horses from friends and riding at the PMC home football games. There were usually four horses ridden at every game. The riders wore a cavalry uniform similar to the that worn by the U.S. Cavalry in the late 1800's. Eventually it was decided to have a mounted troop as part of the Cadet Corps. The two cadets who founded the unit began to recruit additional members. Each new member was required to provide his own uniform and horse. A problem confronting the Troop was where to board the horses. The Unit found an old cow barn which they began to turn into a riding stable. After many months of hard work and sacrifice, the cow barn became a horse stable. By the end of February 1968, the Unit had a sturdy facility with 15 stalls, a horse van, and a Troop of 15 riders, each with his own horse.

The Unit, though growing, had many challenges. Many of the riders had never ridden a horse, let alone owning and caring for one. The task of training the men remained a challenge. During March and April of 1968, the Unit started practicing for a Mothers' Day show that would be part of the Corps' annual Mothers' Day formalities. At this time a riding uniform was selected consisting of a white hat, a gray cadet shirt, a senior belt, yellow ascot, yellow and gray gloves, gray trousers with a yellow stripe, black riding boots, and spurs.

In order to formalize its existence, a constitution was developed that would govern the Unit's activities and organization.

The Troop worked hard to put on a good show for Mothers' Day, which would be the first-time parents would see the Troop in action. As it turned out, the Unit made a big impression on everyone. The Troop, which became known as the PMC Marauders, was a SUCCESS!

There was a quote attached to a photo of the unit which captures the story of the Marauders… "The establishment of the PMC Marauders has brought a much-needed recognition to the Pennsylvania Military College's long and interesting history. The reintroduction of the Cavalry provides a strong tradition to the Corps of Cadets and pride in the inspiration that promoted and successfully completed this task."

John W. Stealey:
Headquarters Company

I played Trombone since the 7th grade as the fat smart kid with big lips and long arms. (I graduated from the fat smart kid club when 12 guys beat me up in the 9th grade). Mom hired the next-door neighbor to beat me up for two hours each Tuesday and Thursday with boxing gloves. He quit two months later, saying I was hitting too hard.

I got even with the local gang when three of them tried to jump me again and I beat the heck out of them. (We became good friends later as I stood up to them.) The football coach saw me fighting. He said, "I could have stopped that, Bill, but you seemed to be doing all right. Do you want to play football for me?" (Moved up to a B+ athlete!)

I played in several High School band organizations. I was never great, but I was loud and as a Civil Air Patrol Cadet and Squadron Commander, I knew my left foot from my right foot and how to stay in step.

I got promoted to Right Guide in HQ Company! Cool! That meant that in the King Rex Parade in New Orleans at Mardi Gras 1966, I got to be at the front of the band where I could hold the Trombone in my left hand with a Bud can in the right. Played the entire march in first position!

Interestingly, for the USAF Academy band the next year I was also at the front of the King Rex parade. My mom was from New Orleans and both times I fell into love very meaningfully for three entire days!

John Vencius:
Pershing Rifles

As Rooks we were presented with the various possibilities for joining extracurricular activities such as Rangers, Battery Robinett, Greek Letter Fraternities, and Pershing Rifles. I was initially inclined to go with the Rangers for obvious reasons, but two other factors weighed in on my decision.

The first was that my cadre sergeant was one Jack Gale, whose pride in Company Q-5 was evident in virtually everything he did, and whose infectious grin (smirk?) belied the seriousness with which he took both his studies and everything Q-5.

The second was recalling my very first introduction to PMC. My cousin was a member of the PMC class of 1963. With my family, I attended the 1963 Mother's Day activities on campus. While the Cadet Corps parade impressed me, the Pershing Rifles' performance was just incredible. That visit drew me to PMC instead of either VMI or The Citadel.

Faced with the choices of activities to pursue, I felt that the Pershing Rifles was the most uniquely "PMC" of the choices. And so I pledged PR, even considering that the pledge period was the entire academic year as opposed to a single semester.

Unfortunately, I didn't survive the final "blackball" of the year and could only watch as my classmates became brothers in the unit. However, with the encouragement of those classmates and my big brother, I came back the next fall, determined to gain my PR Shield and shoulder cord.

Pledging in my sophomore year felt a little strange as I moved around campus sounding more a rook as I called out "Viva La Q-5, Sir" to the brothers, many of whom I had just pledged with a few months prior. But I took it all in stride as I worked at improving my skills and earning my way into the brotherhood. I was also the best and fastest in the pledge class at shining up the buttons on the full dress "alpha" blouses. Lousy at spit shining shoes, but the Master of the Brasso, I think the stuff had gotten into my blood.

By the time spring rolled around and I survived the final blackball to finally become a brother, our Q-5 Drill Instructor (the same Jack Gale who'd previously been my cadre sergeant) took me under his wing to teach me the signature "double spin" to be able to anchor the shorter guys' end of the Machine Gun Line. He kept me at it until I earned the spot, which I held for the next two years.

The downside was that each time we performed, and it came time for it, I was scared out of my mind that I'd mess it up. Luckily, nobody was close enough to hear the huge sigh of relief I let out following after each one.

Corps ?
THE BRIGADIER
A CADET PUBLICATION
FOR CADETS
Whosoever shall pulleth
forth the sword
from this stone
May 1972 A.D.

REFLECTIONS

Dave Neimeyer:
Into Death, With Honor

Part I: Oh, play the fife slowly...

Something was brewing. Vague rumors were popping up left and right, but no one knew for certain. All we really knew was that the fate of the Corps of Cadets was at stake.

It was no secret that the Corps was in trouble. Ten years earlier, the Corps of Cadets at Pennsylvania Military College numbered over six hundred. Now there were barely two hundred and fifty left...only one sixth of the total student body at PMC Colleges.

The Cadets attributed the loss to skullduggery by the college president and the admissions department. There were many proven cases where prospective Cadets had been urged by admissions not to join the Corps, but to enroll as a civilian student instead. To the Cadets, it was a truism to say that President Moll wanted to see the Corps dead and an all-civilian college in its place.

The administration, on the other hand, attributed the drop to the mood of the general public. According to admissions, in the wake of the Vietnam War, no one wanted to go to a military college. No matter what the reason, the Corps had diminished dramatically, and now its survival was threatened.

It was on the sixteenth of March of my junior year when things finally began to break. It was announced that President Moll wanted to meet separately with each Cadet class. This was it. We knew instinctively that the Corps would die or survive depending on what we heard tonight.

At the appropriate hour, we trudged over to the large lecture room in the Kapelski Learning Center. The Seniors were still inside with Moll, so we had to wait outside. I saw Pony Soldier Gerber and walked over to him. "Well, Fred, what do you think's gonna happen?" I asked.

"I don't know," he replied, "But I think that Mole Parsons had the right idea when he transferred to VMI. This place is dying."

"Dazer" Clemens spoke up. "Aw, come on, Gerber. How can you say that. They wouldn't kill the Corps...it brings in too much publicity."

"Yeah, but does it bring in the money? That's what the administration looks for," Fred replied.

"How about the alumni?" I countered. "If they dump the Corps, how many of the alumni will give anything to this place?"

"How many give anything now?" Fred answered. "You know darn well that most of the guys that graduate from here never give anything at all."

"Yeah, but..." I began.

"Hey, here come the Seniors...we can go in now" interrupted Dazer. The Seniors walked out in clusters, talking among themselves.

"Hope you've got good stomachs," one of them yelled. "You'll love this one."

"Yeah," another Senior added. "Better be sitting down when you get the news."

I wanted to ask what they meant, but my classmates were filing inside the lecture hall, so I decided to get the news first-hand. We shuffled and pushed for about five minutes, then everyone was finally seated. In the front of the room, President Moll leaned against a table and played with a handful of coins in his pocket. He had a phony, shifty look. I didn't trust him. Against the door to his right stood Colonel Frey, the Corps Commandant, and Chuck Ketchel, who was Brigade Commander that year. As such, he was the highest-ranking Cadet in the Corps. By the opposite door stood Major "Jungle George" Lynch, the assistant Commandant. Next to him was Bob Sabochik, the Cadet Adjutant. All four of them looked sour. It was no task to see that bad news was coming.

Moll smiled, then stood up and walked forward a few steps. He was obviously nervous. I got the impression that he was afraid we would jump down and beat him up, or something. Maybe he wasn't entirely wrong, either.

"Let me begin by reassuring you of one thing." His voice was smooth and melodious. "The Corps will be back next year. However, things will be changed somewhat." He went on to tell us a story we had all heard several times already. Its basis was always the same:

PMC Colleges was composed of cadet Pennsylvania Military College and civilian Penn Morton College. However, very few people had ever heard of Penn Morton. Consequently, everyone thought PMC was an all-military school. No one ever did explain why, if this was so, the civilian enrollment grew every year.

Moll reminded us that a survey had been instituted to check the feasibility of a name change for the college. We were familiar with this, too. The survey had suggested that the name Pennsylvania Military College be retained, and the overall college name be changed. Moll had promptly commissioned another survey. Tonight, we were faced with his results.

The speech continued. "There will be a convocation tomorrow to announce the name change to the public at large. However, we felt it proper to tell the cadets now because of the added effect on them. As of next year, the Cadet Corps will be known as the Kapelski Regiment of Widener College." At this pronouncement there was a groan from the Cadets, then a few bits of laughter. "He's got to be kidding!" someone said.

Moll smiled nervously, and then continued. "As you all know, Louis Kapelski is a great friend of the Corps. In fact, he is the man who donated this building to the college. That is why we chose his name for the Corps: to honor him for what he has done..."

No doubt President Moll would have gone on for some time, but at this point Ken Wade jumped up. "You don't understand, sir. Sure, Kapelski's a great guy, but that doesn't matter. It wouldn't matter if you named the Corps after George Washington! It can't be done. The Corps is bigger than any one man, no matter who he is!" Ken sat down to our applause. Several others spoke up in agreement with Ken, and soon everybody was trying to make his opinion heard. The meeting began to degenerate this way for a few minutes, then President Moll brought us back to order again.

"Well," he said, "We can argue the point forever, but that won't do us any good right now. I still have to meet with the freshmen and sophomores, so let's get on with the business at hand. Now then, there's no need to worry about your diplomas, or transcripts, or things of that nature. All documents will be changed to read 'Widener College', so you won't be tied to a name that no longer exists."

"Hey, wait a minute!" Someone said. "You mean that my diploma will say 'Widener' and not 'Pennsylvania Military'?"

"That is correct," Moll replied.

"What good does that do me?" The Cadet returned. "I went here for three years. I want mine to say, 'Pennsylvania Military'!"

"But that wouldn't be wise. In the future, the name Widener will mean something, and the name PMC won't. If you get PMC on your diploma, it will be just a scrap of paper," Moll replied.

"It will mean something to me! That's what's important. The name Widener would be just a scrap of paper!" Tempers were rising. Again, several Cadets agreed with the speaker, but their voices were louder now, more demanding. Every time Moll would insist that it would be to our benefit to have Widener on our diplomas, several Cadets would insist that they wanted Pennsylvania Military on theirs. The arguments threatened to get worse, but once again President Moll put himself on top of the situation.

"Well," he said. "If that's the way you all feel, we'll have to look into it. Let's just say that we'll leave that open to interpretation."

The Cadets were somewhat mollified but were not ready to let him off the hook just yet. I spoke up at this point. "Mister Moll, will you put that in writing?"

Some of my classmates snickered. Moll reddened slightly.

"Why?" he asked.

"Well, I don't mean to cast aspersions on your character," I began, "But in the past we've found that you're prone to say one thing and do another. You'll give us one story one day, and a different story the next. You haven't given us any reason to trust you." I gained fervor as I spoke. "Your word to us doesn't mean a thing."

Moll reddened even more. His hand began to work the coins in his pocket even more furiously. In the silence as we waited for his reply, the noise of their clinking together was clearly audible. President Moll sat back down on the tabletop and tried to smile. He failed.

"I don't feel you have any right to make those accusations," he said calmly.

"I feel I do," I answered loudly.

Now Ketchel broke in. "All right, hold it. We're not here to engage in accusations. It's an unpleasant business and I realize tempers are high, but let's not fly off the handle."

I sat down, still somewhat piqued. Dazer reached over and shook my hand. "Way to go, Hobbit. That's telling him."

The rest of the meeting was anticlimactic. A few more questions were asked and answered, and in another ten minutes we walked out through a milling herd of freshmen and sophomores.

"Ready for the big surprise?" a Junior asked of the milling herd.

"Hope you enjoyed your time at PMC?" Another added.

The underclassmen stared at us quizzically. No doubt they wanted to stay and question us further, but they had to file into the lecture hall for their meeting with destiny. We were in as much of a hurry to get away, so the questions would have to wait for later. They were all rhetorical now anyway.

Part II: ... and play the drum slowly ...

Friday dawned somewhat overcast. It fit our mood perfectly. We had our usual morning formation at 7:00, then marched to Mess I as always. The convocation would not be until 9:00 but the fun started much sooner than that. At around 8:00 we heard noises from the quadrangle, so Howie and I poked our heads out the window to see what was going on.

Heads were protruding from nearly every window of the Cadet dorms. Under a barrage of jeers, two security guards were putting the flag up to full staff. The Cadets had left it at half-mast at formation. They finally got it all the way up, and then walked away. As they did so, three freshmen: Rushworth, Cramer, and Gasser, walked boldly out of the dorm, across the street, and up Senior Steps to the flagpole, where they once more lowered the flag to half-staff. The cheers that greeted them from all the Cadets were invigorating. Security looked at the flag, shrugged, and went back into the building. The Cadets had won a minor victory.

At around quarter to nine, Rushworth, Howie, and I walked over to the cafeteria for the convocation. The tables had all been removed and rows of chairs set up instead. Several TV cameras focused on the stage, upon which were set several chairs and a lectern. On the wall behind the stage was a covered banner, quite obvious in its presence and just waiting to be unveiled to reveal…what? The Cadets already knew.

"Let's get those seats in the front row," said Howie, and we readily agreed. "I want a good view of this," Howie continued.

Before long, Colonel Frey and Ketchel came in and took their seats on the stage. Moll followed them in, beaming his customary toothy smile. He walked confidently to the lectern and began to make basically the same speech the Cadets had heard the night before. At an appropriate place he paused and gestured to the covered banner. Two coeds in blue jeans had been standing by, and at Moll's signal they stepped forward and removed the covering from the banner. The name "Widener" stood forth in electric blue letters. It was one of those quirks of fate that the banner was framed by the chairs of Colonel Frey and Chuck Ketchel, thus providing an interesting contrast. As the applause from the audience filled the cafeteria, Colonel Frey clapped once or twice, then gave up and looked disgusted. Ketchel continued clapping half-heartedly, but it was clear he was displeased. Was their reaction a hint of things to come?

The speech resumed and everyone was now informed that the Cadet Corps would be known as the Kapelski Regiment. As had happened the previous night, groans and laughter dominated the reaction. I had had enough. I looked around and saw Ken Wade get up and start for the door. Then Chicken Man Williams and White Hunter Fischer started to leave, too. Then Cadets all over were standing up and walking out. Rushworth, Howie, and I joined them.

We had barely gotten out the door when reporters began popping up all over the place, taking pictures and asking opinions. They got them. Cadets were definitely out to make themselves heard that day.

More and more Cadets were joining our cluster. "What are we gonna do now?" someone asked.

"Hey, I've got an idea!" cried Rushworth. "Let's go get that giant 'Pennsylvania Military College' banner and hang it from Howell Hall."

"Yeah, great…let's go." Someone else agreed.

"Where is it?" A freshman asked.

"Major Lynch keeps it in his office," I answered. "We'll have to get it from him."

We found Major Lynch sitting dejectedly in his office. We knocked and saluted as we walked in. As ranking Cadet present, I was spokesman. "Sir, we were wondering if we could borrow that big Pennsylvania Military banner. In light of what's happened, we figured we'd hang it from Howell Hall and let everyone know how we feel."

Major Lynch smiled, then began to chuckle. "You know I can't give it to you. That's against regulations." He replied. "But if you go back outside for a minute, I'll be leaving my office soon. When I go, you can come back and try to find it. I might not be allowed to give it to you, but if you just happen to find it, that's not my fault."

"Yes, Sir." We snapped a salute and took off. A minute or so later Major Lynch came out of his office and whistled his way past us. He smiled again and motioned towards his office. We needed no further encouragement. We dashed into his office and "found" the banner neatly folded on his desk. Picking it up we raced happily back to the quadrangle, holding our prize up to show our friends. Then we sprinted up to the third (and top) floor of Howell. Before long the great square banner was draped down the front of the dorm, nearly touching the ground. The words "Pennsylvania Military College" stood out in foot-high golden letters against the bright red background. A crowd of Cadets and curious onlookers had gathered in the quad by this time, and as the banner fluttered in the slight breeze, a happy cheer went up. We were determined to stick by our name. The final battle had begun.

Part III: ... and play the death march as they carry me along.

The next few weeks were the busiest and the most confusing any of us had ever seen. After the walkout at the convocation, President Moll had agreed that perhaps "Kapelski Regiment" was not a good name for the Corps. The job now became to find a name suitable to everyone. A faction arose to make the name "Pennsylvania Military College of Widener College." Moll said, "Definitely not. It's too confusing" and was only slightly more favorable towards, "Pennsylvania Military Corps of Cadets of Widener College." A dozen other names arose. The Cadets mulled over Pennsylvania Military Institute, Pennsylvania Corps of Cadets, and even the original name of the school, changed a century earlier: Pennsylvania Military Academy. All rose, gained support, and then floundered. No name was suitable.

In a seemingly amazing contrast to our earlier position, a ground swell began to rise among the cadets to let the Corps die. I was one of those who clung steadfastly to the name "Pennsylvania Military College," yet even I had to agree with those who said, "let the Corps die." Their reasoning had a noble logic about it. The Corps had been the college scapegoat for years. Dwindling numbers had made the Corps a mockery of what it had been. The freshman class of seventy-five men was a shadow of the class that had entered just five years earlier with over two hundred people. The "Men in Grey" were fading away. Many of the Cadets felt that even if we survived this crisis and lost our name in the process, we would be better off dead. We were only prolonging the agony.

The ground swell rose and became a wave. By the time the windy afternoons of April had rolled around, even the most die-hard Cadets agreed that it might be better to end the Corps now, with its name, honor, and traditions intact than to let its heritage be stripped away bit by bit.

April Sixth was a Thursday like any other. At 6:30 PM, the Cadets formed up on the horseshoe around the flagpole and we had our usual retreat ceremony, after which we marched into the cafeteria for Mess III. Supper went as always. Food at PMC hadn't improved much over the years. The Cadets were done eating and were restlessly waiting to be dismissed, when President Moll and F. Eugene Dixon, the head trustee, came in and walked up to the staff table. Captain Ketchel stood up and said a few words to us, telling us, among other things, "We expect you all to act as gentlemen, regardless of what the situation may be." He then handed the microphone to Mr. Dixon, who made a short speech summarizing the flurry of meetings that had been held since the middle of March. He then began to read from a resolution by the board of trustees.

The resolution was what we all expected for some time. There was no way out. It stated, in brief, that the Corps was to be dissolved at the end of that school year and replaced by an ROTC unit. The Corps was dead.

Colonel Frey now stood at the microphone. Some, who sat closer than I, said that he had tears in his eyes as he spoke. "Gentlemen," he began calmly, "The decision is made. The time is now for going back to the books, completing the education you came here for." He paused and seemed to sigh as he looked out at his Corps, then he spoke once more. "I would remind you that you are still Pennsylvania Military College and will be until graduation day. I'm sure that each of you will do your best to live up to the 126 years of tradition so that we can finish this thing with dignity and honor. Thank you very much."

Colonel Frey moved away, Chuck Ketchel reclaimed the microphone that he had relinquished only a few minutes before, and yet we all knew that an era had died in those minutes. It remained but for him to dismiss us as usual. His voice was soft and slightly bemused against the unnatural silence of the Cadets. "I guess the Corps is, literally, dismissed," is all he said.

The Cadets rose in silence and began to slowly move out of the cafeteria. Somewhere across the room a glass fell to the floor and shattered noisily, and the Corps filed slowly through the doors and into the night.

Dave Neimeyer:
Epilogue — And I, With Mournful Tread

I think we all walked away from graduation day that year feeling a little dazed. It had been eerie to stand at attention and watch as the Corps colors were gently rolled up and put away for the last time. It seemed strange to think that I'd be coming back next year and not have the Corps there. I'd be a senior at a college that had known my footsteps for three years, and yet was unknown to me. Even this last gathering of the Corps was a jumble of contrasts.

The program took place inside the newly constructed Schwartz Gym, yet there on the stage sat actor Burt Musten, PMC class of 1903. The oldest living graduate of the Corps in their newest building. I felt a pang of disappointment. If it hadn't been for the weather, the formation would have been held outside. In that case, Juniors would have been given the positions usually held by seniors. As Corps Personnel Sergeant, I would have been given the position of Adjutant for this, the last Corps parade ever. Oh well, it couldn't be helped.

People were everywhere as I walked back to my room. Parents, girlfriends, brothers, and sisters thronged around the dorms. Cadets, half buried under piles of belongings, quickly loaded cars, and prepared to take off for the summer. Others had taken care of that earlier and were even now driving away. Shouts filled the air.

"See ya next year." "Come visit if you get a chance...you know where I live." "Don't forget to write." "Have a good summer." "Watch out for those wild women."

These were my friends. Some were graduating. Others didn't plan on returning next year. Many of these I'd never see again, but I had come to accept that. I bumped into Howie as he came out of the room.

"You still here yet?" I asked. "I thought you'd be gone by now."

"Almost, Hobbit. This is my last load." he replied as he set down his suitcase and shifted a pile of books to his other arm. "Take care of yourself this summer."

"Same goes for you, Howie." I said as I shook his hand. "Don't work too hard."

"Don't worry, I won't. Well, I've got to get moving. See you in September."

I walked on into the room. It was almost empty. I had taken most of my belongings to the car earlier that morning. All that remained now were a few odds and ends. The barren shelves stood forlornly on the wall; their possessions gone. I carefully closed and locked the windows in preparation for summer. It was hot in the room. It had been hot on my first day here. A small roll of dust blew under the bed. I watched it and thought about my three years in the Corps.

Had they been worth it? I wasn't sure. I thought of the friends I'd made. Only a few still remained. Znidarsic had enlisted a few months after McKelvey and was currently fighting in Vietnam. Kajioka was working in the stock room of a hospital in Philly, and the last I'd heard, Kortlang was doing construction work in New York.

Of the one hundred and forty men that had started with me, less than fifty remained. Some were gone under more somber circumstances. Dick Cranston was dead in a car wreck, and Kiley had shot himself. In a few months, they would be joined by Jack Downing, dying of a cerebral hemorrhage, and Tom Williams, losing his life in a hunting accident. Now even the immortal Corps was dead, and the thin grey line drew to a close.

And yet...Mole Parsons was at VMI, but I could still remember the hilarious way he used to sing, "If you want it, here it is, come and get it." Ken Okamoto was at the University of Miami, yet I remember his reaction the first time he saw snow, as he bounced back and forth across the corridor yelling, "It's snowing! Hey guys, it's really snowing!" his usual composure lost completely.

I remembered how Crazy Charlie, Kaj, and I used to rappel off of Kirkbride Hall and drive the civilians crazy. I remembered Znidarsic's crazy laugh as he and McKelvey raced down the hall after pulling another prank on Jim World.

I picked up my odds and ends. In the hall I turned and kicked the door shut, then headed for the car. Thinking back on those three years, I realized that I had made good friends and had good times. Whatever else happened, I had my memories. I knew then that it had been worth it.

James H. VanSciver:
What Are They Doing Now?

It's been over fifty years since these young lads created the memories found in this book. What have they now been up to?

Nearly forty of the Class of 1972 and their wives flooded back to Widener University for their 50th Reunion on October 15 and 16, 2022. Most bivouacked at the Concordville Best Western on the evening of October 13 in preparation for the weekend's festivities, which were the work of a 13-member committee (Jeffrey Bendit, Michael Campbell, Ku Chin, Craig Glassner Greg Haugens, Paul Lewis, Philip Lewis, Scott McGinnis, David Newcomb, Edward Rogers, Bill Speer, Clifford Trumbo, and Jimmy VanSciver) after nearly two years of planning.

Friday's agenda began at 9:00 A.M. when Alumni Auditorium opened its doors and visitors could make their way to the PMC Museum. Once inside, they were bedazzled by the Class of 1972 display which featured class members in various activities, including training, formations, sports, academics, and recreation. Ron Romanowicz, from the Class of 1968, provided expert testimony to any and all questions regarding the museum collection.

Classmate Paul Lewis next conducted a respectful and informative wreath laying ceremony at 10:00 A.M. which honored the class's fallen members. Immediately thereafter LTC James Pascoe provided an update regarding Widener University's Army ROTC program.

Beginning at 11:00 A.M., narrator Greg Wall teased memories from a panel of Paul Ketchel, Breck Cook, John Andreas, Philip Lewis, and Jimmy VanSciver with questions such as, "What lessons did you learn at PMC that you were able to apply to your life after graduation?" and, "What is the craziest situation in which you were involved, or you saw while at PMC?" Answers ranged from the serious to the humorous as the respondents offered their rejoinders to the queries. Noon saw everyone gather at the University Center for a festive luncheon before returning to the hotel to prepare for the evening banquet.

Friday evening's banquet began at 6:00 P.M. at the Concord Country Club with an open bar, continued through a program, a buffet meal, awards and recognition, and a cash bar until 10:00 P.M. Attendees were treated to a professionally developed program, designed, and donated by Paula and Jimmy VanSciver and bags of candy and a newspaper clipping from the 1950s as well as floral arrangements created by Hannah Campbell, wife of Mike Campbell.

Emcee Jimmy VanSciver, with the assistance of Craig Glassner, Scott McGinnis, and Greg Haugens, took attendees through a diverse itinerary which included introductions of the reunion committee. Craig Glassner explained the Fallen Classmate Table, read the name of each fallen classmate, Jeffrey Bendit, James Brickley, Charles Driggers, Joseph Edwards, John Fassett, Robert Frutchey, George

Ginovsky, Arthur Hafner, Paul Hydutsky, Robert Leach, Walter Lenox, Hubert Lynch, William Marsele, Robert Poltarak, Anastasio Ruiz, James Tarantola, James Vandever, and Denis Williams (each followed by a bell ringing) and explained a project he headed that will guarantee that the legacy of Pennsylvania Military College and the Class of 1972 will continue in perpetuity.

Christine Edwards was honored for her attendance in representing the wives of fallen classmates and was presented with a special sweatshirt. Classmates in attendance were next asked to close their eyes while a special gift was presented. When they opened their eyes, they were shocked to find a perfectly produced challenge coin, presented in a black velvet bag, in front of them. This was the result of the efforts of classmate Bill Speer, who had the vision, the drive, and found the resources, to bring it to fruition.

Scott McGinnis took attendees on a trip "Down Memory Lane," and Greg Haugens was introduced to explain plans for future activities with the class after which the meal began. After door prizes were presented and recognition had for classmates who traveled the farthest and had the most grandchildren, David Wray was called to the podium. Wray has the distinction of being the final graduate of the final class of Pennsylvania Military College. He also was also presented with a special sweatshirt. Merriment continued after the 10:00 P.M. hour as classmates enjoyed each other's company.

It was back to the PMC Museum on Saturday morning at 9:00 A.M. for pastry, fruit, coffee, and juices. Perhaps the most challenging aspect of the day was securing the cooperation of the classmates for two pictures, one at the flag in front of Old Main and the other on the Senior Steps. It took all of the creativity and patience of photographer Justin Jackson to accomplish this fete, but he did so with grace and dignity.

Most class members participated in the Memorial Bench Dedication Ceremony for Colonel Richard Mulhern, Class of 1971, which began promptly at 10:30 A.M. in the Alumni Garden.

Many advantaged themselves of the golf cart transportation system to make their way to the PMC Village Recreation Center for the tailgating experience. At noon, nearly forty 1972 Alumni made their way to the James Quick Stadium in preparation for the Broom Drill. The Class of 1972 formation dwarfed that of other classes. As they stood parallel facing the stadium on the left hashmark, small leaves began falling from the trees behind them. As the afternoon sun shone on the leaves, they likened to flakes of gold flittering down behind the members of the Class of 1972. How fitting! A message from God.

Next came the coin toss with Billy Burris, Bill Cole, Craig Glassner, Ed Storey, and Jimmy VanSciver participating. The group had selected Cole to flip the coin in the air but, after being introduced to the captains from both teams, the referee showed the team captains the heads and tails, stepped back, and to Cole's dismay, pitched the circular item up into the afternoon sunlight.

Some classmates attended the college reception at Lathem Hall, which began at 4:30 P.M. after which it was off to the weekend's final activity, a cash bar and dinner at the Concordville Inn.

Bittersweet goodbyes were made as the members of the Class of 1972 prepared for their trips home. It was a weekend filled with precious memories, enlightened fellowship, and tasty food.

Burt Mustin said at the graduation of the Last Class of 1972, "There were thirteen of us in my graduating class and twelve of us are no longer with us."

Everyone agreed and Scott McGinnis proclaimed, "We have become the Class of 1922." The history and contributions of those associated with Pennsylvania Military College are not forgotten.

Stories and Vignettes from PMC

PMC Cadet with Widener Lion
© Newman 2020

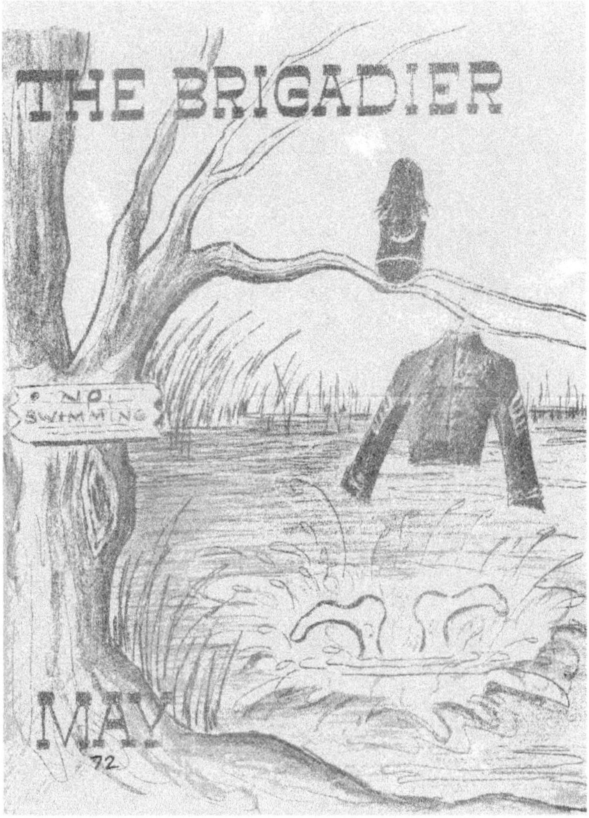
THE BRIGADIER
NO SWIMMING
MAY
72

ABOUT THE AUTHORS

Alan Hilkene "Hilk," Cadet #388
PMC: 1950-1954
Positions held at PMC: Sgt Junior year, Lt Senior year
PMC Organizations: Pershing Rifles, Intramural sports

Jack Kane, Cadet #658
PMC: 1954-1958
Post PMC: US Naval Engineer, LTC, Bronze Star (2), Legion of Merit, Program Manager

Bruce David Hubbell, Cadet #291
PMC: August—November 1962
Rank: PMC Rook
Post PMC: Software Engineering and Massage Therapy

Larry Liss "Super Jew," Cadet #337
PMC: 1959-1963
PMC Organizations: Pershing Rifles

Freddi Carlip (wife of Harry), Cadet #123
PMC: 1961-1965
Positions Held at PMC: Achieved rank of Cadet 2LT, German Club,

Rep. Club, Band, NROTCBA, Alpha Psi Omega, Intramurals, swim team,

Post PMC: Systems Analyst, Manager of Data Processing, VP of Systems

William R. Moller, Jr. A/K/A Rick, Cadet #601
PMC: 1961-1965
Positions Held at PMC: Cadet 2 LT, HQ Company (Band) Public Information Officer); S-3, 5th Rgt, Pershing Rifles; Theta Chi; DMS; DMG;

Post PMC: Mortar Platoon Leader-Fort Knox; IOBC, ABN, RGR Schools-Fort Benning; Security Chief World-Wide Armed Forces Courier Service (ARFCOS)-Washington D.C. (Personal Courier for POTUS); Spec Ops Team Ldr-RVN. Separated Active Duty as O-3; Various banking interests after service.

Jack Wilson (As told to son Tom Wilson)
PMC 1961-1965

W. David Eckard, III (Dave), Cadet # 187
PMC: 1962-1966
Positions Held at PMC: Corporal, Battalion Operations Sergeant, Lieutenant, Rifle Team, Alpha Sigma Phi, Student Council
   Post PMC: CPA, CFO

Brian P. LaBar, Cadet # 323
PMC: 1963 — 1967
Positions Held at PMC: Cadet Captain Company B, Football 1, Young Democrats, American Chemical Society, Tau Kappa Epsilon
   Post PMC: Two years in the Army including 11 months in Vietnam, Chemist in a pharmaceutical QC lab for Warner Chilcott, Di-

rector of Purchasing for Parke Davis Pharmaceutical, Director of Purchasing and Marketing Logistics for Warner Chilcott and Director of Chemical Sourcing for Watson/Activas Pharmaceutical.

Art Liss, Cadet #340
PMC: 1963-1967
Positions Held at PMC: BN XO, 2nd BN, Track 1967 MAC Champions

Post PMC Career: LT U.S. Army 1968-1970, President of: The San Jose Life Underwriters Association 1978, The Vancouver (WA) Life Underwriters Association 1992. Oregon National Guard responsible 2003-2019. North Bank Masonic Lodge #182, Historian on Larry's Medal of Honor case from April 2008 to the present.

Byron Wood Daniels, Cadet #97
PMC: 1964-1968
Positions Held at PMC: A & R Sergeant, Executive Officer Battery Robinett, Judo 1, SAM 2, AFCEA 2, Signal Club 2 and Rangers 3, Kappa Epsilon Fraternity

Post PMC: 2LT MI, Army Colonel (O-6), Fifth US Army General Staff: Emergency Planning Liaison officer to the state of South Dakota, auditor for the Federal Government US Department of Energy & Internal Revenue Service, Hurricane Evacuation Specialist

David M. Fiedler (Dave), Cadet #157
PMC: 1964-68
Positions Held at PMC: 4-year cadet private, Battery Robinett Commander, President AFCEA Chapter

Post PMC—3 years Active Duty (1 in Vietnam), 33 years Electronics Engineer U S Army, 26 years USAR/NJARNG Ret LTC/ Chief Signal Officer NJARNG

Stories and Vignettes from PMC

Alfred J. Peck (Al), Cadet #434
PMC: 1964-1968
Positions Held at PMC: Sergeant, Senior Private, Football, Chorus, TKE, Cultural Affairs
   Post PMC: Vietnam (Purple Heart), Social Worker (MSW Fordham 1975), Various directorships in Social Services

Thomas D. Caracciolo, Cadet #43
PMC: 1965-1969
Positions held at PMC: Corporal, Squad Ldr, Sergeant, BN Operations Sgt, 2nd Lt, Platoon Ldr, Cross Country, Track Teams, Triathlon Team, TKE Fraternity
   Post PMC: Graduated as a 2nd Lt, Infantry, 2 years active duty at Ft Ord, CA, accountant, building contractor.

Thomas J Dougherty III, Cadet #429
PMC: 1965-1969
Positions held at PMC: Mother's Day Corporal, Color Corporal, Platoon Sgt Cadre, Color Sgt, Private, Tau Kappa Epsilon
   Post PMC: Real Estate and Marketing, Dept of Health Education and Welfare

Daniel C. Gascoyne "Gas," Cadet #543
PMC: 1965-1969
Positions held at PMC: Corporal, Platoon Sgt., Co XO F CO (Honor Company), Pershing Rifles '65-'69, Theta Chi '67-'69. 3 years in the US Army, Infantry Officer, retired Captain, metals business for 45 years, Executive Vice President of two Billion Dollar firms. Currently retired in North Palm Beach, FL., Ocean City, NJ., and Higganum, CT.

Mark L Richards, Cadet #399

PMC: 1965-1969

Positions Held at PMC: Mother's Day Corporal, squad sergeant, lieutenant

Post PMC: Commissioned US Army Infantry, CPA, CFO of a large teaching hospital, Adjunct instructor St Joseph's University, Author of five published novels on the Roman legions

John W. Stealey "Wild Bill," Cadet #466

PMC: 1965-1969

Positions Held at PMC: HQ Company, Rook Right Guide in the Cadet Band

Post PMC: USAF Academy 1966 to 1970, USAF from 1970 till 1990, entrepreneur 1982 to present in the computer game business

Frederick H. Beals, Jr. "Rick," Cadet# 134

Year at PMC: 1966-1969

Positions Held at PMC: Mother's Day Corporal, Foxtrot Company,Pershing Rifles Company Q-5

Post PMC: Switzerland hotel school, 4 years sour-chef for two Swiss style restaurants, financial services business on the retail side, play trumpet with an Octoberfest-style band, playing with the part-year Brunswick County Orchestra

Mark Billen, Cadet #50

PMC: 1966-1970

Positions held at PMC: PMC Mounted Troop 1966-70, Varsity Tennis 1969-70

John E. N. Blair, Cadet #51

PMC 1966-1970

Positions held at PMC: Theatre PMC, Alpha Psi Omega, 15th Regimental Headquarters, Pershing Rifles, Canterbury Club, Society for the Advancement of Management: Member, Association of the United States Army

Post PMC: United States Army (Lieutenant Colonel), Rolls-Royce Owners Club, Comedy Writer for NATIONAL LAMPOON, Author of Legal Briefs for New York City law firms, Owner, Blair Farms, Board Member, Washington Township Municipal Association, Worshipful Master, Acacia Lodge No. 586, F. & A. M., Committee Member, Tuscarora District, Mason-Dixon Council, B. S. A.

Don Cooper, Cadet #129

PMC: 1966-1970

Positions held at PMC: Rook Echo Company, Cpl. Alpha Company Sgt. Battalion Staff, 1Lt.—Mess Officer, Rangers, Lamda Chi Alpha

Post PMC: U.S. Army Military Police—Germany, Veterans Administration—Philadelphia (74-04), Superior Court of New Jersey–Camden (04-18)

John Czekner Jr., Cadet #156

PMC: 1966-1970

Positions held at PMC: Lieutenant Platoon Leader Headquarters Company

Post PMC: US Army, real estate agent.

Dave Esto (Birdman), Cadet #195
PMC: 1966-1970
Positions held at PMC: Corporal, Color Sergeant, Corps ExO, Baseball: '67, '68, '69, Ranger Platoon: '68, '69, '70
Post PMC: 40+ years in the high-tech semiconductor industry

Terry Fadem, Cadet #187
PMC: 1966-1968
Positions held at PMC: Corporal, Band, Lacrosse Club
Post PMC Career: Lecturer Wharton Business School

Gerald Ferguson (Ferg), Cadet #638
PMC: 1966-1970
Positions held at PMC: Corporal, BN Operations Sergeant, Captain-Company, Baseball: Team Captain 1969-70, President Cadet Government 1969-70, Sr. Class Treasurer
Post PMC: 3.5 Yrs. Army Active duty (Germany), 35 Yrs. DuPont Co.

William C. Feyk, Cadet #218
PMC: 1966-1970
Positions held at PMC: Company Commander, Captain Headquarters Company, Band, Lacrosse Club
Post PMC Career: United States Army Service

Abraham J. Gale "Jack," Cadet #224
PMC: 1966-1970
Positions Held at PMC: Platoon Sergeant in Bravo Company, Executive Officer of Alpha Company, cadre leader my last year at PMC, Varsity letter in Tennis, Associate Editor of The Dome Newspaper,

Brother of Company Q-5/Q-15 and Drill Instructor my last year, Greek Fraternity Brother
　　Post PMC: Attorney

Bob Kukich, Cadet #292
PMC: 1966-1970
Positions held at PMC: HQ Co Platoon Sergeant, HQ Co XO, Golf Team 2-4; Band 1-4; Treasurer, Interfraternity Council; Secretary, Senior Class; Member, Phi Epsilon Pi.
　　Post PMC: US Army Field Artillery 1970-92; Computer Sciences Corporation 1992-2010.

David Edward Ling "Ding," Cadet #306
PMC: 1966-1970
Positions held at PMC: Four Year Cadet Private (due to low grades, as such, I believe I was the "Goat" of our class with a 1.74 enough to graduate, Sports, PR, Band, Battery Robinett, Mounted Troop, Rangers, Tau Kappa Epsilon
　　Post PMC: US Army LTC; corporate America (STI); Florida contract medical investigator/inspector (AHCA); EM Director (Santa Rosa County, FL); DoD civilian (DIA), now spending my retirement days back in FL.

Stuart Perlmutter "Stu," Cadet # 428
PMC: 1966-1970
Positions held at PMC: Lieutenant, Platoon Leader Headquarters Company, Band
　　Post PMC: Furniture Retailer

Clyde Tinklepaugh, Cadet #358
PMC: 1967-1970
Positions Held at PMC: Ranger Platoon, Tau Delta Phi

Mike Campbell & Hannah Campbell, Cadet #70
PMC: 1968-1972
Positions Held at PMC Played trombone in HQ Co. Was a happy private
  Post PMC Career: Army from as German linguist trained to listen in on East German radio traffic. Worked in kitchens at Fort Indiantown Gap feeding Vietnamese refugees in 1975. Became a Teamster truck driver in 11/1976 and retired in 06/2013

Joe Edwards "Derf," (As told by his Wife Chris), Cadet #107
PMC: 1968-1972
Positions Held at PMC: ZBT Fraternity, DJ for the radio station, Band (drummer)

Maris Eshleman, Cadet #108
PMC: 1968-1972
Positions Held at PMC: Cadet Corporal, First Sergeant and First Lieutenant, Corps Academic Officer, Band, Associate Editor of the Dome (Student Newspaper), Chairman, Social Affairs Committee, Intercollegiate Conference on Government, Model UN
  Post PMC: MA in Political Science, Univ of Louisville, JD Suffolk Univ Law School, MS in Info and Telecom Systems, Johns Hopkins Univ. Retired US Army 2000, Retired Booz Allen Hamilton 2013 and now live on a sailboat in the Caribbean.

Vito Greco
PMC: 1968-1972

Greg Haugens, Cadet # 163
PMC: 1968-1972
Positions Held at PMC: Platoon Sgt, HQ and TKE
   Post PMC: ADT Transportation Corps, Roadway Express Trucking, coils (US Steel) metal scrap.

Steve Kenevich
PMC: 1968-1972
Position held at PMC: Platoon Sergeant

Paul S. Lewis, "The Frog," "Froggie," "Frogman," Cadet #250
PMC: 1968-1972
Positions held at PMC: Mother's Day Corporal, Cadre '69-'70, Lieutenant Platoon leader '71-'72, Swim Team
   Post PMC: 2LT, Field Artillery. 2nd Armored Division at Ft. Hood, TX. University of Texas. Master's degree in Geological Sciences, worked in oil and gas for Pennzoil in Houston, Austin Geological Society.

Scott McGinnis, Cadet #267
PMC: 1968-1972
Positions Held at PMC: Private, Corporal, Platoon Sgt, Private
   Post PMC: Navy, Commander (RET O-5) in 1994, senior level sales and marketing positions, retired and work part time at TSA at Evansville Regional Airport.

Bob Schneider Schneido, Cadet #392
PMC: 1968-1972
Positions Held at PMC: Band Supply Sergeant, Band Commander (Cadet Captain) 1971—1972, Band 1968—1972, 15th Battalion

HQ Commander, 1972 Pershing Rifles, PHI EPSILON FRATERNITY (ZBT after merger)

Post PMC: Field artillery officer, Lance Missile XO, 42nd Artillery Group Asst S-3/Liaison Officer, 175 mm Battery Commander, Penn State University—ROTC Instructor, Air Force Materiel Command—Program Manager IT and Resource Manager, Adjunct Faculty, Sinclair Community College, Edison State Community College, Park University, Mount Vernon Nazarene University, Indiana Wesleyan University

Gary Sisco, Cadet #418
PMC: 1968-1972
Positions Held at PMC: Rook, Echo Company, 2nd Year—Private, Bravo Company, 3rd Year—Platoon Sergeant, Bravo Company, 4th Year—Captain, Alpha Company, Ranger Platoon.

William Speer "Chucker," Cadet #488
Years at PMC: 1968-1972
Positions: Squad Corporal, Athletics and Recreation Sergeant, A&R Officer (Captain), Lambda Chi Alpha, Baseball, National Education Association (president).

Post PMC: Middle/high school teacher/department head, basketball (head coach), baseball, cross country head coach, bass fishing guide (TX) and tournament fisherman, author of "Broomsticks to Battlefields: The Cadets of Delaware Military Academy in the Civil War and Beyond," adjunct instructor American Military University, historian for American Cruise Lines, Project Manager: Army Signal Corps GWOT project, MI history video project, NC & GA National Guard video projects.

Stories and Vignettes from PMC

William J. Troy "Tiger," Cadet #453
PMC: 1968-1972
Positions Held at PMC: Sergeant, Squad Leader Delta Company Cadre 1971, Cadet Captain Commander, C Company 1972, Ranger Platoon, Lambda Chi Alpha Fraternity
    Post PMC Career: US Army and US Army Reserve 1972-2000, Retired Lieutenant Colonel, Northrop Grumman Corporation 1984-2016, Retired Supply Chain Program Manager.

James H. VanSciver "Clammer," Cadet #466
PMC: 1968—1972
Positions Held at PMC: 1st Lt., Class Vice-president, president, football, baseball, TKE, Sportswriter for The Dome, Mounted Troup
    Post PMC Career: Public school educator teacher/coach, assistant principal, principal, director, and superintendent, professor, published four children's books, an educational leadership book, and published a novelty book, pitched in semi-pro baseball leagues.

John A. Vencius "Johnny V," Cadet #111
PMC: 1968—1972
Positions Held at PMC: Color Corporal, Corps Sergeant Major, Platoon Leader, Pershing Rifles
    Post PMC Career: U.S. Army, Armor, 1-72 Armor, 2d Infantry Div., Korea 1977, 2-5 Cav, 1st Cav Div, Defense Contract Management Agency, Contract Specialist (with intervening positions in the IRS, Navy, and VA)

Ed Albertson, Cadet #9
PMC: 1969-1973
Positions held at PMC: Cadet Corporal, Cadet Sergeant, Cadet Captain (S-4), Pershing Rifles HQ, Cadet Government Association,

HQ (Band), Pi Gamma mu Honor Society, Alpha Chi Honor Society, Center for the Study of the Presidency, Distinguished Military Student, Distinguished Military Graduate

Post PMC: US Army Regular Army, US Army Reserve, Defense Consultant at BDM on AWACS Aircraft, Programmer at Southwestern Bell), Programmer Manager at AT&T (9 years), Sales at Huthwaite, Vice President & Partner at Carew International.

John Sermertzides
PMC: 1969-1970

Douglas P. Cervi (Art) "Hulk #383
PMC: 1969-1973
Rank/positions held: Cpl. squad leader, Varsity Football Tri-Captain Senior year

Post PMC: 41 years high school history teacher, Head wrestling coach, assistant football and baseball coach. Currently Adjunct Professor Stockton University teaching Holocaust/Genocide Studies. Executive Director of the New Jersey Commission on Holocaust Education, Captain New Jersey National Guard (retired)

Jim Hulitt "Bowser," Cadet #132
PMC: 1969-1973
Positions held at PMC: Private, Sergeant, Beater & Blower (Band), Pershing Rifles Regimental Staff

Post PMC: USAR, Transportation, Conrail Operating Dept, Regional Transportation Manager for Sunoco.

Dave Neimeyer "Hobbit," Cadet #201

PMC: 1969 –1973

Positions held at PMC: Staff Sergeant, Ranger Platoon, Editor "Brigadier," Lambda Chi Alpha

Post PMC: US Navy 1972-1993; retired LCDR, genealogy business, college adjunct faculty.

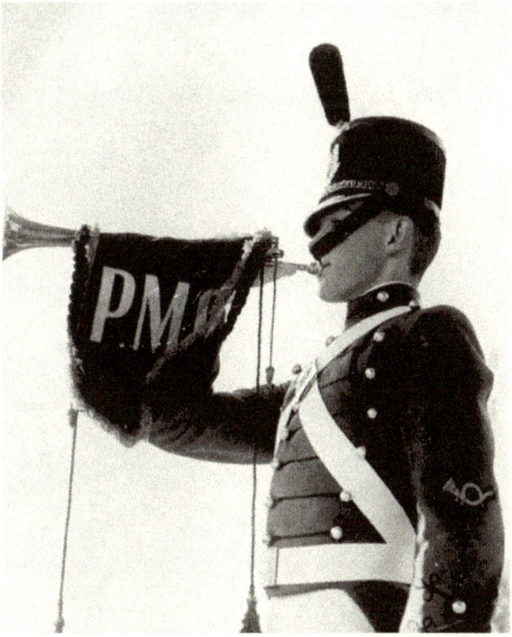
PM

INDEX (AUTHOR STORIES)

Alan Hilkene "Hilk," Cadet #388 [1, 335, 350]

Jack Kane, Cadet #658 [179]

Bruce David Hubbell, Cadet #291 [8, 9]

Larry Liss "Super Jew," Cadet #337 [2]

Freddi Carlip (wife of Harry), Cadet #123 [180]

William R. Moller, Jr. A/K/A Rick, Cadet #601 [6, 182, 183, 233, 234, 237]

Jack Wilson (As told to son Tom Wilson) [8]

W. David Eckard, III (Dave), Cadet # 187 [11, 12]

Brian P. LaBar, Cadet # 323 [15]

Art Liss, Cadet #340 [250]

Byron Wood Daniels, Cadet #97 [21, 25,]

David M. Fiedler (Dave), Cadet #157 [17, 18, 24, 28, 30, 31, 37, 39, 40, 42, 147, 148, 149, 151, 154, 155, 159, 161, 163, 183, 185, 186, 190, 192, 235, 238, 241, 246, 254, 255, 257, 258, 259, 261, 322]

Alfred J. Peck (Al), Cadet #434 [12, 34, 243]

Thomas D. Caracciolo, Cadet #43 [44]

Thomas J Dougherty III, Cadet #429 [160]

Daniel C. Gascoyne "Gas," Cadet #543 [324, 328, 333, 352]

Mark L Richards, Cadet #399 [54]

John W. Stealey "Wild Bill," Cadet #466 [45, 46, 47, 48, 49, 50, 319, 360]

Frederick H. Beals, Jr. "Rick," Cadet# 134 [337]

Mark Billen, Cadet #50 [358]

John E. N. Blair, Cadet #51 [51, 267]

Don Cooper, Cadet #129 [62, 164, 195]

John Czekner Jr., Cadet #156 [353]

Dave Esto (Birdman), Cadet #195 [58, 59]

Terry Fadem, Cadet #187 [353]

Gerald Ferguson (Ferg), Cadet #638 [57, 59, 61, 63, 262, 266, 268, 270, 271, 323]

William C. Feyk, Cadet #218 [353]

Abraham J. Gale "Jack," Cadet #224 [64, 356]

Bob Kukich, Cadet #292 [157, 193, 268, 334, 336]

David Edward Ling "Ding," Cadet #306 [263]

Stuart Perlmutter "Stu," Cadet # 428 [52, 56, 353]

Clyde Tinklepaugh, Cadet #358 [328]

Mike Campbell & Hannah Campbell, Cadet #70 [197, 199, 201]

Joe Edwards "Derf," (As told by his Wife Chris), Cadet #107

Maris Eshleman, Cadet #108 [81]

Vito Greco [333]

Greg Haugens, Cadet # 163 [203]

Steve Kenevich [99]

Paul S. Lewis, "The Frog," "Froggie," "Frogman," Cadet #250 [77, 79, 97, 100, 102, 119, 144, 299]

Scott McGinnis, Cadet #267 [82, 90, 118]

Bob Schneider Schneido, Cadet #392 [68, 74, 165, 166, 176, 287, 291, 295]

Gary Sisco, Cadet #418 [282]

William Speer "Chucker," Cadet #488 [80, 82, 89, 94, 100, 101, 168, 169, 299]

William J. Troy "Tiger," Cadet #453 [70, 198, 272, 278, 285, 291, 296]

James H. VanSciver "Clammer," Cadet #466 [65, 69, 73, 74, 77, 87, 92, 95, 97, 102, 276, 286, 289, 292, 305, 309, 311, 320, 326, 378]

John A. Vencius "Johnny V," Cadet #111 [361]

John Semertzides [303]

Ed Albertson, Cadet #9 [143, 176, 316]

Douglas P. Cervi, Cadet #383 [113, 114,

Jim Hulitt "Bowser," Cadet #132 [145}

Dave Neimeyer "Hobbit," Cadet #201 [104, 114, 120, 124, 128, 133, 135, 140, 141, 170, 207, 211, 216, 220, 221, 222, 226, 313, 315, 365, 376]

Printed in the USA
CPSIA information can be obtained
at www.ICGtesting.com
LVHW091959100224
771306LV00007B/886